Oak Associates

TEL (03) 5472-7077
FAX (03) 5472-7076

Aoki Bldg. 3F
4-1-10, Toranomon,
Minato-ku,
Tokyo 105

12-12-13 発

Japan – A Modern Retail Superpower

Japan – A Modern Retail Superpower

By Roy Larke and Michael Causton

palgrave
macmillan

First published 2005 by
PALGRAVE MACMILLAN
Houndmills, Basingstoke, Hampshire RG21 6XS and
175 Fifth Avenue, New York, N. Y. 10010
Companies and representatives throughout the world

PALGRAVE MACMILLAN is the global academic imprint of the Palgrave Macmillan division of St. Martin's Press, LLC and of Palgrave Macmillan Ltd. Macmillan® is a registered trademark in the United States, United Kingdom and other countries. Palgrave is a registered trademark in the European Union and other countries.

ISBN-13: 978–1–4039–9670–1 hardback
ISBN-10: 1–4039–9670–9   hardback

This book is printed on paper suitable for recycling and made from fully managed and sustained forest sources.

A catalogue record for this book is available from the British Library.

Library of Congress Cataloging-in-Publication Data
Larke, Roy, 1962–
    Japan, a modern retail superpower / by Roy Larke and Michael Causton.
        p. cm.
    Includes bibliographical references and index.
    ISBN 1–4039–9670–9 (cloth)
        1. Retail trade–Japan–Management. 2. Consumers–Japan.
I. Causton, Michael, 1965– II. Title.

HF5429.6.J3L368 2005
658.8'7'0952–dc22   2005046344

10   9   8   7   6   5   4   3   2   1
14 13 12 11 10 09 08 07 06 05

Transferred to digital printing in 2006

For Wati,

For Yuko

This book is dedicated to all the non-Japanese companies and entrepreneurs who have braved the Japanese market with open minds and open hearts and who have taken the time and made the effort to understand and learn. We know it is hard work. We also know it is worth it. For those who have yet to make the effort, we hope this book encourages you.

Contents

List of Tables

List of Figures

List of Case Studies

Preface

Japan: Why Bother?

Some might wonder why go to the trouble of producing a book on Japanese retailing. Reading newspaper reports from everywhere else in the world, you might imagine the Japanese economy is about to default, that consumers are not spending, and retailers are either already bankrupt or surviving solely because of friendly bankers. If you do a search on Google for the words "Japan lost decade", there are over 1 million results. In other words, most overseas pundits have written Japan off.

For those who have actually visited, however, it is clear that these same pundits have spent very little time on the streets of Tokyo or Osaka recently, or checked the results of the best specialty store retailers over the past two or three years.

In Japan, as in any market, it is important to distinguish between the theatrics and posturing of the political arena and the financial markets on the one hand, and the more concrete world of consumer goods distribution and consumption on the other. Yves Carcelle, head of Louis Vuitton worldwide, put it like this:

> Economists have been saying that Japan is a risk for 10 years. You have to distinguish between the Japanese people and the banks. The Japanese have money. The Japanese banking system does not. We've been asking ourselves the same question for a long time: Will it collapse? And year after year, I watch the Japanese continue to consume more and more Vuitton products.(JapanConsuming, 2002b)

It is not just luxury goods companies that are doing well in Japan. Yes, Daiei, Sogo and Nagasakiya collapsed, but the cause of their demise was less about a poor economy and much more about poor management. More specifically, it was due to an inability to react to changing consumer conditions and expectations; many retailers fell into the expensive trap of over-expansion in the late 1980s that led to unsustainable debt levels. For others, it was simply conservative management, lack of innovation, and a refusal to accept change.

Anyone who visits Japan regularly and is even indirectly involved in retailing would agree with this. We can say it with authority because of the wealth of brands and retailers that contradict this story of stagnation and decline. Some retailers and consumer goods brands are achieving record growth. There are examples of significant success in almost every retail sector: supermarkets,

GMS chains, convenience stores, specialty apparel, drugstores, electronics, home centers, variety stores, discounters, and, yes, even department stores. Within each sector, the list of companies posting healthy growth in both sales and profits is long. If the entire market was really in a slump, how would you account for the performance of these retailers?

Such performances are at odds with the background of macro level statistics produced by government bureaus that show negative growth overall. There is a good reason for this. In general these statistics include data for all retailers within a sector. As many observers of Japan will know, this means the inclusion of hundreds of thousands of mom and pop stores which still account for around 45 per cent of retail stores. This type of retailer is famously unproductive and in decline. Remove this group from the statistics and the picture looks a lot brighter. Better yet, ignore the general trends in department store retailing, and things look brighter still.

Efficient retailers are gradually taking over market share and replacing this unproductive mass of general small stores with modern retailing. These new leaders of retailing are doing well in Japan because they are meeting consumer demand with imagination and supplying it efficiently. As they grow to maturity, many are even expanding overseas.

This is a lengthy way of saying something that should be obvious: Japan is one of the most promising consumer goods markets in the world with a fast-changing retail market. Japanese consumers are also the wealthiest consumers by savings. According to government statistics for 2003, the average working household had total savings of approximately ¥17 million. In families where the household head was over 65 years of age, this figure rose to an incredible ¥26 million. Japanese have plenty of money but, as many innovative retailers have found out, the key is finding ways to make them part with it. Some retailers are struggling simply because consumers are bored by them.

This book attempts to distinguish clearly between the winners and losers for consumer mind share. It provides readers, whether academic, student, vendor, buyer, advisor or investor, a complete map of what was, until now, a very complicated maze. At the same time, it shows clearly the sectors, and companies within sectors, which will lead the retail industry in the future.

We would like to take this opportunity to thank the many people who have helped us learn about and understand Japan over the years. There are far too many to list in full, but we would particularly like to thank Professor John Dawson of Edinburgh University, Professor Masao Mukoyama of UMDS, Professor Richard Harrison of Kobe University and Bertrand de Streel, the other half of CFN.

Most of all, we would like to thank our wives, Wati and Yuko, for the long patience through hours of writing, editing and complaining about Microsoft Word. Thanks to you all, and to all the people we don't have room to mention here.

Tokyo, 2005

Foreword

Retailing in Japan has often been characterized as being "different" to other places, dominated by historical relationships and practices, focused around the protection of vast numbers of independent, small shops. Yet, whilst there is an element of truth in this, the retail sector also contains some of the world's best and leading retailers, both Japanese (e.g. Seven Eleven Japan) and non-Japanese (e.g. Wal-Mart, Gap and Tesco). Underneath this stereotypical view of Japanese retail distribution, major changes have been taking place, involving rethinking and restructuring of supply relationships and operational practices on both vertical and horizontal dimensions. This process involves both Japanese and non-Japanese companies. This coming together and restructuring of ancient and modern in a rich and large consumer society offers both commercial and academic potential.

Unlocking this potential is not necessarily easy or rapid. International retailers have in the past perhaps squandered some opportunities in Japan (e.g. Boots, Carrefour). However international approaches to aspects of retailing (e.g. supply chain, data collection and use, branding) are recognized as being significant and of interest. Change in retailing in Japan will not be driven by the "British-ness" or "American-ness" of an imported retail offer, but by excellence, knowledge and appropriateness in a changing Japanese market. The issue is not westernization of Japanese retailing, but modernization. Academics are also realizing the scope for study of a different set of questions about retailing in Japan, though some remain wedded to the old themes.

The fact that Japan is the world's second largest economy with a population of nearly 127 million is sometimes used to suggest that the difficulties dogging the economy since the early 1990s are only relative and not to be taken too seriously. Anyone who walks down one of the bustling streets in Tokyo full of shoppers and crowded restaurants can be forgiven for asking "What recession?" There are many who will emphatically say "Don't believe all the negative press. It's not that bad; in fact opportunities abound if originality and expertise are offered". After all Louis Vuitton has never had it so good in Japan (allegedly one in six Japanese own a Louis Vuitton item, 35 per cent of worldwide sales are in Japan and 30 per cent of other worldwide sales are to Japanese overseas).

However it is also true that Japan's consumer and wider economy has been in trouble for over 15 years. Consumer spending has been in decline. Japan has been in a recessionary and deflationary situation. Whilst sometimes overstated, Japan has significant problems. Yet, despite the retail disasters of the department store chain Sogo and leading general merchandise chains Daiei and Mycal amongst others, there are pockets of excellence in Japanese retailing. The market since the mid 1990s has attracted record numbers of foreign retail businesses. The consumer market remains large and affluent. The issue is to persuade consumers to spend on your products and services and to do so at a profit through being efficient and effective retailers, in control of products, branding and supply and retail operations.

Japan perhaps has a two-tier or two-speed economy. One tier consists of highly competitive internationally oriented manufacturers that have restructured their operations to remain profitable. The second tier consists of traditionally more domestically oriented companies that have not been as exposed to international competition. Retailing and wholesaling, whilst part of this second tier, has however become increasingly receptive to change agents. Some change agents have been international such as international retailers entering Japan, international retail practices observed globally and in Japan, and offshore manufacturing with its impact on price and quality dimensions. Others have been internal as some Japanese retailers and wholesalers have recognized the need and seized the opportunities to change. Organizations such as Fast Retailing, Aeon, Yamada Denki and Cainz, as well as a host of other large and small retailers are transforming the retail, wholesale and distribution landscape of Japan. They are modern, efficient and effective businesses. Lots of independent small shops still exist, but the battle to modernize is well under way.

I have been fortunate enough to visit Japan on a number of occasions over the last 12 years. Its sense of difference and peculiarities provided me with instant attractions. I have been aware both academically and personally of some of the changes underway. But short casual or even focused visits are unable really to get the depth of knowledge and understanding required to fully comprehend retailing behaviors and change in a country. When that country is as special as Japan, and when change is as socially, politically, culturally and economically contested as it is in Japan, then there is no substitute for real expertise, gained from living and breathing the changes underway.

This volume is thus both timely, given where Japanese retailing is currently positioned and authoritative, given the depth of knowledge and detail exhibited by Roy Larke and Michael Causton. Their work with Japan Consuming and in this volume is based on a deep lived experience of Japan, Japanese consumers and Japanese retailing. Through a painstaking description of the Japanese retailing and wholesaling sectors, they paint a picture of real change and an exciting future. They described some of the problems, including denial, counter-strategies, power balances and inadequate management. But they also point to those retailers which have transformed their own businesses, the retailers around them and their supply chains which could become powerful players in the Asian region and further afield. Their comprehensive study is a vital and accessible landmark on this journey, though with its strong personal views on aspects of Japan, it may not find favor everywhere.

The situation described is witnessing an increase in retailer power, increased concentration, a move away form general merchandising and positive change in consumer thinking and reactions. This is a new distribution system being created. It will transform Japanese distribution, though it is of course not a total replacement of the old ways. Similar changes are occurring in other countries.

There is therefore much to be learned from this volume, whether you are a business (thinking of) operating in Japan or elsewhere where change is happening, or an academic interested in change and dynamism in retail structures. The authors are to be congratulated on their work. It will be of interest and use to many.

Leigh Sparks
Professor of Retail Studies
Co-editor, International Review of Retail, Distribution and Consumer Research
Institute for Retail Studies,
University of Stirling,
Stirling, Scotland, UK

Introduction

1

Japan's Retail Market in Context

Japan is currently undergoing its most significant transformation in history. Many people continue to hope that this statement applies to Japan as a whole. Be that as it may, it is certainly true for retailing and distribution.

Throughout the past 40 years, distribution in Japan has been a major issue. At first, as Japan exploded into the modern world to enter the elite group of top industrialized nations, domestic distribution was merely of academic interest. The same economic miracle that turned just another Asian nation into the world's second richest country also changed the distribution system, introducing all of the main formats found in most industrialized economies. Japan saw self-service supermarkets and general merchandise chains, niche specialty retailers, and even convenience stores all appear up to the early 1970s, when the economy was in its fastest period of growth.

At the same time, these new, corporate, chain retailers were unlike most of their counterparts in the West because, on the whole, they took a back seat in the supply chain. Manufacturers ran marketing in Japan. Marketing was done the "push" style to pump product, along with its assorted marketing paraphernalia of advertising and even in-store merchandising, down the channel to convince the consumer she just had to buy it. This approach is still used to a significant extent, and manufacturers still tend to believe they should have complete control over supply chains.

It took a very long time before retailers began to realize that leaving it to manufacturers was not always the best way. Unfortunately, by the 1990s, when retailers saw the first major downturn in the consumer market since WWII, many were already heavily tied into the system and unwilling or unable to strike out on their own. Even today, some retailing sectors still suffer from the attitude of companies who take too little direct interest in vital aspects of their businesses. Even now, some still take the traditional stance that they set prices according to supplier requirements, effectively giving up control of their own bottom line.

Luckily, an increasing number of retailers, both by desire and necessity, have seen the light and are taking an interest in their own supply chains and all issues related to them. These companies are increasingly powerful, and their success has pushed others to follow suit. For most it has been a leap into the unknown, with all the worries and insecurity that entails, but it was long overdue.

Retailers discover retailing

This trend of retailers becoming involved in, or even taking full control over, marketing channels really summarizes almost all the important current developments in Japanese retailing today. It is something that has happened gradually over the past 10 years and will continue for the fore-seeable future. It is also something that has widespread consequences for all aspects of modern distribution in Japan and retailing in Asia too.

There is also a significant number of retailers who have taken a further step and are beginning to actually cater directly to consumer needs, something they have always claimed to do, but in reality had mostly left up to manufacturers. Again, speaking generally, these are also some of the most successful retailers around today, and they stand out as examples to the rest. The retail companies actively involved in media advertising, merchandise development, and new store format innovation are the ones leading the pace in Japan, just as they do in all other advanced nations. Throughout this book, we take our examples and case studies predominantly from this group of new leaders.

Some Japanese observers continue to myopically mislabel this change as Westernization rather than modernization. One of the major trends, that of internationalization, is frequently lamented as unchecked "globaliza-tion" of Japanese distribution, with Western companies very much the vil-lains of the plot. This overlooks the fact that in much of Asia, it is Japanese companies who are leading a similar rush to global standards – the same standards they are implementing in the domestic market (see Chapter 12). On the whole, it is not the retail companies themselves who are lamenting this change or seeing it as a step backwards. Retailers understand their predicament and many agree that, while Japan should always maintain its own cultural identity, within the business of distribution, management styles and operational techniques should not be rejected simply because they are not their own. Rather, as with so much in Japan's history, overseas ideas are there to be adapted and adjusted to Japanese needs.

Modernization and concentration

The major trends described below are all leading from, or are a consequence of, this overall modernization of retail systems in Japan. One of the main trends is the significant polarization occurring between retailers that offer high end, branded merchandise, and those offering generic, low priced goods, with those in the middle being squeezed out of existence. This concentration at the extremes has brought with it more intense competition; the consequence of this is diversification of formats and even a push into overseas markets.

At the same time, as is far better known, more and more overseas companies are setting up in Japan. As always, of course, it is the successful cases that generate the most publicity, but there is also a significant number of companies coming to Japan and repeating the same mistakes of numerous predecessors. It is in light of such repetition that the authors of this book began their work in Japan more than 10 years ago. It is too easy to follow the trends as dictated by bureaucrats and journalists, when, in reality, a little independent study can reveal a markedly different picture entirely.

Finally, and most significantly of all, there is a gradual concentration within the retail sector as a whole, again to the extent that some would contrast Japan with other industrialized nations. This is appearing most clearly in certain key sectors. Over the next decade, it is a trend which will continue to pick up pace as other sectors also race to form a more modern structure, developing a greater number of large, corporate chains, and fewer regional independents.

Perhaps the best example of this trend can be found in apparel retailing. A profound change occurred in the balance of power within apparel retailing in the late 1990s and early 2000s. The catalyst for this change was the rise of the SPAs (Specialty Private Apparel chains: see Chapter 9 for details), a group of single brand chains of which Fast Retailing's Uniqlo brand is the most well-known. After two decades as an unknown discount apparel retailer in Yamaguchi, Fast Retailing suddenly took its Uniqlo brand to the top of sales rankings and broke all records for year on year growth in sales and profits. Today it is the second most profitable retailer in Japan. Put simply, Fast Retailing took control over all aspects of distribution from production to retail stores, and of branding and marketing, and, most importantly, it focused on retailing and the needs of the consumer. It is a model that has been copied throughout Japanese retailing, starting with apparel. The success of this model has had a profound effect on the entire retail industry and one that is still not fully understood as companies continue to develop and improve on what Fast Retailing started.

Arguably, Uniqlo was able to become so pervasive and was so visible for one very simple reason: branding. Fast Retailing was only the second Japanese retail company to turn itself into a brand. The only serious attempt previously was Mujirushi Ryohin – ironically a brand name that actually means "non-brand" (see Chapter 12), but even Muji never took the final step into marketing and developing its brand. Before Uniqlo, apparel retailing, like the rest of Japanese distribution, was dominated by the apparel manufacturers and wholesalers, with only basic marketing over which retailers had no control. Fast Retailing changed all this.

Today, all of Japan's leading retailers are attempting to find a better balance of power between themselves and their suppliers. In the past, retailers were locked into agreements that favored the manufacturers because, unless they acquiesced, producers would simply stop the supply of product (see Chapter 6). Department stores were Japan's most visible and exclusive retailers, but even they found themselves increasingly handing over floor space to be managed by suppliers, effectively becoming mere shop windows with little control over pricing or merchandising. In short, suppliers offered retail chains a comfortable, easy life with steady sales and a reasonable, but limited return. Wholesalers and manufacturers supplied sales staff and dictated everything including prices, advertising, shelf positioning, and all other forms of promotion, and then rewarded the retailers with bonuses and rebates more for cooperation than for performance. These conditions have not completely disappeared, but such a system is no longer sustainable because retailers have finally come to realize that they can do much better on their own.

Given this background, it is no surprise that Fast Retailing and others like it managed to expand so quickly and acquire such pervasive visibility in the market. It was a chain designed from the ground up to push the brand through product, store design, and marketing, with a focused target market. Today, Japan's best retailers can be considered as "modern" simply because they are at last attempting to control their own businesses and their own destinies, working with suppliers, but not being dictated to by them. For the older and larger retail companies this switch has caused major upheavals and it is something they have grappled with since the mid-1990s. Some simply could not change and a number of the very largest companies from only 15 years ago have now collapsed. Those that have changed, however, are Japan's new retail leaders and can be found in every single merchandise sector.

As a result of retailers beginning to understand the value of becoming brands in their own right, Japan is currently experiencing a major shift away from general merchandise towards more specialty retailing focused on much narrower merchandise sectors. Again, apparel retailing is the primary example, but the same trends have now taken hold in almost every sector. Japan's new specialty retailers are not necessarily small format store operators, and they are certainly not small firms, except in apparel, but they are always focused on the type of merchandise and store formats that they know best and, in most cases, the retailers themselves brand them. General merchandise chains and department stores still exist and, at least in a small number of cases, have managed to find new strategies that allow them to prosper, but it is in specialty retailing, with its ability to entertain and excite consumers, where real growth is now occurring.

It is easy to show the decline in general merchandise retailing. Between 1991 and 2003, sales at department stores declined by 24.7 per cent and a net 52 stores closed nationwide. Even so, sales space at department stores increased by 11.3 per cent during the same period to more than 7.751 million sqm. Sales for members of the Japan Chain Store Association grew by 25.5 per cent, but this was largely due to a net increase of 1,734 new stores and an increase in sales space of 97.4 per cent. For both formats, sales densities, as measured by sales per 1,000 sqm, fell by 32.3 per cent and 36.4 per cent respectively, clearly illustrating just how poorly general merchandise retailers performed (see Figure 1.1.).

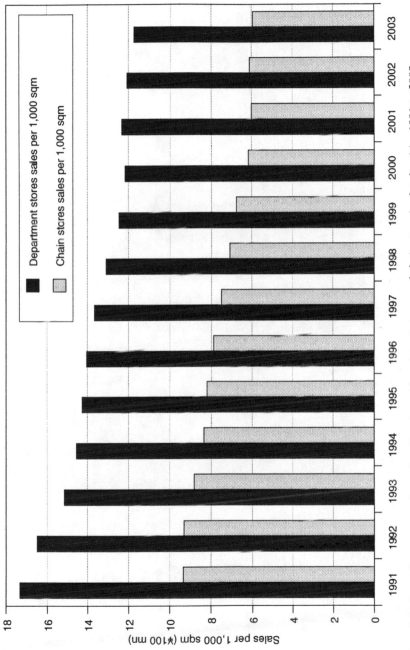

Figure 1.1 Large format general merchandise stores (department stores and chain stores) sales densities 1991 to 2003
Source: Shukan Toyo Keizai (2004a)

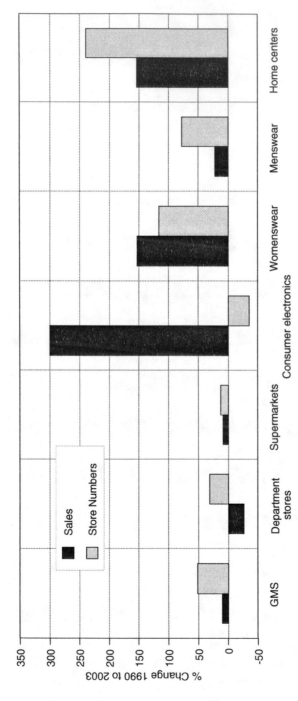

Figure 1.2 Proportional change in sales and store numbers for leading three retailers in main retail formats, 1990 to 2003
Source: Nikkei Ryutsu Shinbun (1991), NMJ (2004)

Because of the predominance of small, independent retail stores that mingle with specialty retail chains in the general statistics, it is far more difficult to show the growth of specialty retailing in general terms. In addition, most leading retailers in the various merchandise sectors have been replaced since 1990 and several new specialty sectors such as casual apparel and discount retailing have now been created. Taking the leading three retailers per sector and comparing average percentage changes in sales and store numbers, it is clear that, once again, specialty retailing has improved much more than general merchandise retailing (see Figure 1.2).

Figure 1.2 shows the leading retailers for both 1990 and 2003, with all seven comparable sectors showing positive changes with the exception of department stores where even the largest firms have declined. But the magnitude of change between GMS chains and supermarkets, and then the four specialty sectors is remarkable. Even in men's apparel retailing, where there has been little change in leading retailers, growth rates are more than three times those for GMS formats.

Through direct control, retailers have also become more competitive. Top end premium retailing, such as that offered by overseas luxury fashion brands, is still very popular in Japan. In fact, the branding appeal of such upscale retailers has actually helped them achieve incredibly high levels of performance even while most retailing in Japan declined about them. Today, however, by controlling their own margins, Japan's modern retailers are also able to offer far higher value both in their pricing and their merchandise quality, and have made significant adjustments towards what they know consumers actually want, rather than simply offering what manufacturers hope to sell.

Traditional retailing declines

While some academic observers prefer to dismiss the idea of Japanese retailing modernizing in this way, the trend is further confirmed by the massive decline in traditional retail business models and formats. This is most clearly seen in department store and independent store retailing, both of which are the most traditional of all formats. Department stores are discussed at length in Chapter 5, but it is worth briefly considering the fate of small, independent stores.

Japan still has a vast number of small stores. The three-yearly Census of Commerce carried out by METI (Ministry of Economy, Trade and Industry, previously called MITI: Ministry of International Trade and Industry, itself a name change of paramount significance) recorded 1,300,043 retail stores in 2002. This is an amazing figure, higher than in the USA where there is twice the population and 25 times the land area. But the 2002 figure represents a net fall of some 305,540 stores since 1991 alone. That is an average net fall of 76 stores per day for 11 years. Between the previous two surveys in 1999 and 2002, the rate was even higher at 98 stores per day.

Back in the early 1990s, the fate of independent retailing was a significant political and social problem. From the 1930s onwards, various Japanese governments took measures to protect small retailers from competition with large, corporate chains through a series of increasingly restrictive laws. Similar legislation remained in place right up until 2000, but in the end, the effect of the legislation was greatly reduced in 1990 when Japan responded to pressure from the US to make large store development easier and the process more transparent. With the one hugely important exception of Toys 'R' Us, the move did not, as the US government had hoped, encourage more US retailers to enter the market, but it did allow GMS chains to expand rapidly, adding 1,369 stores and 9.6 million sqm of sales space between 1991 and 2000. In addition, as part of the growing success of specialty retailing and convenience store retailing there was a shift in emphasis from independent private businesses to dynamic chain organized businesses in the retail sector. Many independent retailers were run as low profit, family operations and a large number that closed did so because younger generations were unwilling to take over from their parents.

One of the important aspects of independent retailing, however, is the way a large proportion of small stores are organized into local shopping associations called *shotengai*. There are numerous types of *shotengai*, but many are easily spotted in regional cities because they are pedestrian only streets covered over with a roof – this in itself providing evidence of the level of organization and investment that has gone into the street's development. Around Tokyo, roofed off shopping streets are less common, but local independent retailers still band together into associations. Ginza has its own *shotengai* association, and there are other famous examples such as Takeshita Dori in Harajuku and Sugamo in northern Tokyo. Elsewhere in Japan, Osaka boasts a 3 kilometer long, covered *shotengai* stocked with local retailers, department stores, and even famous luxury brands. Kobe too has its Sentagai *shotengai*, which is also several kilometers in length and has a full range of formats.

Such streets are found in almost every small town and regional city and, until 1990, were the main business and retail districts. Today, however, these streets are in rapid decline as large format retailing opens in the suburbs, and even small format, specialty chain stores prefer newer, smarter locations in shopping buildings and shopping malls (see Chapter 12). Many regional cities have experienced a hollowing out of their city centers as a result and it is common to see shops boarded up in the regions. Sad though this situation may be, it is now only the older generation of Japanese academics that still have very much interest in the fate of the independent retailer in Japan. Not only has the world moved on, but even their younger academic colleagues have realized that corporate chains are now where the action is. Japan still has far, far too many small retail shops, and this is the main reason why people refer to the market as being over stored. In reality, the number of stores will continue to decline very rapidly indeed and for a long time into the future.

Overseas retailers: a few successes put the many to shame

Despite the image of Japan as a difficult market, its size has at last attracted an increasing number of overseas retailers to the country. The number of newly established overseas companies operating retail stores grew significantly in the 1990s (see Figure 1.3). By 2000 there were some 205 non-Japanese companies operating retail stores in Japan (see Shukan Toyo Keizai, 1999). Of these, 79 were American in origin, while 29 were French, 22 British, 11 German, and 10 Italian. A third, 77 companies, were involved in apparel, accessories, cosmetics or jewelry. Undoubtedly, the most successful as a group were the French and Italian luxury fashion brands, most of which have operated in Japan since the late 1970s or early 1980s. In contrast, more than half of the American companies active in 2000 had entered after 1990.

The two most successful overseas retailers to date are Toys 'R' Us and Gap. Toys 'R' Us was the first major retailer to make inroads into the market despite fierce local opposition, and had a significant and overriding influence (see Chapter 3). It began the work that companies like Gap and Wal-Mart are continuing in forcing local vested interests to accept the necessity and inevitability of increasing entry of overseas retailers. Toys 'R' Us was the first to challenge and break the manufacturer hold over supply chains and prove that a store format similar to, but adapted from, a Western model could work outside the luxury brand sector.

Other than Toys 'R' Us, Gap is the only other directly operated chain in Japan that has a long-term record. From the outset, Gap understood the necessity of operating in the market through its own subsidiary. Choice of location, pace of expansion, direct communication with consumers, building up a substantial local workforce with retail skills, control of brand marketing and retention of income within the group, are all obvious advantages to direct operations. Brands like Louis Vuitton, Chanel, Giorgio Armani, Bvlgari and others have all seen the benefits too.

Despite the overwhelming interest in the Chinese market, Japan is still the most important market in the world for luxury brands. Japanese consumers have a seemingly unending demand for brands and status symbol products. This is an often quoted, but little understood fact that has received surprisingly little academic study.

Figure 1.4 presents a series of results gleaned from trade press over a period of five years that give estimates of Japan's share of worldwide sales for numerous leading brands. It is not uncommon for top brands to gain 10–15 per cent of global sales from Japan alone. In Louis Vuitton, Prada, and Dak's case, it is much higher. Louis Vuitton is rumored by trade press to have as much as 65 per cent of its sales coming from Japanese consumers;

12

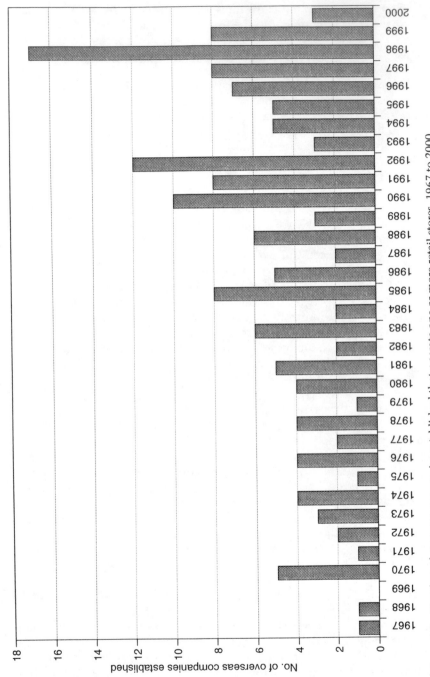

Figure 1.3 Number of overseas companies established that operate one or more retail stores, 1967 to 2000
Source: Shukan Toyo Keizai (1999)

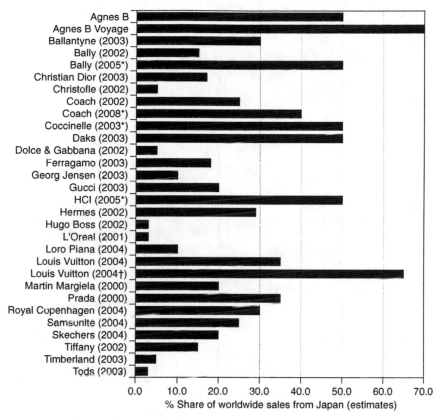

Figure 1.4   Estimated share of worldwide sales coming from Japan for leading brands as reported in trade press, 2000 to 2005
Notes:* reported target; † Louis Vuitton sales from all Japanese consumers worldwide
Source: Trade press

35 per cent in Japan and another 30 per cent from Japanese tourists overseas. On the back of this success, LVMH Group is currently building Christian Dior as the successor to Louis Vuitton even though sales in the latter do not yet show signs of waning. Dior already has an estimated global sales share from Japan of about 18 per cent.

Even though many companies achieve such astounding success in Japan, others have failed to understand the intricacies of the market or to learn from the lessons of their peers. Since 2000, several international retailers have had widely reported exits from Japan. Some left within two years of arriving, some within one year. Boots, Sephora, Office Max, Dairy Farm, Jigsaw, Warehouse, REI and others have all left the market. Aeon Group particularly has had numerous partnerships with overseas companies and some, such as Body Shop, Laura Ashley, and Claire's Accessories, have been successful, but others like Office Max, Rooms to Go, and Oasis, have been dissolved.

In addition, there are many retailers from overseas who are not in the market but should be. Some others are now here but it is too early to say whether they will succeed. These include Tesco, Inditex and Ikea. There remain many others that could succeed in Japan.

Case Study 1.1:   International retail giants take on Japan

In December 1999, there were only two food or general merchandise retailers operating in Japan from overseas, Carrefour and Costco. Since then, Wal-Mart entered with the acquisition of a controlling stake in Seiyu in 2002, and Tesco entered in 2003 with the complete acquisition of C2 Network. German cash and carry retailer Metro also entered in 2003 through a joint venture with Marubeni, but having only opened two stores, both of which it has been careful to keep strictly within the wholesale sector not allowing general consumer access, so far it is difficult to count this as a retail operation.

Wal-Mart, Carrefour, and Tesco are the world's largest retailers and the most international. Unsurprisingly, they have been treated with outright suspicion by domestic suppliers and, thanks to a remarkably hostile press, even by consumers. Each chose a different market entry strategy. Carrefour chose to enter independently. It began with three experimental stores, all in the true hypermarket format, all including a small shopping mall and restaurant area, and all designed to be supplied by domestic Japanese food wholesalers. This format of store was unknown in Japan, the nearest equivalent being Daiei's Hypermart format that had failed so conspicuously due to its large size and poor merchandising. For this reason, consumers flocked to the newly opened stores, visiting in their tens of thousands every day and causing overload at cash registers and service counters. Carrefour offered prices lower than Japanese consumers had ever seen before, even undercutting the much loved Uniqlo by selling fleeces at ¥500 each and oven toasters for ¥1,800, the latter even being Japanese brands like Sharp. Moreover, Carrefour introduced the first low price guarantee ever promoted in Japan, giving consumers the chance to get their money back if they found the same product cheaper elsewhere.

The euphoria did not last, however. Japanese press went out of their way to suggest that, despite all the quantitative evidence, Carrefour was no cheaper than its domestic rivals. Japanese suppliers made life difficult for the French retailer, either by outright refusing to deal with it or making delivery schedules less than certain. The head of one leading wholesaler even went as far to say he would only deal with Carrefour if Aeon and Ito-Yokado allowed and only if Carrefour guaranteed not to undercut wholesale prices (Nikkei Ryutsu Shinbun, 2001). The press also gleefully reported rumors of aggressive dealing by Carrefour, and Kokubu, the leading food wholesaler (see Chapter 4), outright refused to supply the chain.

It took Carrefour three years to add more stores to its network. By 2004 it had three stores around Tokyo and five in Kansai. Newer stores showed clearly that the company had learned a lot from its four years in the market and, again, were phenomenally successful in the short-term with queues of cars waiting for parking for two to three hours every weekend.

Case Study 1.1:   International retail giants take on Japan – *continued*

Yet nothing Carrefour tried was seen as right. The parking was free so people went by car; the company was French so it should only stock French product; the prices were low so quality was clearly poor; stores were too big so Japanese legs got tired. All such complaints were as ridiculous as they sounded, but with just eight stores, Carrefour was never going to beat its journalist critics. Despite clearly showing it had come to terms with many of its problems, faced with shareholder demands for better performance worldwide, Carrefour announced a withdrawal from Japan in early 2005, selling off its sites to Aeon with a deal that Aeon would also get access to some Carrefour own brands – the same ones that Japanese press had so vehemently described as unsuitable for Japanese tastes. Such pressure from boardrooms back in Europe has been a burden to more than a few overseas entrants and provides plenty of ammunition for critics to say foreigners do not understand Japan and how long it takes to be accepted there. In Carrefour's case, however, withdrawal after so much effort and hard work is clearly a missed opportunity.

On the other hand, Carrefour's performance in Japan was important for the entry of both Wal-Mart and Tesco. Whichever company had made the first move into the market would have faced similar, overwhelming opposition, particularly in the supply chain. With Carrefour taking the brunt of such outcry, both Wal-Mart and Tesco went for a different entry strategy.

In April 2002, Wal-Mart acquired a small, 6 per cent stake in Seiyu, the fourth largest GMS chain and previously part of the Saison Group. This small stake cost Wal-Mart a mere ¥6 billion, but with it came two conditions. First, Wal-Mart took an option to acquire up to 66 per cent of Seiyu over the next three years. Second, dealmaker and existing Seiyu shareholder Sumitomo Shoji expanded its own stake in Seiyu to 15.6 per cent. In other words, Wal-Mart not only acquired Seiyu, it also acquired a new partner. Sumitomo not only remains Seiyu's second largest shareholder but it is also the operator of one its main rival chains, Summit. Although Wal-Mart instills fear in competitors no matter where it goes, by working with an existing Japanese chain, it has avoided a lot of the criticism faced by Carrefour. Not that the Japanese press is kind, however. Despite clear improvements in Seiyu's operations since the takeover, with Wal-Mart actually saving the company from bankruptcy, mediocre final results in FY2003 and FY2004 have also been pounced on as evidence that Wal-Mart also does not understand Japan. In reality, improving on Seiyu's dismal past record will take quite some time and Wal-Mart is first improving back office operations and supply chain efficiency.

Tesco entered the market in 2003 with the outright acquisition of a small supermarket chain in Tokyo called C2 Network. The move had even Japanese analysts scrambling to find out more about the company that operates around 80 stores, most under the name Tsurukame. The British retailer later pulled off something of a coup by also winning rehabilitation rights to another small Tokyo supermarket chain called F'rec. Since then, however, Tesco has quietly stayed out of Japanese press for most of the time, possibly a sensible move given the criticism of its international rivals.

See Chapter 3 for more details.

Retailing in Japan: the next 10 years

All too often it is easy to become enthralled or blinded by the stories of doom and gloom surrounding Japan's economy as a whole. It often seems the more one digs deeper into the stories of poor performance, apathy, and general despondency, there is no end to the bleak outlook.

Such gloom mongering may have its place, particularly in spurring politicians into action, but it can be over emphasized. Overseas retailers already in Japan are well aware of the opportunities, as are the international suppliers who they work with. Not surprisingly, they aren't telling, happy as they are to keep this rich market to themselves. Walking around Japan, stores are full. Look carefully and, yes, at many department stores for example, you won't see the manic shopping common in the 1980s, but visit the more interesting and more professional retail chains and it is difficult, even impossible, to reconcile the throngs of shoppers and high sales figures with flat growth in the economy in general.

Japanese retailing is undergoing incredible change – perhaps the widest ranging and most significant change ever to have occurred in the distribution sector of an advanced industrial country. This change has been prompted partly by the consumption downturn in the poorer and more conservative retail sectors, by the entry of efficient, ambitious overseas firms, by deregulation, and also by the simple growth in management ability and strategic foresight at a small number of the most advanced firms. The success of Uniqlo, Comme Ca, Toys 'R' Us, and even ¥100 Shops has little to do with chance and a lot to do with Japan's retail industry coming of age.

These changes are so far reaching that there is a certain amount of inertia and even opposition still to be overcome, but we believe that it has a momentum that is now unstoppable. Japan is not a retail market to have pity for. It is one that offers as much, probably more opportunity, than most in the world. No matter what business you're in, it is a market that will offer unlimited interest and challenge over the next decade.

Japan: a modern retail superpower

In the past, retailing and distribution in Japan has been presented as different from other industrialized countries. In some ways this is true. Japanese consumers of course have their own tastes and shopping habits, stores are operated differently with, for example, a higher emphasis on customer service, and there are other unique attributes over and above the actual merchandise on offer.

As recently as 1990, distribution in Japan was clearly organized and controlled at the behest of manufacturers and wholesalers. Retailers made their money from volume alone and from cooperating with the channel leaders. Rightly or wrongly it was a model that was very different to other advanced economies at the time. Today, however, retailers make their own money through creativity, innovation, branding, marketing, and, simply, through being better retailers. Their day-to-day operations are still based on the local Japanese culture, but their overall strategic goal is the same as in the West: to make money. Moreover, the way they make their money is also the same as in the West. Japanese retailing has modernized and there is no turning back. In fact it has now gone the extra step of expanding outside the confines of the domestic market with many of the best firms active throughout Asia and some even in Europe.

In this book we aim to present a more accurate picture of how Japanese retailing has developed and to illustrate the important trends and features of the system today. The book is split into four main parts.

Part I consists of Chapters 2 to 4, in which we consider some history and background details. Chapter 2 introduces the consumer market, the demographics and basic facts about consumer spending. Chapter 3 considers the historical development of retailing in Japan. Finally, we look at the whole-sale sector and how that has changed and developed in recent years and particularly the influence and role of the general trading houses or *Sogo Shosha*.

In Part II, we introduce food and general merchandise retail formats. In Chapters 5 to 8 we cover department stores, general merchandise stores, supermarkets, and convenience stores. Not all the companies we describe in these chapters are failures or even performing poorly, but the chapters do progress from the relatively poor to relatively good. With a small number of significant exceptions, department stores are in long-term decline, as is much of the GMS chain sector. Supermarkets are the new specialist food retailers that are now only just beginning to modernize and be organized in large scale chains. Convenience stores have been around for more than 30 years in Japan and are the quintessential retail success story, based firmly on the local culture, but clearly specialist and niche market in nature.

In Part III, we cover a broad spectrum of specialty retailing much of which has not been presented before in the literature available in English. Chapter 9 looks at apparel retailing in considerable detail. Chapter 10 covers drugstores, consumer electronics, and home centers, three types of retailing that have grown from almost nothing since 1990. Finally in Chapter 11 we present a summary of other important specialty merchandise sectors. Throughout this section the theme of success through controlled specialty retailing appears again and again. There is still some way to go in various sectors, for example men's apparel, footwear and books, but on the whole these categories are proving beyond doubt that Japan is now far from being the traditional, archaic distribution system that it once was.

Finally, in Part IV, we look at the expansion of Japanese retailers overseas. Japan itself has generated considerable noise concerning the entry of overseas retailers into its own market, at the same time sympathizing loudly at the destructive nature of "foreigners" entering the less developed markets of East Asia. The fact that, outside Japan, Japanese firms themselves are actually foreigners too, is largely overlooked. The growing success of numerous Japanese retailers is now such that they are bursting out of their domestic market and expanding rapidly overseas. Many fully expect to match the achievements of Western companies in China and there are several cases of Japanese retailers already dominating in other Asian markets. The very best Japanese retailers are also looking to enter Europe and North America with one or two firms already leading the way.

In terms of population or long-term, theoretical market potential, Japan clearly cannot be compared to the likes of China, but equally it should not be ignored. Japan is still the second richest consumer market. International retailers have made some headway here in the 1990s and early 2000s, but there is still a surprisingly large number of capable Western retailers that have not even attempted the market, leaving Japanese firms living happily behind the myth that Japan is too difficult and too expensive. Those days are over. The Japanese market is open and Japanese retailing is now as good as any in the world.

Part I

The Background to Japanese Distribution

2
The Japanese Consumer Market

Discussion of Japanese consumers is worthy of a whole book in itself. In this chapter, we offer the basics in terms of demographic and economic data and key consumer characteristics. Providing a full survey of consumer trends, groups and purchasing behaviors is outside the scope of this book. Given the complexity of the subject, even providing basic guidelines could mislead without indepth and therefore long caveats. Accordingly, this chapter provides data on incomes and savings, demographics, macro trends and information on a number of important consumer groups.

Over the years, numerous authors have claimed consumers in Japan are something that they are not: different from anywhere else in the world (for example Hoshino, 1990; Larke, 1991; JETRO, 1987; JCCI, 1989). Of course, Japan has its own cultural tastes, preferences and attitudes, some of which may even be unique, but no more than any other country. Japan is not an easy market by any means, but while adjustments are necessary for any market, the success of an increasing number of overseas retailers in Japan illustrates that the market can be understood.

Given the barrage of negative commentary from the mainstream press about the problems of the Japanese structural economy, it is also important to remember that Japan is one of the richest countries in the world with consumers to match. Consumers want and expect high quality, but they are equally concerned with value for money, entertainment, and personal gratification. Admittedly, Japanese probably eat more raw fish than other nations, but their taste for high quality brands, modern marketing and other tricks of the commercial trade varies little from anywhere else.

Facts and figures

The Japanese population currently consists of some 127 million people and 47 million households (see Somucho, 2004a). Although Japan has approximately the same land area as Germany, some 60 per cent of this is mountainous and uninhabitable. Overall, population density is only around 200 people per square kilometre, but rises to an average of 1,000 people per square kilometre when this uninhabitable land is accounted for (Asahi Shinbunsha, 2004b).

Prefectures (Major cities in brackets)

1. Hokkaido (Sapporo)
2. Aomori
3. Akita
4. Iwate
5. Yamagata
6. Miyagi (Sendai)
7. Fukushima
8. Ibaragi
9. Tochigi
10. Gunma
11. Saitama (Saitama)
12. Chiba
13. Tokyo (Tokyo)
14. Kanagawa (Yokohama)
15. Niigata
16. Toyama
17. Ishikawa
18. Fukui
19. Yamanashi
20. Nagano
21. Gifu
22. Shizuoka
23. Aichi (Nagoya)
24. Mie
25. Shiga
26. Kyoto (Kyoto)
27. Osaka (Osaka)
28. Hyogo (Kobe)
29. Nara
30. Wakayama
31. Tottori
32. Shimane
33. Okayama
34. Hiroshima (Hiroshima)
35. Yamaguchi
36. Tokushima
37. Kagawa
38. Ehime
39. Kochi
40. Fukuoka (Fukuoka & Kitakyushu)
41. Saga
42. Nagasaki
43. Kumamoto
44. Oita
45. Miyazaki
46. Kagoshima
47. Okinawa

Main Regions

A. Hokkaido
B. Tohoku
C. Kanto
D. Chubu
E. Kansai
F. Chugoku
G. Shikoku
H. Kyushu
I. Okinawa

● Major city (over 1 million)

0　　　　600km
Approx. scale

Figure 2.1　Map of Japan

Table 2.1 Comparison of major urban areas in Japan, 2000

Conurbation	Land Area sq km	Ratio %	Population People	Ratio %	Households No.	Ratio %	Businesses No.	Ratio %	Retail Sales ¥ mn	Ratio %
Tokyo Area [1]	11,708	3.1	31,662,748	25.3	12,590,060	27.7	1,547,893	23.0	37,942,806	26.5
Osaka Area [2]	11,449	3.0	16,078,081	12.8	6,650,917	14.6	964,651	14.4	19,286,928	13.5
Nagoya Area	5,152	1.4	6,700,598	5.3	2,335,607	5.1	377,777	5.6	8,086,015	5.6
Fukuoka Area [3]	3,319	0.9	3,618,244	2.9	1,398,785	3.1	189,774	2.8	4,209,382	2.9
Sapporo Area	11,774	3.1	2,794,668	2.2	1,176,462	2.6	127,813	1.9	3,413,788	2.4
Hiroshima Area	8,064	2.1	2,290,355	1.8	896,586	2.0	121,429	1.8	2,827,522	2.0
Sendai Area	6,710	1.8	2,210,254	1.8	753,957	1.7	112,143	1.7	2,557,835	1.8
Large city sub-total	72,943	19.3	85,051,273	67.9	33,852,076	74.4	4,595,905	68.4	101,820,586	71.0
Japan Total	377,837	100.0	125,257,061	100.0	45,498,173	100.0	6,717,025	100.0	143,325,065	100.0

Notes:
[1] Including Yokohama and Kawasaki metropolitan areas
[2] Including Kyoto and Kobe metropolitan areas
[3] Including Kitakyushu metropolitan area
Source: Asahi Shinbunsha (2004a)

Japan has 12 cities with populations that exceed 1 million (see Figure 2.1). Seven of these are along a Pacific Coast corridor that stretches between Tokyo and Kobe. Even taken alone, the Tokyo conurbation accounts for around 30 million people or 25 per cent of the total population (see Table 2.1). Three more cities cluster around Osaka, again a total market of close to 10 million people. Two more, Fukuoka and Kitakyushu, are located in northern Kyushu, and the rest, Hiroshima in southern Honshu, and Sendai and Sapporo in the north, make up smaller, but significant markets.

The concentration of population in these few areas is Japan's single key demographic feature. Overall, more than 80 per cent of the population lives in urban areas, but close to 50 per cent lives in that single 600 km corridor on the Pacific Coast. Consequently, more than a few international companies entering the market have chosen to target these few cities alone, and many do not even venture outside Tokyo. For luxury brands, which often rely on the major department stores as their primary sales route, this is a reasonable strategy. But even in such cases, it demonstrates a rather short-term view of the country. Targeting all of the 12 major cities is, however, a viable and highly feasible option, and today even the luxury brands have large stores in all the top 12.

In other ways too, Japan's demographics are similar to a typical industrialized economy. It has clearly definable and significantly large baby-boom generations, and, related to this, a rapidly aging population overall.

Japan's so-called senior and junior baby booms, those people born immediately after the war and their children who were born in the early 1970s, make up close to 29.7 per cent of the total Japanese population when defined in the broadest terms (see Figure 2.2). Both are significant consumer demographic clusters in terms of lifestyle and psychographics.

The senior baby boom was the first generation of Japanese to be born after the Second World War. Not only that, they were in their late teens and early twenties during the 1960s as Japan went through a period of social reform and market modernization. The 1964 Tokyo Olympics was a major turning point for the prosperity of Japan. They were the first generation to eat McDonald's, drink Coca-Cola, and learn to enjoy life (see Fields, 1983).

Then, as salarymen (a term used for any salaried employee), this was the same generation that pulled Japan to the peak of its economic prosperity. They worked as hard if not harder than their parents, becoming the driving force of the export engine. Better educated than ever before, they were dedicated to the success and health of the nation. In this way, they had inherited all of the traditional values and patriotic feelings of their parents, but combined these with materialistic consumption and the desire for economic success. Such spirit was the subject of much research in the era when the Japanese business model was seen as the one to emulate (see Ohmae, 1991), but it is also one that remains uncommon in a modern industrial economy.

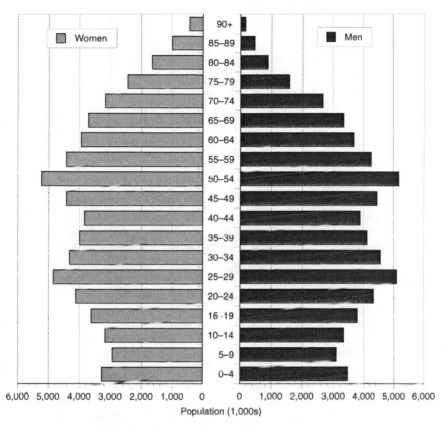

Figure 2.2 Japan's population by age and sex, 2000
Source: Somucho (2001)

There are few countries outside the former Soviet bloc where a social system has developed that so uniformly denigrates the needs and rights of the individual in favor of the company or country as a whole (see Doi, 1973; Kendrick, 1990). The self-sacrificing nature of Japanese society, encouraged as it is by both the political and the education system, was channelled through the senior baby boom generation into economic performance. Some now argue that Japan is finally changing, partly as a result of no longer being the leading manufacturing nation and so requiring that it competes on the terms of other countries rather than its own, but for all but the youngest consumers, there is still this strong sense of cooperative identity within the group, and the advantages of a more individualistic outlook have yet to be realized by the majority.

The aging population problem

Today, the people of the senior baby boom generation are in their late fifties, and include many of the top tier of Japanese industry. Over the next 10 years, they will progress into their retirement years, and, in doing so, become proportionally the largest senior market in the industrialized world. Japan already boasts the longest longevity rates in the world, and at the same time the birth rate continues to decline. As a result, the population pyramid is due to become top-heavy. By 2025, the 15–65 workforce will shrink to only 58.7 per cent of the total population, with those over 65 accounting for 25.8 per cent (see Figure 2.3).

This large proportion of senior consumers represents a major challenge to Japan. Its pension and health care systems are already under tremendous pressure, and economists prefer not to talk about just how bad this will become. Many young people are aware of the problem, and this awareness is often blamed in the popular press for a lowering of the traditional Japanese work ethic among the younger generation (see Nakamae, 1998). Indirect taxation in the form of the Consumption Tax was introduced at 3 per cent by the Nakasone government in 1989 and later increased to 5 per cent in 1999, but even in one of the most expensive countries in the world, this level remains far too low to provide sufficient extra income for the welfare system. In the mid-2000s, as the Japanese economy continues to stutter, the Koizumi government was so concerned with getting people to spend at all costs, further increases in the tax, while necessary, are politically impractical. In addition, it is a fear of the future, particularly long periods of unemployment or retirement, that is prompting consumers to hold on to their cash (see below).

The aging population also represents an opportunity, of course, but one that few companies are taking any great advantage of at present. There has been an increase in welfare and medical services aimed at older people during the past 10 years, but despite the huge proportion of the population about to become senior citizens, Japanese companies are only now offering services aimed at their needs. Whereas in the US, the senior market is targeted as an active, lucrative consumer segment, in Japan it is still seen mostly as one that needs improvements solely in healthcare and other welfare services. There are some examples of products for the more mature consumers, but they are rare. It is certain that such a market will develop in Japan and very soon, providing opportunities for a great many companies. In most cases, it will be mainly domestic companies that benefit as Japanese of this age group tend to remain highly Japan-centric in attitude and purchasing habits, but nimble international firms will be able to reap reward from tapping the market as suppliers and consultants.

27

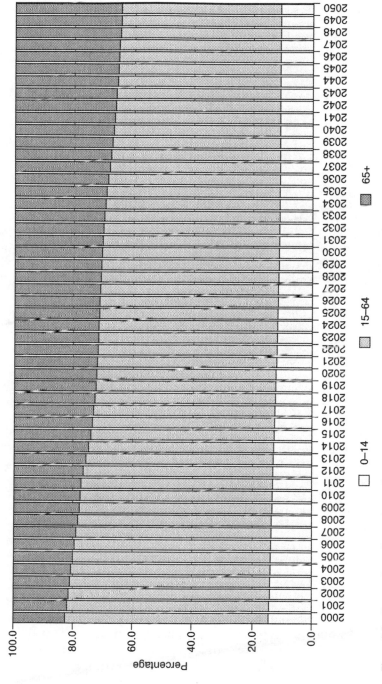

Figure 2.3 Proportion of population by age groups for current and future population of Japan, 2000 to 2050
Source: Kokuritsu Shakai Hoken Jinko Mondai Kenkyusho (2001)

The junior baby boom and other young generations

The junior baby boom generation are the children of the senior baby boom. Like their parents, these consumers have never known war personally, but even more they are now two generations removed from suffering of almost any kind. Unlike their immediate seniors who grew up during the oil crisis of the 1970s, and their immediate juniors, who today face the prospect of the first Japanese post-war generation not to automatically find employment, the junior baby boom are a generation that never knew hardship. They have enjoyed Japan at its most prosperous, and those at the older end of the 20–34 year-old group are currently the mainstay of Japan's young salaried workforce.

This affluence has given this generation a remarkable propensity to consume. Their parents strove for a better home and a better life, but the junior baby boom are more interested in lifestyle and enjoyment of the present. They have not developed into the lazy, non-working rebels that Japanese sociologists love to predict with every passing generation; rather they work almost as hard as their parents, but at the same time they have learned to mistrust the spirit of unthinking patriotism and loyalty to the group. They are more self-centered, more time focused, and expect quicker reward. It was they who began the Western practice of career changing and job-hopping, something that their parents would never do and still frown upon, but something that has become normal and accepted over the past 10 years. The trend began as many were forced to seek new jobs during the economic slowdown of the 1990s, but both young employee and company alike soon recognized the benefits of gaining personal skills and selling them in an open labor market. This, as described below, is one of the most significant changes in Japanese society since the War.

In between the senior and junior baby booms is a gap of low birth rate – the waist of the population pyramid in Figure 2.2. This generation, now in its thirties and early forties, was known during its youth as the *shinjinrui* – literally the new people types (see Fields, 1986). *Shinjinrui* were labelled, like all youth in Japan, as rebellious and different. Academics predicted it would be the first generation to change traditional social norms. Of course, it didn't happen. This generation has turned out to be just as work orientated and overtime prone as their forebears. For some sociologists, such a result is seen as almost disappointing. They may get a second chance, however, as Japan is set to have long periods of low birth rates and increasing numbers of single person families (see Figure 2.4).

Something similar is now occurring with the teenagers and students of today. Like the *shinjinrui*, they too come from a low birthrate generation, much smaller in numbers than the junior baby boom that preceded them. They are Japan's grunge generation. Branding and materialistic consumer behavior is still the norm, but now brands need to be cool and trendy, and

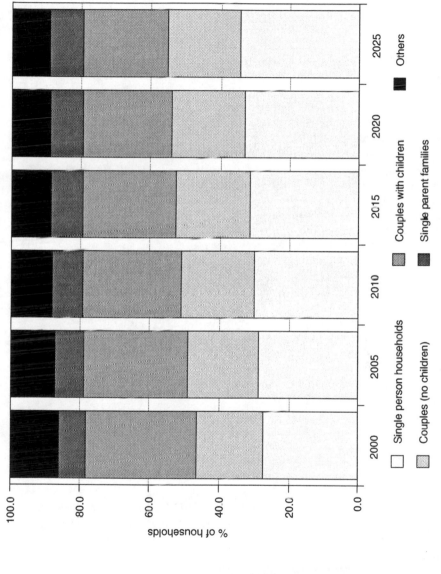

Figure 2.4 Japan's households by household numbers, 2000 to 2025 projections
Source: Kokuritsu Shakai Hoken Jinko Mondai Kenkyusho (2001)

allow for some adaptation to individual taste. More relaxed styles (older generations would say, scruffiness) are also now OK as long as they are fashionable, and purchase of the leading brands, simply because they are the leading brands, is no longer automatic (JapanConsuming, 2002a)

As a result, instead of broadly following trends in the USA and Europe, younger consumers have developed their own unique fashion sense. This is often described as a mixture of grunge, rap, and reggae, but with a distinct Asian flavor. It is coupled with homegrown Japanese music and other youth culture. A key indication that this is a new development is the spread of Japanese youth culture to other parts of Asia. Japanese music, fashion, and TV have become popular in Hong Kong, Taiwan, Singapore, and, suddenly since 2004, even in South Korea. Many fashion brands and pop bands are also finding their way into the lucrative Chinese market and are being well received.

Again, sociologists are quick to insist that the latest youth generation will change Japanese values (Kingston, 2004). Again, they are seen as less willing to work, more individualistic, and far more leisure orientated. This may well turn out to be no more than wishful thinking but there are several signs to suggest more optimism (Kingston, 2004: pp. 257–305). Many Japanese freely and frequently admit to a need for Japan to change its group orientated, rather static social structure in favor of something more dynamic and flexible. The fear of individual responsibility at all levels of life and business is something that has caused the country some problems over the past decade (Kerr, 2002; Nakamae, 1998), but at the same time, such behavior is also something that has defined Japan, is both a strength and a weakness, and it is unlikely to change quickly.

Socio-political considerations aside, this generation, comfortable in themselves, with the freedom to experiment with their working life and leisure time, and backed up by generations of prodigious savings, is an important and discerning consumer market.

The hidden, not lost, decade

In general terms, household spending patterns mirror those in other industrialized nations. Food expenditure, for example, continues to fall as a proportion of the total, while communication expenses grow along with expenditure on such things as education, medical, and leisure (see Table 2.2 below). Japanese consumers spend a large, but rapidly falling amount on apparel, and on social exchanges such as gifts. They also have a famously high propensity to save.

The 1990s saw household income and expenditure remain totally flat. The most significant change, however, was the large increase in monthly household savings rates. Figure 2.5 shows the growth in savings values between 1980 and 2003. At their peak, working households were saving

31

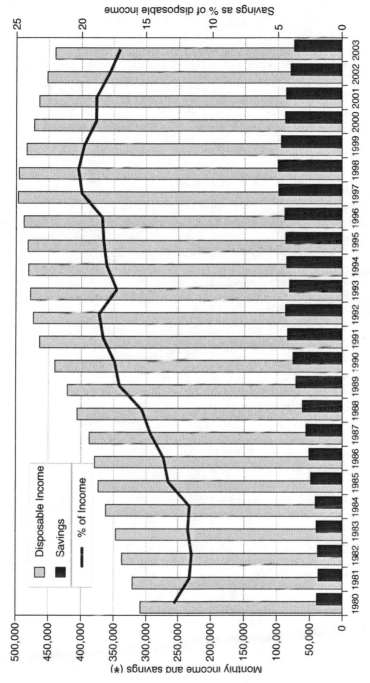

Figure 2.5 Monthly disposable income and savings for working households, 1980 to 2003
Source: Somucho (2004b)

more than ¥100,000 a month in 1998, amounting to some 20 per cent of monthly disposable income. This figure has fallen more recently, but even in 2003, the average was ¥75,000 a month or more than 17 per cent of income. As a result, in 2003, the total average savings for all households were a little over ¥17.8 million, with working households holding an average of some ¥13.6 million. This compared with an average annual income per working household of ¥7.69 million.

Unlike in some Western nations where consumer debt is a problem, Japanese consumers have a lot of money in the bank waiting to be spent. The problem has been finding ways to convince them to part with it. As illustrated in Part 2 of this book, the success that some companies have had while others failed also points to consumer boredom just as much as towards lack of confidence.

Consumer confidence has, however been a problem. In the 1990s, unemployment rose for the first time since the War. By the end of the decade, official figures put unemployment at around 4.5 per cent on average. Rates were lowest in Tokyo at around 3.8 per cent, but rose steadily out in the regions, exceeding 5.5 per cent in Hokkaido and 5.4 per cent in Kyushu. Along with increasing acceptance of career changes, job-hopping and head-hunting, all new concepts for most adult Japanese, the term "restructuring" (or *resutora*) entered the evolving Japanese vocabulary. People, for the first time, truly began to fear for their jobs and for the sustainability of their personal income. This added further to the desire to save rather than consume, and represents a problem that the government has failed to solve.

Compared to the United Kingdom of the 1980s or even much of Europe today, for example, an employment rate of 4 to 5 per cent does not seem overly high. Indeed, a number of Japanese economists also believe that a move away from full employment and more towards a more leisure-based society would be a preferable solution to Japan's long-term problems, despite the major cultural and social shift this would still entail (see Nakamae, 1998). Nevertheless, unemployment means rejection from the group, and for men in particular, is a far more serious problem than simply lack of income. Some men find it very hard to admit to their families that they have lost their jobs because work is the man's primary role. Both men and women in society cling to this belief, and without work, a man's personally perceived value can drop to alarming degrees. Such a comment may seem needlessly emotional to some, if it were not for recent suicide statistics (see Figure 2.6). Suicide rates are generally higher for men than women, and for older people rather than younger, but between 1996 and 2000 alone, suicides of men aged 50–59 alone rose some 76 per cent. This age group corresponds with the age of men most likely to lose their jobs as a result of restructuring and it is easy to speculate that the large increase is at least partly to blame on unemployment trends. Male suicide now stands at an all

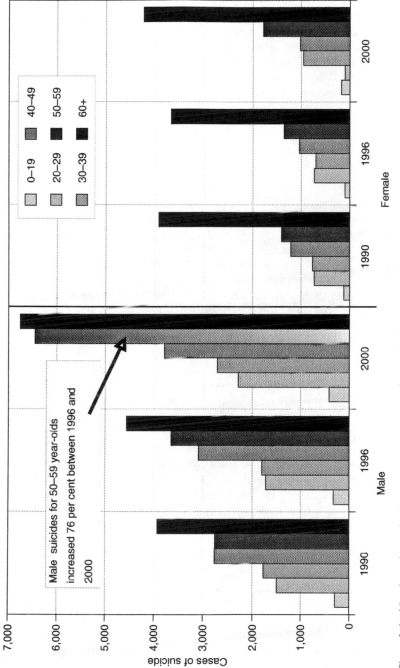

Figure 2.6 Number of suicides by age and sex, 1990, 1996 and 2000
Source: Asahi Shinbunsha (2004b)

time high with more than 34,427 cases in 2003 beating the previous record set in 2000.

Both the savings and unemployment rates are problems of great concern and urgency for any government. In Japan, where the social consequences of losing a career job are so significant, it is a problem that cannot be ignored. It also indicates how hard Japan needs to work to reform its social and economic structure, and, some would say, its attitude to work as a whole. The types of problems it faces also show that simply resurrecting the systems of the past are unlikely to solve the problem in the long run.

Category spending patterns

As already noted, Japan's overall spending patterns resemble that of a typical advanced economy. Table 2.2 illustrates changes in spending for the main product categories that come under government statistics. In 2003, the average working household spent some ¥325,823 per month. Of this, the main categories were food (21.9 per cent) and Other Consumption (24.2 per cent). The proportion of expenditure on food has been falling steadily for the past decade, and fell in total volume for seven of the past 10 years. "Other Consumption" represents a wide range of items including pocket money and spending on obligatory gifts that are given at mid-year and end of year seasons in recognition of favors done or expected. The volume spent on such items has also been falling in recent years as it is seen as an unnecessary expense.

Considered over the past 20 years, apparel spending has fallen by a larger proportion than any other category. This is partly due to the rapid and, from a distribution perspective, significant fall in prices as well as a general fall in volume of spending. Since 1992 spending on apparel has fallen by large percentages every year.

Categories where households are spending more include housing, utilities, medical expenses and transport and communications. In 2003 housing costs had fallen to similar levels to 1993, although economists expect rents to begin to rise again in the near future. The proportion of expenditure given over to housing and rent is small due to the fact that so many Japanese actually own their own homes. On average, utility costs actually are higher than rents. They remain at a high level in terms of overall expenditure, but have remained stable due to price stability in the 1990s.

Transport costs have risen in recent years, but only marginally as, for average households, expenditure on gasoline remains a minor expense and commuting expenses have stayed static. For communications, however, mobile phones and, more recently, high speed Internet services, have a high and increasing diffusion rate that have swollen this expenditure category. It is not uncommon for individual consumers to change mobile phone models twice a year, and, although younger consumers spend more,

Table 2.2 Monthly expenditure for working households, 1985 to 2003

	Disposable Income	Total	Food	Rent	Utilities	Furniture & Household	Clothing	Insurance & Medical	Transport & Communications	Education	Leisure	Other Consumption	Non Consumption
												Consumption Expenditure	
1985	360,642	289,489	74,369	13,748	17,125	12,182	20,176	6,814	27,950	12,157	25,269	79,699	71,153
1986	367,052	293,630	74,889	14,215	16,912	11,388	20,554	6,985	28,819	13,118	26,142	80,109	73,422
1987	369,214	295,915	73,431	15,170	15,655	12,632	20,834	7,255	30,069	13,570	26,072	81,227	73,299
1988	382,517	307,204	74,827	15,722	15,701	12,235	21,715	7,753	31,210	14,522	28,109	85,410	75,313
1989	390,904	316,489	76,794	15,846	15,887	12,388	22,577	8,092	32,217	15,349	29,585	87,753	74,415
1990	412,813	331,595	79,993	16,475	16,797	13,103	23,902	8,670	33,499	16,827	31,761	90,569	81,218
1991	430,380	345,473	83,051	18,234	17,642	13,944	24,451	8,776	34,659	17,129	32,861	94,726	84,907
1992	442,937	352,820	83,445	20,191	18,094	13,560	24,033	9,125	35,304	18,625	34,279	96,164	90,117
1993	447,666	355,276	82,477	20,258	18,674	13,144	23,134	9,586	38,561	18,269	34,799	96,373	92,390
1994	439,112	353,116	81,513	22,446	19,150	13,239	21,963	9,474	37,301	18,988	34,549	94,491	85,996
1995	438,307	349,663	78,947	23,412	19,551	13,040	21,085	9,334	38,524	18,467	33,221	94,082	88,644
1996	442,679	351,755	78,131	24,679	19,971	12,811	20,438	9,858	40,611	18,511	33,804	92,939	90,924
1997	455,815	357,636	79,879	24,114	20,841	12,599	20,264	10,386	41,552	19,162	34,295	94,543	98,179
1998	446,581	353,552	80,169	22,242	20,839	12,186	19,081	10,565	41,295	18,766	34,484	93,926	93,029
1999	436,943	346,177	78,059	22,614	20,680	12,110	18,876	10,880	40,610	17,813	35,284	89,246	90,766
2000	429,109	340,977	74,889	21,674	21,124	11,208	17,192	10,865	43,660	18,214	33,831	88,320	88,132
2001	421,479	335,042	73,180	22,168	21,072	11,319	16,192	10,760	43,955	17,668	33,522	85,206	86,437
2002	416,427	330,651	73,396	21,528	20,740	10,801	15,823	10,456	43,544	17,499	33,142	83,721	85,776
2003	409,903	325,823	71,606	22,248	20,712	10,378	15,450	11,498	44,622	18,021	32,303	78,985	84,081

Notes: To 1992 only the income of male household heads was included. After 1992 spouse income was also included, making figures incompatible with older statistics.
Source: Somucho (2004b)

the amount spent on fees and usage has increased monthly for a number of years.

Medical and education expenditure have both increased overall in recent years largely due to a greater number of services available and consumers' willingness to pay for such things rather than to buy more tangible goods. Spending in these areas is often seen as an investment for the future, whether for the consumers themselves or for their children.

Summary: consumers are consumers

It would be a mistake to expect Japanese consumers to act precisely as consumers do in other countries. It is equally a problem to consider them a unique, more complicated group than elsewhere. Statistical data describing consumers in Japan is freely available and the number of companies offering skilled market research services has increased in recent years. Consumers can and should be understood to the fullest extent. The old, deliberately misleading adage that consumers in Japan are different and, therefore, difficult is now largely accepted as the smokescreen it always was, although it is still surprising how many overseas firms are taken in by it.

As in every country and culture, where Japanese consumers do differ is largely in their most micro of behaviors. For supermarkets and other food related companies, consumer tastes and preferences are vital and culturally determined, as are purchasing rates and volumes. For household and interior goods firms, an understanding of household norms and behaviors is equally important, but even here there are many similarities to the rest of Asia. For apparel firms, sizes and branding are crucial, but, yet again, little different with the rest of Asia. In fact, Japanese body sizes are now probably closer to the European average than that of China or Korea.

True, it is easy to misunderstand, and equally clear that even Japanese retailers have a hard time, but there is little excuse to ignore the problem as just being too difficult to solve. The signs of falling confidence caused few changes in retail strategy in the early 1990s largely because the largest firms were so tightly tied into systems that put consumers last behind the needs of suppliers. For the majority of firms, consumers were simply workers spending their salaries, so, of course, firms decided they understood the market because they thought they were themselves the market. This mistaken attitude has now evaporated thanks to the efforts of companies like Aeon, Fast Retailing, and Yamada Denki. Whereas in the past, the Japanese market employed a scattergun approach, presenting consumers with such a huge variety of both products and retail stores that some could not help but succeed, this has now been adapted to a much more modern, efficient system of providing a more focused, targeted market response to actual consumer requirements.

This situation has generated a positive spiral, with competition forcing retailers to make more effort to win over consumers. In the traditional distribution system, manufacturers dominated supply chains, effectively reducing competition at the retail stage to a minimum, ensuring that retailers obeyed pricing and merchandising rules, and meaning there was little need for retailers to think much about branding and store marketing. With the frenetic pace of economic growth before the 1990s this did not matter. Retail supply was still keeping pace with demand. Retail expansion continued in the 1990s but met with a mature economy with flat income growth. As consumer confidence plummeted, for the first time in Japanese history, retail capacity exceeded consumer demand. Japanese consumers now had more choice than ever and competition increased. The second half of the 1990s brought five years of bankruptcies, mergers, deregulation, and liberalization in response to this tougher environment. At the same time, the market has seen the dramatic arrival of genuine store branding, improved merchandising and lower prices.

Today high household savings rates are now declining gradually. In the past 10 years or so, an increasing number of retailers have engineered ways to encourage consumers to part with their jealously guarded savings, and, on seeing these results, all but the most conservative or debt-ridden firms have made attempts to copy the strategy. Saving is still high compared to the West, and consumer confidence remains patchy in the mid-2000s, but equally, long years of postponing spending have also increased the level of consumer boredom, which the better retailers have now moved to alleviate.

Consumers have rewarded those retailers that have responded, making more educated and better informed choices than ever before. This trend will continue. For the most part, the leaders of the new generation of confident, more self-assured consumers are rejecting aggressive or complacent marketing techniques. Retailers and brands will have to continue to work harder for consumer attention. Having said that, all things are relative and, in many sectors, retail competition remains at a low level. There is still a lot of opportunity for better operated, modern retail businesses in Japan simply because it remains a relatively rare phenomenon. The situation is changing rapidly, but both domestic and overseas firms that look closely and intelligently at the market will see niches yet to be filled.

3
Development of Modern Retailing

Japan is a modern, industrialized nation in every sense. The retail and distribution system still receives occasional criticism as being somehow different from those in other advanced countries, but it is now rare to hear claims that it operates as some form of non-tariff barrier to trade, unlike the case in the early 1990s (see Czinkota and Kotabe, 1993; Maruyama et al, 1989). The overall structure of distribution is different to Europe and the US but most differences are insignificant from the point of view of corporate business, existing largely at the micro level. As this book aims to illustrate, in many sectors, retailing in Japan is as advanced or even more advanced than in other countries. The level of sophistication, efficiency and, very importantly, profitability in convenience store retailing, home center retailing, increasingly at leading GMS chains and apparel retailers all indicates how much Japanese retailing has changed since the mid-1990s. This chapter provides a brief historical perspective of Japanese retailing and the overall macro level trends and statistics for the industry.

Quantity not quality

As already noted in Chapter 1, Japan has a lot of shops. Every three years, the Ministry of Economy, Trade and Industry (METI, but formerly MITI: the Ministry of International Trade and Industry) conducts a detailed Census of Commerce. It provides an overall and long-term picture of how Japan's distribution system is changing. The most recent complete survey was completed in 2002.

Tables 3.1 and 3.3 show results of the most recent Census. Retail sales space continued to grow during the three years (an extraordinary, limited Census was carried out in 1999), up 5.1 per cent to 146.4 million sqm from 133.878 million sqm in 1999, although in the same period overall retail sales fell 6.1 per cent to ¥135.12 trillion. The number of retail outlets peaked back in 1982 at over 1.6 million shops, but even after 20 years of decline, in 2002 Japan still had 1,300,043 outlets. The average size of a single retail store had grown to a startlingly unimpressive 17.6 sqm, and the average annual sales per store were just ¥960,087, not even a subsistence income. As mentioned in

Table 3.1 Retail sector statistics from Census of Commerce, 1991 to 2002

Census Results	1991	89–91 % Change	1994	91–94 % Change	1997	94–97 % Change	1999	97–99 % Change	2002[1]	99–02 % Change
Businesses	1,294,532	-4.0	1,197,039	-7.5	1,109,679	-7.3	1,013,937	-8.6	885,196	-12.7
Outlets	1,605,583	-0.9	1,499,948	-6.6	1,419,696	-5.4	1,406,884	-0.9	1,300,043	-7.6
Employees	7,000,226	2.2	7,384,177	5.5	7,350,712	-0.5	8,028,558	9.2	7,973,599	-0.7
Sales Space (sqm)	109,901,497	7.7	121,623,712	10.7	128,083,639	5.3	133,869,296	4.5	140,641,482	5.1
Sales (¥ mn)	142,291,133	23.9	143,325,065	0.7	147,743,116	3.1	143,832,551	-2.6	135,125,323	-6.1
Averages										
Outlets/Business	1.24	3.2	1.25	1.0	1.28	2.1	1.39	8.5	1.47	5.8
Employees/Outlet	4.36	3.1	4.92	12.9	5.18	5.2	5.71	10.2	6.13	7.5
Sales Space (sqm)/Outlet	15.70	5.4	16.47	4.5	17.42	5.8	16.67	-4.3	17.64	5.8
Sales (¥ mn)/Outlet	1.29	15.1	1.18	-9.0	1.15	-2.1	1.07	-6.9	0.96	-10.6

Notes:
[1] Business numbers for 2002 estimated by authors
Source: METI (2003)

Chapter 1, the rate of decline has actually increased, with a net average of 98 stores per day going out of business between 1999 and 2002.

Overall, each outlet serves just 97 people in Japan, or, alternatively, there are 10 shops per 1,000 people. Both figures are significantly different from what would be expected in Western Europe or North America. Of course, most of these shops are small, independent retailers. As shown in Figure 3.1, non-incorporated retailers, which can be assumed to make up the majority of small, independent retailers, accounted for 44.9 per cent of total stores in 2002, but only 25.8 per cent of employees and only 11.5 per cent of sales. This situation is not as extreme as in the wholesale sector (see Chapter 4), but as in other industrialized nations it does illustrate the declining importance of small business retailing.

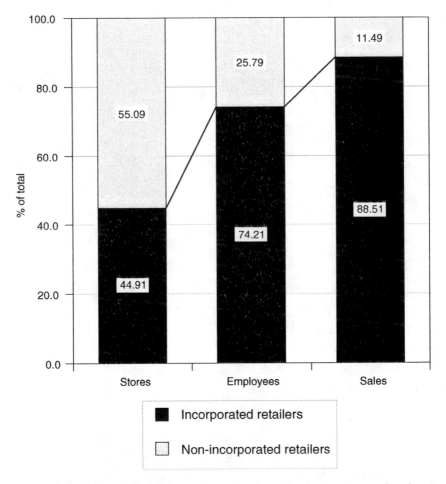

Figure 3.1 Relative share of stores, employees and sales for incorporated and non-incorporated retailers, 2002
Source: Calculated from METI (2003)

The main retail sectors

METI distinguishes eight major business sectors in retailing (Table 3.2). These are determined largely by size of store, proportion of sales within the three major categories of food, apparel and household goods, service format (self-service or full-service) and general industrial categorization. These definitions are used in some other chapters of this book. In many cases, however, they are too broadly based on product category rather than retail format, so we expand on the METI definitions wherever possible. They do provide a useful overview of the broadest types of retail format operating in Japan, however, and allow analysis of the volume of business within each major type.

Table 3.3 provides a detailed statistical breakdown of all of the broadest retail formats in Japan. These are useful summary figures showing the number of department stores, general merchandise stores, and convenience stores, along with their relative market share, employee numbers and sales space. Interpreting data for specialty stores is more difficult because of the overlap between chain-operated specialty stores and small independent stores. Depending on store size and on the operator's definition of self-service as opposed to full-service, a specialty apparel store might appear in either the Specialty Self-Service or the Specialty Store section. It is even possible that different stores from the same retail chain could appear in different business categories. The approach of counting stores rather than businesses is adopted in the official statistics because of the large number of very small stores, but is often unhelpful.

What is clear from Table 3.3, however, are the growing and declining sectors. Whereas both the department store and the general merchandise self-service categories declined overall, larger stores did significantly better than smaller ones. Apparel self-service specialty stores saw store numbers increase, with sales rising 20 per cent and sales space up 18 per cent, reflecting the improvement in sales densities as well as market share. Food specialty stores declined in number and turnover but sales space actually increased, illustrating the increase in large store numbers from companies like Aeon and Ito-Yokado (see Chapter 6).

The "Other Retail" and non-self-service categories, which signify smaller retail stores, also declined. These make up 22.7 per cent of all retail stores and are generally the smallest independent retailers. This section alone saw sales decline but in reality this decline includes some aberrations due to changes in counting methods in the most recent survey.

Several sectors within the industry also enjoyed rapid expansion, notably home centers, supermarkets and drugstores. From 1999 to 2002, the home center category (see Chapter 10) alone saw sales space increase 44.1 per cent and sales growth of 27.9 per cent. Drug and cosmetics retailers (see Chapter 10) added 20.2 per cent more sales space but saw sales growth of

Table 3.2 Retail Business Classifications used in METI Census of Commerce for 2002

Classification	1. Department Stores		2. General Merchandise Stores		3. Specialty Merchandise				4. Convenience Stores	
	Large scale	Others	Large scale	Medium scale	Apparel	Food	Household	(of which home centers)		(of which 24 hour operations)
Self-Service	No		Yes		Yes				Yes	
Product Category	No less than 10% and no more than 70% of sales from any of apparel, food or household		No less than 10% and no more than 70% of sales from any of apparel, food or household		70% or more apparel	70% or more food	70% or more household	Under 70% sales from 5991–2, & 6022 combined	Dealing with food and drink	
Sales space	Over 3,000 sqm (6,000 sqm in designated cities)		Over 3,000 sqm (6,000 sqm in designated cities)			Over 250 sqm			Between 30 sqm and 250 sqm	
Operating Hours									More than 14 hours a day	24 hours a day
Notes	Employing 50 people or more. Industrial classification 551		Employing 50 people or more. Industrial classification 551						Includes stores not only in 5791	

Table 3.2 Retail Business Classifications used in METI Census of Commerce for 2002 – *continued*

5. Drugstores	6. Other Specialty	7. Specialty Stores			8. Semi-Specialty Stores			9. Other retailers (of which general merchandise)
		Apparel	Food	Household	Apparel	Food	Household	
Yes	Yes		No			No		No
Industrial classification 601, selling items from 6011		90% or more from 561–4, 5691–2, 5699	90% or more from 572–7, 5792–7, 5799	90% or more from 5811–4, 582, 591–2, 599, 601–7, 6091–7, 6099	50% or more apparel	50% or more food	50% or more household	
	All other self-service stores except 2, 3, 4, & 5 above				Except stores included in 7 above			Stores not included in 1, 7, 8 above

Notes:
Self-service stores operated at least 50 per cent of floor space as self-service
Industrial classifications are Apparel (56), Food (57), Household goods (58–60)
Definitions for 'Home Centers' and 'Drugstores' were introduced in 2002

Source: Adapted and translated from METI (2003, p. 9)

Table 3.3 Key statistics for main retail categories in Census of Commerce, 1997 to 2002

	Store Numbers			Employees		
	1997	1999	2002	1997	1999	2002
Total	1,499,948	1,406,884	1,300,043	7,384,177	8,028,558	7,973,599
Department stores	463	394	357	205,493	168,343	139,193
Large department stores	398	365	318	199,282	165,289	131,646
Other department stores	65	29	39	6,211	3,054	7,547
Self-service stores	1,804	1,670	1,672	272,426	320,422	383,668
Large self-service stores	1,360	1,461	1,503	232,669	296,905	363,675
Medium self-service stores	444	209	169	39,757	23,517	19,993
Specialty self-service stores	25,171	33,381	37,037	627,593	996,008	1,134,143
Apparel	3,111	4,780	6,324	34,712	52,755	77,694
Food	16,096	18,707	17,692	497,556	742,991	782,817
Household	5,964	9,894	13,021	95,325	200,262	273,632
(of which home centers)		2,911	4,356		83,154	125,639
Convenience stores	28,226	39,561	41,769	302,233	536,429	596,332
(of which 24 hour open)	13,431	25,911	32,431	198,063	425,378	515,744
Drugstores		10,917	14,673		69,288	113,982
Other self-service	84,874	77,667	66,163	404,890	452,890	439,496
(of which general merchandise)		1,020	782		9,810	8,708
Specialty stores	930,143	921,801	774,905	3,917,056	4,188,124	3,661,906
Apparel	147,478	134,329	106,122	461,566	423,411	344,659
Food	263,681	249,287	204,081	1,028,615	1,063,048	947,080
Household	518,984	538,185	464,702	2,426,875	2,701,665	2,370,167
Small retailing	427,099	318,161	361,238	1,643,860	1,280,899	1,494,219
Apparel	65,733	54,928	65,569	251,302	227,449	251,247
Food	185,509	131,465	140,107	605,638	471,793	515,568
Household	175,857	131,768	155,562	786,920	581,657	727,404
Other retailers	2,168	3,332	2,229	10,626	16,155	10,660
(of which general merchandise)		3,331	2,085		16,105	9,524

Table 3.3 Key statistics for main retail categories in Census of Commerce, 1997 to 2002 – *continued*

	Sales (¥1 billion)			Sales space (1,000 sqm)		
	1997	1999	2002	1997	1999	2002
Total	143,832.6	135,125.3	143,325.1	121,623.7	133,869.3	140,641.5
Department stores	10,640.3	9,705.5	8,021.2	7,124.1	7,290.2	6,825.5
Large department stores	10,364.5	9,517.6	7,649.8	7,057.4	7,262.6	6,797.1
Other department stores	275.8	187.9	371.4	66.7	27.6	28.4
Self-service stores	9,335.9	8,849.7	8,917.0	11,394.3	13,393.0	14,879.8
Large self-service stores	8,069.3	8,264.2	8,463.6	10,168.6	12,753.4	14,358.2
Medium self-service stores	1,266.6	585.4	453.3	1,225.7	639.6	521.7
Specialty self-service stores	17,134.9	23,121.2	23,631.6	17,239.7	28,864.1	34,774.9
Apparel	891.4	1,270.7	1,583.3	1,882.4	3,264.7	3,941.2
Food	13,197.7	16,748.0	15,903.2	10,410.1	15,569.2	16,396.6
Household	3,045.8	5,102.5	6,145.1	4,947.2	10,030.2	14,437.1
(of which home centers)		2,402.4	3,073.2		5,250.1	8,386.2
Convenience stores	4,011.5	6,127.0	6,713.7	2,764.3	4,090.2	4,481.0
(of which 24 hour open)	2,350.1	4,665.4	5,718.6	1,440.8	2,854.5	3,603.2
Drugstores		1,495.0	2,495.7		1,843.0	3,227.1
Other self-service	8,343.3	7,561.6	6,808.2	8,227.6	8,674.2	8,135.8
(of which general merchandise)		258.7	191.3		394.6	312.9
Specialty stores	61,018.3	62,643.5	52,166.8	48,222.1	47,331.6	43,291.9
Apparel	7,319.0	5,926.6	4,414.7	9,532.1	8,785.3	7,231.0
Food	10,451.6	9,206.8	7,389.3	8,804.4	8,097.2	6,869.1
Household	43,247.7	47,510.0	40,362.8	29,885.6	30,449.1	29,191.7

Table 3.3 Key statistics for main retail categories in Census of Commerce, 1997 to 2002 – *continued*

	Sales (¥1 billion)			Sales space (1,000 sqm)		
	1997	1999	2002	1997	1999	2002
Small retailing	32,579.2	23,958.4	26,141.5	26,417.3	22,029.3	24,768.3
Apparel	5,038.6	5,041.4	4,224.1	6,521.1	6,518.5	6,843.5
Food	9,429.7	6,680.2	6,758.1	9,046.8	6,399.7	7,204.3
Household	18,110.9	12,236.8	15,159.3	10,849.5	9,111.1	10,720.5
Other retailers	261.7	370.7	229.7	234.3	353.7	257.2
(of which general merchandise)		369.8	174.2		353.7	221.5

Notes:
Figures for the 1999 survey supplement omitted stores in the 1997 survey
Due to counting changes in the 2002 census, 1999 figures have been adjusted for comparison
Source: METI (2003)

66.9 per cent. Most other sectors had a much tougher time, particularly the department store sector (see Chapter 5) where sales fell 17.4 per cent in the same period. Another statistic that comes as no surprise is the saturation in the convenience store sector (see Chapter 8). Although sales were up 9.6 per cent, there were close to 40,000 outlets by 2002, with most new stores replacing poor performing locations.

As mentioned above, the rapid net decline in small stores at 98 per day shows better than any statistic the speed and extent that Japanese distribution is modernizing and moving towards models common in other industrialized nations. The fragmented, independent retailer based structure of Japanese retailing is a thing of the past. Traditionally, much of this excess capacity has been soaked up by expanding, modern chain operations. The convenience store sector in particular has been very successful at converting small retail locations, and indeed their owners, into franchisees (see Chapter 8). Other saviors have been food chains like McDonalds, Dennys, Subway and Starbucks. Unfortunately for the independent stores that remain, some of these retail sectors are also fast reaching saturation. Overall, 1.3 million retail shops is still a lot of shops for a country with a land area only slightly larger than Germany. The Census statistics clearly show the long-term trend of falling store numbers, and a major shift from small, independent retail businesses to larger, incorporated companies.

The rise of the general merchandise stores

Although the Japanese retail system is rapidly modernizing, there have long been many large, corporate retail companies. Many of these have operated in the traditional distribution system for far too long, dominated and dictated to by manufacturers and acting as shop windows for manufacturer planned and marketed product. Those that have failed to keep pace with this new shift to retailer control of channels have found life more than a little difficult in recent years. In addition, during the 1980s, some of the largest firms sought to escape the confines of the retail business through wide ranging diversification, the result of which was heavy debt burdens. In order to understand why this came about, it is useful to briefly consider the last 30 years and how corporate retailing in Japan developed.

Up to the 1970s, Japan's largest and most powerful retailers were still nationwide department store chains such as Mitsukoshi, Daimaru, Takashimaya, and Matsuzakaya. These companies trace their history back, not in decades, but in centuries. Both Mitsukoshi and Matsuzakaya proudly claim their retail origins from the early 1600s, the beginning of the Tokugawa period in Japan. Others, including Takashimaya and Sogo, began life in the middle of the 19th century. Not surprising, then, that these were the biggest and the most influential retailers for the first half of the

20th century. Restrictive legislation on the opening of large stores was aimed originally at curtailing this power (see Larke, 1994).

In the 1950s and 1960s, however, Japan's chain stores came to life and spread quickly around the country. The leading companies at the time were Daiei, Ito-Yokado and Uny. Aeon, or Jusco as it was then, was still a much smaller operation (see Larke, 1994; Meyer-Ohle, 2003).

In 1972, Daiei became Japan's largest retailer, surpassing Mitsukoshi and other large department stores for the first time. This was seen as a major change to distribution and prompted alterations in the so-called Large Retail Store Law in 1974 in order to strengthen the restrictions not just on department stores, but also on general merchandise stores.

The remainder of the 1970s continued with the rest of the Japanese economy quickly overcoming the OPEC crisis and gearing up to the height of its power as an export driven nation. By 1980, the largest retailers were all chain stores, and in 1982, for the first time since WWII, MITI's Census of Commerce recorded a fall in the number of retail stores overall. It took another 10 years, and significant pressure from overseas politicians, notably in the US, to push Japan further towards a more modernized distribution system, but at this point, the decline of the fragmented system of small unit retailing and wholesaling had begun. As already mentioned, small store numbers have been falling for the past 20 years, and, despite changes in survey counting, numbers of wholesale outlets have followed the same downward trend as a result (see Chapter 4).

The consequences of the collapse in asset prices

The next major stage in the development of the distribution system was the end of the Japanese economic boom in 1990–1. Debate still rages even today about what really happened in the 1980s and how the economy overheated, but, in hindsight, few people disagree that the crisis could have been avoided. For retailers, the sudden and dramatic switch from a vibrant and consumption based economy to a stagnant and savings based one was a shock that even the best companies took some time to recover from. Fifteen years on, the better companies have emerged lean and efficient, but others have suffered a 15-year decline, and their continued survival would be impossible in almost any other economy. There remain a lot of questions over why retailers found it so difficult to reinvent themselves and adjust to the new economic conditions, and why some so clearly still have not done so. Several major companies declared bankruptcy in what became the largest shakeout in the history of Japanese distribution, and others are certain to follow. This would have happened faster and more pervasively if these retailers had been exposed to market forces and a more critical credit analysis by the banks.

The demise of companies that led retailing in the 1970s and 1980s can be traced to several major factors, but all originate in significant failings in management and long-term strategic direction. At the end of the 1980s, Daiei, Saison Group, and, to a lesser extent, Jusco, Mycal and Uny, were all following similar strategies of far reaching expansion and diversification. In every one of these cases, firms sought to expand their retail portfolios. Even the profitable and often lauded Ito-Yokado was no exception. But in both Daiei and Seibu's cases, diversification took on a whole new meaning. Both companies acquired restaurant chains, overseas farming facilities, restaurants, hotel groups, and even pro baseball teams. Saison's key retail investments included Seibu Department Stores, Parco, Loft and, the Seiyu GMS chain, which in turn owned Familymart and Mujirushi Ryohin (Muji). It operated a major construction business, a helicopter leasing firm, and numerous hotel interests. Daiei similarly ran Printemps Ginza, Lawson, numerous franchised restaurant businesses including Big Boy, Volks, Wendy's Hamburgers, Sunday Sun, Jolly Pasta, and the Hub. It also acquired radio and TV stations in the Kobe area, and ran both marathon running and volleyball teams in addition to the Daiei Hawks pro baseball team.

Such strategies are no longer an option for large retailers. For Saison Group, the crisis came early with the takeover of the Intercontinental Hotel chain in the late 1980s. Since then Saison has been almost completely restructured, and the group has been largely broken up. The latest development in this 10-year process was the acquisition of Seiyu by Wal-Mart. Familymart and Loft were sold, and Seibu Department Store was merged with Sogo under the Millennium Retailing banner in 2004.

Daiei's problems are also now no longer its own. With ¥2.1 trillion in total debts, including ¥1.6 trillion in interest bearing debts, Daiei had been restructuring since the early 1990s, and many of its better businesses had been sold off: Lawson to Mitsubishi, Oriental Hotels to Goldman Sachs, and even its Akashi hypermarket store to Carrefour. In late 2004, after a long struggle with the government, the Daiei Board submitted to bank pressure and entered administration under the IRCJ (Industrial Revitalization Corporation of Japan).

The IRCJ is a semi-private, government backed body that was set up precisely in order to help Japanese firms with serious debt problems find a way to restructure and survive. It has gained a reputation for tough action in its short life, taking responsibility for Misawa Homes, Utsui Department Stores, Kanebo and a number of others before receiving the job of turning around Daiei.

The IRCJ selected Marubeni and Advantage Partners as the official rehabilitation sponsors in March 2005 and Daiei lives to fight another day although it is probable that its name will eventually be wiped from the Japanese retail landscape. The primary reason for Daiei's long survival was the dubious advantage that, in terms of volume, it was the second most indebted company in Japan, meaning that banks and government alike made extraordinary efforts to avoid allowing the chain to fall into formal bankruptcy. In 2002, it even received an oral vote of confidence from Prime

Minister Koizumi indicating that Daiei was indeed just too large to fall. In the end, it was simply a matter of time.

Daiei may be the last large retailer to undergo the ignominy of IRCJ administration, but it certainly was not the first to go bankrupt. Nagasakiya failed in 1999, quickly followed by Sogo and Kotobukiya in 2000 and Mycal in 2002. All were top 20 retail chains at the time of their failure. For Seiyu the takeover by Wal-Mart almost certainly allowed it to avoid a similar fate.

Over the next decade only a few GMS chains will survive. Aeon and Ito-Yokado will lead and there is a chance one or two international retailers will join them (see Chapter 6). In the department store sector, a core group of top chains are tightening their grip on the sector as it shrinks dramatically overall. By the end of the decade, it is likely we will see only four or five firms in effective control, operating increasingly upscale and services-oriented stores (see Chapter 5).

Convenience store and grocery chains, along with a vast group of specialty chains across each of the main sectors of apparel, drugstores, consumer electronics, home centers, and discount retailing, will come to dominate sales rankings. Although the convenience store sector is fast reaching maturity, recent developments, as outlined in this book, show that the sector has potential for further growth (see Chapter 8).

As the 2002 METI Census indicated, the specialty sector is expanding at a rapid pace. Each of the main categories of specialty store is seeing a small number of efficient, fast-growing companies emerge as leaders in both the sector and retailing as a whole. In general, they are characterized by:

- Independence from manufacturer and wholesale suppliers
- Efficient supply chains
- Strong, centralized management
- Industry leading operating margins
- Professional and usually imaginative merchandising
- Better branding and store marketing
- Consumer orientation and better value
- Good access to a variety of funding sources with less dependence on banks

Companies such as Shimamura, Sanei International, Onward Kashiyama, World and Fast Retailing in apparel have taken over from small wholesaler dependent traditional stores. The same can be said for consumer electronics chains like Yamada Denki, Japan's fastest growing retailer, drugstores like Matsumotokiyoshi, home centers like Cainz and so on across most merchandise categories. These chains are reshaping distribution for many non-food sectors, forcing the decline of wholesale distribution practices that have been a hallmark of Japanese consumer goods markets for four decades.

Large Store Law: gone but not forgotten

One of the most significant factors in the development of corporate retailing in Japan over the past 30 years has been a series of Laws that were enacted to curtail the activities of retailers operating large format stores. As long ago as 1937, Japan enacted the Department Store Law, aimed specifically at reducing the expansion of department stores and at protecting small retailers. The Law was reintroduced in 1956, after the American Occupation, but was soon obsolete thanks to the growth of the new GMS chains. Daiei's jump to the top of the retail sales ranking in 1972 prompted the Law's abolition and its replacement with the Large Retail Store Law (LRSL). This new legislation required special governmental and local authority permission to open any store over 1,500 sqm. In 1979 and again in 1982, it was further amended to apply similar restrictions to stores as small as 500 sqm. Retailers required permission to open such stores, and faced restrictions on opening hours and opening days as laid down by the LRSL.

The crux of the LRSL was the requirement for retailers to hold special explanatory meetings in the area around proposed new developments and gain a consensus from interested parties. Naturally, such parties included strongly opposed small, local retailers and, although usually only active behind the scenes, existing large store retailers. Only after consensus was achieved were applications accepted. Not surprisingly, the number of large stores opened in Japan between 1972 and 1992 was a steady, but slow trickle. Companies complained, with total justification, that the LRSL made the application process unnecessarily long. Although the often quoted claims of applications taking 10 years or more were unconfirmed and largely the fantasy of the Law's political opponents, it is certainly true that a process of 3–5 years was enough to make many applications fall by the wayside.

In 1992, largely due to tough US pressure to deregulate the distribution system, the LRSL was again adjusted, with a new application process introduced to make the procedure both transparent and relatively quick. From the initial announcement of intent to the actual opening of a new store, the retailer could be guaranteed acceptance of the application within 12 months, and interested parties were required to cooperate in the consensus building process.

Finally, in June 2000, the LRSL was abolished and replaced with the current Large Store Location Law (LSLL). Despite initial complaints by large retailers, the latest law is quite different from the LRSL. Throughout its 55 year history, the chief aim of the LRSL was to protect small retailers at the expense of large retail formats. By contrast, the new LSLL aims to enforce environmental, noise pollution, and traffic control standards on new retail developments. Developers are required to undertake planning and assessment in relation to these issues. In addition, greater control has been given to local authorities, and areas where retail development is permissible are laid down in city planning documents. The new law applies to all stores over 1,000 sqm, or 3,000 sqm in six designated largest cities.

The long shadow of the LRSL

The deeper, historical effects of the original LRSL on the distribution system in Japan, have never been properly studied, probably as the majority of academics felt compelled to support the Law in the first place. The suggestion that such legislation was harmful to the free market development of retailing would have been seriously politically incorrect. Today, with the Law gone, its true impact is of purely historical interest, but impact there most certainly was.

First, the development of the convenience store sector and, to a large extent, its success, can be considered a direct result of the LRSL, although not a result legislators intended (see Chapter 8). Due to the restrictions on opening large format stores, all of the big retail groups set out to develop small formats instead. Convenience store chains were lavished with large amounts of investment that would have otherwise found its way into GMS chains simply because they had little choice. In addition, convenience store chains were built with little regard for traditional aspects of the distribution system. Information systems, supply chain management, wholesale and supplier contracts, and logistics systems were built from scratch with the goal being to introduce the most advanced and efficient practices in all areas. Traditional wholesale systems were completely bypassed by the larger firms. It is easy to speculate that the development of such sophisticated and efficient small format chains actually did more damage to small independent retailing than larger formats ever would have.

Secondly, although less significant, it can be argued that the slow development of large format stores up to 1992 meant that retailers continued to build stores in great numbers after that date despite poor performance of the economy as a whole. Japan has more than enough retail shops overall, but there is still a shortage of large formats in many regional areas of the country and plenty of room for expansion. This situation continues to the present time, with only Aeon and Daiei among the large-format retailers having nationwide coverage.

The new LSLL is being reviewed in 2005, but few changes are expected. New store applications have maintained a steady pace of 30–40 a month after a brief period of adjustment in the summer of 2000. This rate of around 300 new applications a year is likely to be seen as quick enough by most planning authorities (see Figure 3.2).

The LSLL and similar legislation will continue to be a point of interest for any retailer in Japan that is looking to open medium to large sized stores. This applies equally to international retailers. On the other hand, similar

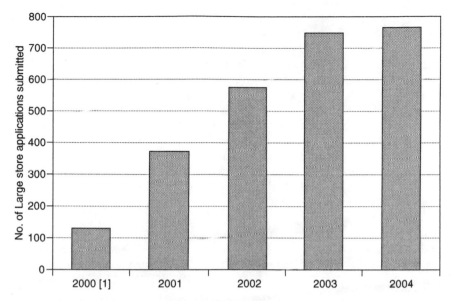

Figure 3.2 Applications to open new large retail stores under the Large Store Location Law, 2000 to 2004

Note: [1] 2000 figures for July to December only

Source: Calculated from Store Japan Online (2005)

laws and regulations exist in many major markets, and most retailers will not find the process unduly worrying or a major barrier.

International retailing in Japan

International retailers have been operating in Japan ever since the War. In the late 1950s, US supermarket chain Safeway opened several stores in the Tokyo area, only to exit Japan's underdeveloped economy soon afterwards. Since then, there have been three main waves of overseas retailer entry into Japan. The first began with the early entry of overseas brands in the early 1960s. Most came to Japan through domestic import agents, wholesalers and other intermediaries. Later, as Japan's economy reached prosperity for the first time since the War, consumers discovered their ongoing taste for luxury designer brands, and general trading companies became the most common brokers.

This second period of international retail development took place over the 1970s and 1980s, and, again, relied mainly on domestic Japanese companies to arrange and manage market entry. Japan was an export driven country, and barriers to import were numerous. Not least, Japanese companies and government alike were more than happy to emphasize cultural problems and the steep learning curve needed to enter the market. With only a few significant exceptions, of which Louis Vuitton stands out as a key leader, overseas brands either placed themselves in the hands of Japanese firms, or, at best, signed joint venture agreements and attempted to build a working relationship with a Japanese agent. During the years of high prosperity in the 1980s, poor management was easily masked by impressive sales.

The final period began, as with many modern aspects of distribution in Japan, with the bursting of the economic bubble. The 1990s saw a major increase in the number of international companies opening up stores in Japan (see Table 3.4). While in the earlier stage, most imported retailing came from Europe and Asia, this last phase opened the market to US owned retail companies and brands.

Table 3.4   Examples of overseas retail entry, 1990 to 2003

	Company	Head Office	Sector	Entry mode	Notes
1990	Virgin Megastore	UK	AV software	JV (Marui)	
	HMV	UK	AV software	Independent	
	Body Shop	UK	Cosmetics	Licence (Aeon)	
1991	Toys 'R' Us	USA	Toys	JV (McDonalds Japan)	
1992	Kinko's	USA	Printing etc.	JV (Sumitomo Kinzoku)	
	Disneystore	USA	Toys, Disney goods	Independent	
	LL Bean	USA	Outdoor wear	Licence (Seiyu & Matsushita)	Independent 2001
1993	Nike	USA	Sportswear	Independent	
	Eddie Bauer	USA	Apparel	JV (Sumisho Otto)	
1994	Land's End	USA	Outdoor wear	Independent	
	Claire's Accessories	USA	Accessories	JV (Aeon)	Wholly Aeon managed
	Esprit	Hong Kong	Apparel	Independent	
1995	Dairy Farm	Hong Kong	Supermarkets	JV (Seiyu)	Withdrew 1996
	Tie Rack	UK	Apparel	Licence JR Kiosk	
	Gap	USA	Apparel	Independent	
	Mango	Spain	Apparel	JV	Now 98% Mitsui Bussan
	Timberland	USA	Apparel	Inchcape	Independent 1999
1996	Warner Studio Store	USA	Gifts and collectibles	JV (Daiei)	Withdrew 2000

Table 3.4 Examples of overseas retail entry, 1990 to 2003 – *continued*

	Company	Head Office	Sector	Entry mode	Notes
	Sports Authority	USA	Sports goods	JV (Aeon)	
	Pier 1 Imports	USA	Household goods	Licence	Fate unknown
	Saks Fifth Avenue	USA	Apparel	Independent	
1997	Office Depot	USA	Office products	JV (Deodeo)	Independent 1999
	Office Max	USA	Office products	Licence (Aeon)	Withdrew 2001
	Footlocker	USA	Footwear	Independent	Withdrew 2000
	Next	UK	Apparel	Licence (Xebio)	
1998	Walgreens	USA	Drugstore	JV (RX Network)	Never realized
	Rooms to go	USA	Interior furnishings	Licence (Aeon)	Withdrew 2003
	JC Penney	USA	General Merchandise	JV (Deodeo)	Withdrew 1999
	Athlete's Foot	USA	Footwear	Licence	
	Viking Office Products	USA	Stationery	Independent	Merged with Office Depot
	Zara	Spain	Apparel	Merger with Bigi Group	Independent, 2004
	Mail Boxes etc.	USA	Office services	Licence (Family Mart)	Itochu controlled
1999	Costco	USA	General Merchandise	Independent	
	Boots	UK	Cosmetics & toiletries	JV (Mitsubishi Shoji)	JV dissolved 2000
	Oasis	UK	Apparel	Franchise licence (Aeon)	Cancelled 2003
	Sephora	France	Cosmetics	Independent	Withdrew 2000
	Hager Clothing	USA	Apparel	Independent	
	Liz Claiborne	USA	Apparel	JV (Aeon)	Dissolved 2003
2000	Carrefour	France	General Merchandise	Independent	Withdrew 2005
	REI	USA	Apparel	Independent	Withdrew 2001
	Giordano	Hong Kong	Apparel	Independent	Second attempt
2001	Metro	Germany	General Merchandise	JV (Marubeni)	
	QVC	USA	TV shopping	JV Mitsui Bussan	
	Dolce & Gabbana	Italy	Apparel	Independent	New subsidiary
	Bally	Switzerland	Footwear	Independent	Cancels JV
2002	Wal-Mart	USA	General Merchandise	Acquisition of Seiyu	Sumitomo involved

Table 3.4   Examples of overseas retail entry, 1990 to 2003 – *continued*

	Company	Head Office	Sector	Entry mode	Notes
	Coach	USA	Bags	JV (Sumitomo Shoji)	New JV
2003	Tesco	UK	General Merchandise	Acquisition of C2-Network	
	Hamley's	UK	Toys	JV/franchise	
2005	Liz Claibourne	UK	Apparel	License	

Source: Compiled by authors from numerous sources

The number of companies entering the retail market from overseas continues to expand in the early 2000s. Japan still lacks many large, internationally active retail names on its shopping streets and there is plenty of room in the market for concepts and retail formats that consumers can at present only enjoy on overseas trips. With the exception of Gap and Toys 'R' Us, there are still very few mass market specialty retailers from the US and Europe in Japan that have any size.

As well as a gradual increase in the number of overseas brands and retailers entering Japan, the other major trend, particularly from the end of the 1990s, was the growing number of existing operators who rethought their distribution policy. Brands like adidas, Yves Saint Laurent, and Giorgio Armani all decided to dismiss their Japanese partners and operate directly in the market. Almost without exception, the brands taking this step saw rapid improvements in results. The shift to direct distribution escalated rapidly in the early 2000s, as the need to control brand positioning and the lure of increased margins made direct control a much more compelling proposition. At the same time, many international brand owners realized that Japan was not the impenetrable and indecipherable market they had assumed, and the example of firms like LVMH showed them the benefits of making the effort to understand it. They also saw that the added layer between the brand owner and consumer that existed in joint ventures and license agreements left overseas firms without a proper understanding of market trends, resulting in damage to brands that took years to correct (Sensu Report, 2000). The shift to direct operations was also aided by the spate of mergers and acquisitions of leading brands and retailers in Europe and the US during the late 1990s and onwards. When LVMH or Gucci acquired a brand, they immediately set about updating and streamlining their distribution in key markets including Japan. Since the new owners had themselves already benefited from shifting their existing brands to direct distribution in Japan, they naturally favored a similar approach for their new businesses.

On the other hand, there are more than a few companies that found Japan too hard to handle. There are many reasons for failure, a botched market entry strategy, poor understanding and lack of research, open domestic antagonism, bad luck and, in some famous instances, poor management. In most cases, failure has come surprisingly quickly, partly because many firms did not have the shareholder backing or resources to tough it out for more than three years. In recent years, REI, Boots, and Sephora are just three examples of overseas retailers that really should have succeeded in Japan but did not, although the reasons for withdrawal were different in each case.

Despite these setbacks, there is a general trend towards success among international firms entering Japan. Japanese politicians and even consultants cling to the myth that the market is difficult and archaic, and there are still more than a few international retailers who have been put off by such claims, despite the fact that they are 10 years out of date at least. The history of retailer market entry is also littered with examples of astonishingly poorly judged joint ventures, very commonly with overseas firms tying with a major Japanese competitor. The protestations of lack of co-operation or even outright obstruction these firms take to consultants and their overseas embassies in Tokyo are nowadays met with the cynicism they deserve.

As already noted, however, such failures are increasingly outnumbered by successes. The size of the Japanese market actually warrants far more overseas retailers taking a look. As noted in Chapter 1, many of the leading luxury brands garner large shares of their total worldwide sales from the Japanese market, emphasizing how important Japan can be and that the investment, while long term, is usually justified. The number of non-luxury brands is much smaller but no less successful, and include Gap, Laura Ashley, Body Shop, Tower Records, HMV, Virgin Megastores, and Starbucks. Some of these, notably Starbucks, have even made success out of sensible joint ventures.

There are some notable cases of international market entry in Japan and we look at a few of the important ones below.

Toys 'R' Us Japan

The most successful international retailer in Japan at present is Toys 'R' Us (TRU). Seen, rightly, as the first US test of the Japanese distribution system, TRU now operates 200 stores nationwide and has been profitable since 1995. It succeeded where others failed, partly through being in the right place at the right time. In 1991 the US government was determined to open the market and saw distribution as a key issue. TRU joined with another long-term US success in Japan, McDonalds, and established a joint venture. In many ways, the company took a Japanese management style, promoting many local managers to senior positions, and instigated store designs and merchandising developed specially for the Japanese market that have proved highly successful. Admittedly, the chain has almost no domestic competition, with only department store toy sections providing anything like the range of product that a typical, small format (compared to the US) TRU store can. The company even grew to the extent that it could bypass the traditional toy wholesale system that caters to the needs of large and powerful manufacturers like Bandai and Tomy. Toys 'R' Us Japan is now so dominant that it can dictate its own distribution policy and, as such, is still unique among overseas retailers operating in Japan.

Costco and Metro

Costco and Metro both studied the Japanese market for some time. By the end of 2004, Costco had five stores in Japan: its first a purely experimental store in Fukuoka, followed by Tokyo stores in Makuhari and Machida, and recent additions in Amagasaki in Osaka and Kanazawa in the north. It progressed with a gradual, but steady development of its market. Customer footfall at its two Tokyo stores are reported to be strong and the company claims to achieve almost the same basket price as it does in the US, around ¥10,000 per sale. Merchandise, on the other hand, is more difficult with much of the product available resembling a Costco from the US. Often, stores carry few Japanese brands in categories where domestic suppliers are strongest, including beer and some packaged food categories. The company remains optimistic, however, and plans more stores in price conscious consumer markets like Osaka and the outlying regions (JapanConsuming, 2003 July–August).

By 2004, Metro, which entered in a joint venture with Marubeni, had only two stores operating, both around Tokyo. The German chain took an extremely cautious approach to the market, possibly after seeing what happened to Carrefour, and maintained a low PR profile. It has also been at pains to insist its stores are cash and carry wholesalers and so no threat at all to local retailers. Unlike Costco, which will provide membership to most people willing to pay the fee, Metro strictly screens membership applications and only allows bone fide businesses to shop at its stores.

Despite adding a team of salesmen to visit local restaurants and other businesses around its stores, Metro has found this positioning a hard one to maintain. Metro is also competing with companies that have very long relationships with existing suppliers, most of whom are more than happy to deliver product in even tiny amounts direct to their clients' doors. Why should restaurateurs and small grocery retailers make the effort to visit Metro themselves when the merchandise comes to them? Equally, early press reports suggesting that Metro prices were little better than at local GMS chains were damaging even if slightly misleading. As a result, there is still a question mark over how much Metro plans to expand in Japan, as well as whether it can maintain its friendly stance towards local competitors.

Carrefour

The most recent and significant developments in international retailing in Japan were the entry of Carrefour in 2000, Wal-Mart in 2002, and Tesco in 2003. These three companies represent the first general merchandise retailers to attempt the Japanese market with any serious intent. Others, such as Dairy Farm in the mid-1990s, made abortive attempts through joint ventures with competing partners.

Although few Japanese experts would ever agree, Carrefour did far, far more to promote the cause of international retailing in Japan than any other company, before finally pulling out in 2005. Opening three stores between December 2000 and January 2001, the world's second largest retailer took on the Japanese wholesale system by taking an aggressive stance with suppliers, and generated a lot of bad press early on. Major food wholesalers including the largest, Kokubu, publicly announced they would not deal with Carrefour. Disagreements in negotiations were officially mentioned, but it is more than likely that Carrefour's insistence on having control over retail pricing was too much for the traditional wholesaler to accept.

Consequently, the first Carrefour stores opened to major public interest with thousands of customers visiting the stores in the early days. They found a disappointing merchandise mix. Where they expected and hoped for exclusive French products and brands, instead they found second class Japanese ones. Admittedly, Carrefour offered innovations in their bakery sections, an impressive rotisserie chicken display that attracted long queues, and unheard of sales techniques such as vegetables being sold by weight not volume. It also introduced the first low price guarantee at a large format retailer, although consumers mostly ignored this as being too unbelievable to be true.

The public interest did not last long. As Carrefour continued to fight with its suppliers, employ only French store managers, and attempted to teach French merchandising techniques to bewildered Japanese employees, problems soon arose and Carrefour stores quickly became rather quiet. In hindsight, however, the worst mistake Carrefour made was that it was perceived to be too cheap by Japanese consumers expecting sophistication, and therefore luxury, from a French retailer. The press went out of its way to attack Carrefour's claims of having the lowest prices in Japan, and no matter how ridiculous or biased the articles, consumers believed their own journalists far more than either the foreign retailer or even their own eyes. Carrefour struggled to keep its core 800 lines of merchandise as cheap as any competitor. Naturally, competitors simply took them on, having as they did both greater volume and the backing of leading Japanese wholesalers and brands. While Carrefour attempted to position itself as the cheapest retailer in Japan, consumers expected something very different. For Japanese consumers, Carrefour, with its second tier Japanese brands, was suspiciously cheap. It achieved some record sales in small, one-time only merchandise promotions where prices were cut to levels customers had never seen before, but on the whole, it left many consumers with a sense of disappointment. This only added to an innate sense of suspicion, as everyone knew full well that this was not a Japanese company.

To its credit, Carrefour began to understand this problem and took steps to rectify it. After almost two years of experimentation in its three existing stores, Carrefour expanded rapidly and by mid-2004 had eight stores. It kept its 800 lines of lowest price items, but it also expanded the ratio of French lines including Carrefour retail brands. Carrefour discovered that Kansai consumers are far more price sensitive and have fewer shopping options compared to Tokyo, and opened four new stores in the region. Once again, these stores were swamped with customers and a huge initial success while all the time the press continued to heap criticism on the whole operation.

In the end, boardroom pressure due to major problems with Carrefour's business in Europe, the easier option of expansion in China, and the low overall volume achieved over five years in Japan, all contributed to the announcement of Carrefour's withdrawal in March 2005.

Despite this, Carrefour's entry in 2000 was almost undoubtedly the most significant change in Japanese retailing to occur since the chain stores first overtook department stores 30 years ago. In one fell swoop, Carrefour opened the door to others. It showed that retailers can and often should take control of their own supply chains, and that they should have control over retail pricing. Subsequently, both Wal-Mart and Tesco have entered through acquisition, but they enter a market that is now receptive to retailers taking control of their supply chains. Even as recently as 2000, large retailers would never admit in public to any pressure on suppliers. In reality, large Japanese retailers are as aggressive towards smaller producers and wholesalers as any international firm, but it is only recently that they are assessing their position vis-à-vis major suppliers. Carrefour made such policies legitimate. Much of the restructuring of the wholesale sector would have happened anyway, but it is arguable that it was Carrefour that forced the change earlier than expected. Aeon is leading this change (see Chapter 6), and it is fitting, if somewhat ironic, that Aeon should benefit from Carrefour's withdrawal by acquiring its eight store locations for itself.

Wal-Mart at last

Equally, while it is unlikely that the entry of Carrefour was a direct stimulus to Wal-Mart in its acquisition of Seiyu in 2002, it certainly helped pave the way. In April 2002, Wal-Mart acquired a small, 6 per cent stake in Seiyu, the fourth largest GMS chain and previously part of the Saison Group. This small stake cost Wal-Mart a mere ¥6 billion, but with it came two conditions. First, Wal-Mart took an option to acquire up to 66 per cent of Seiyu over the next three years. Second, dealmaker and existing Seiyu shareholder Sumitomo Shoji expanded its own stake in Seiyu to 15.6 per cent. In other words, Wal-Mart not only acquired Seiyu, it also acquired a new partner in the form of one of the world's largest trading groups.

On the whole, however, Wal-Mart is keeping a low profile as it works on upgrading the logistics and management control of Seiyu and integrating these with its worldwide supply and information network. The possibility that Wal-Mart will not take up its full 66 per cent ownership option still exists, but there are few reasons why it would not and plenty of others to keep Wal-Mart in Japan. It acquired a second round of shares, bringing its shareholding to 37 per cent in 2003 and in March 2005 announced that Seiyu would be a 50 per cent owned subsidiary by the end of the year. Wal-Mart's influence in Japan is already greater than any other overseas retailer; the cost of initial entry was comparatively low; and, with domestic retailers still finding their feet in a more competitive, post-1990s market, Wal-Mart has a real opportunity to quickly establish a strong position.

There are only a few outstanding questions and doubts. First, the Japanese economy remains shaky, but, failing a total economic meltdown that would leave most retailers running for cover, Wal-Mart's discount emphasis is still likely to find a market. This combines with its technological ability and experience as a retailer which, in turn, will be its main strength in dealing with and changing the traditional food wholesale system. There will be opposition at first in the supply chain, but Wal-Mart's buying base of 400 stores in Japan along with global buying muscle, is going to be a powerful argument against even the most reluctant suppliers. In this way, it is already well ahead of the position that Carrefour had at the time of its withdrawal.

Secondly, the entry of other international chains such as Tesco (see Case Study 3.1) is further opening the market to non-traditional methods and practices that will benefit larger retailers no matter what their origin. The same trends are now being further promoted by Aeon and, gradually, other domestic retailers.

Finally, but most importantly, the relationship between Wal-Mart and joint Seiyu owners Sumitomo Shoji will be a deciding factor. While Wal-Mart is the largest and, arguably, the most powerful retailer in the world, Sumitomo Shoji is one partner who can meet this strength – especially in its home market. Sumitomo has its own retail interests along with ambitions to grow. Partnership with Wal-Mart will allow the acquisition of a wide range of know-how and this is more than likely to find its way into the rest of Sumitomo's retail operations, something that has happened with similar joint-venture agreements in the past. Sumitomo and

Wal-Mart may well prove to be a perfect match of retail and supply chain expertise that could change Japan quickly and permanently. It would mean implementing business practices in the distribution system that Japanese wholesalers and manufacturers have long sought to avoid. It would mean that Sumitomo takes a direct role in the modernization of Japanese distribution.

Case Study 3.1:   Tesco in Japan

With the entry of Tesco in July 2003, Japan became host to five of the world's leading food retailers. Tesco joined Costco, Carrefour, Wal-Mart, and Metro. But Tesco used a different market entry model from its competitors. While the other four chains have followed tried and tested models, seeking to impose well used formats from overseas on the different Japanese market, Tesco acquired a small food wholesale and retail operation. Interest from major trading houses, wholesalers, regional supermarkets and even Daiei were all considered, but Tesco chose C2 Network, a minor player in the Tokyo super-market market. In addition to taking a different approach to competitors, in Japan Tesco also adopted a different approach to what it had in other markets, ditching its preferred hypermarket format and going for small format, food orientated operations.

C2: a well groomed candidate

Outside a few suburbs of Tokyo, C2 was actually as little known in Japan as it was in the West. The company originated way back in 1947 as a small whole-saler, developing into a cash and carry operator. Hanamasa, a leading meat and fresh produce cash and carry in Tokyo, is another part of the C2 group-ing, and food wholesaling continues to be a minor but important part of its business.

In 1995, C2 did something almost unprecedented for a wholesaler in Japan: it discovered retailing. From then until acquisition, it built up a chain of 78 stores, of which about 26 were wholesale cash and carry outlets. Its store fascias include Tsurukame, Tsurukame Land and Kamechuru, each varying from 100 to 1,000 sqm, with the wholesale arm directly related to C2 trading under the name Foodlet Tsurukame. The majority of Tsurukame outlets are innovative and suc-cessful, but they are not your typical Japanese supermarket. Whereas fresh produce is usually the core of food retailing in Japan, Tsurukame only sells fresh produce through in-store tenants. Its own products are packaged groceries. This has led some initial reports to compare C2 to convenience stores and in Western eyes, a 300 sqm Tsurukame would indeed resemble a convenience store, but in Japan it is too big, has too much fresh food, and isn't designed to sell product on a three times a day turnaround as all Japanese convenience stores are. C2 executives claim that packaged groceries make up 50 per cent of the total Japanese food market, totaling some ¥21 trillion. Of that the Tokyo market alone accounts, the company says, for ¥6 trillion. As a result, fresh food is outsourced to other tenants within C2 stores so that C2 itself can concentrate on packaged items.

Case Study 3.1: Tesco in Japan – *continued*

C2 has several characteristics that attracted Tesco. Most important of all, it was a company with a business philosophy and style that would have been very recognizable and comfortable for Tesco, precisely because it is so Western. It emphasized shareholder value and profit as its main corporate objectives, and had a management approach that was geared towards delivering these objectives. While only C2 and Tesco can answer the question, C2's large volume of English language company literature and expert PR and investor relations people also make it look like a company that was carefully grooming itself for an overseas entity like Tesco to move in and take over. Like Tesco in the UK, C2 also offered a range of own brands and follows the usual strategy of aiming for quality comparable with national brand alternatives, but at lower cost and higher margins. The target for C2's own brands was set at a gross margin of 30 per cent and in 2003 its own brands were reported to account for 30 per cent of gross profit, with C2's ultimate aim to boost this to more than 50 per cent at some unspecified future date. With Tesco already selling more than 50 per cent of merchandise under its own Tesco labels at home, this is a strategy it could relate to.

A strategic acquisition

Some readers may be surprised that Tesco did not go for a larger format partner, but the choice of the small, food focused retailer makes sense in Japan's mature market. Food retailing remains highly fragmented and will be one sector to see major growth and consolidation over the next few years (see Chapter 7). Indeed Tesco has already taken advantage of this by buying another small firm. In 2004, it took over Fre'c, a small chain of 28 stores based mostly in Saitama and Chiba. The move came about after Fre'c went into rehabilitation under the Industrial Revitalization Corporation (IRCJ). Tesco's C2 won the rights to restructure the firm and, as with the increasing number of cases of this kind, that means Fre'c will become part of C2's current operations.

Acquiring a successful small company and building on a strong foundation makes good strategic sense in complex foreign markets. In particular, and unlike Carrefour, Tesco will have less of a struggle with local suppliers and be able to tap into C2's existing wholesale network. Its existing philosophy of retail branding also syncs nicely with what Tesco already does best. While the company today may be a full-fledged retail operation, its history as a wholesaler and its strong direct sourcing capabilities will help Tesco work around resistance from the top Japanese wholesalers. This gave the fledgling venture crucial breathing space to begin to expand to the kind of size where top food suppliers will find it harder to ignore and refuse to sell to Tesco/C2. Once this stage is reached, Tesco should be in a good position to expand much faster across Japan, both organically and through further acquisition.

A strong foundation for future growth

By acquiring C2, Tesco gained a small but firm foothold in the second largest consumer market in the world. More importantly it did so in food, a sector in which it traditionally excels. Through the C2 acquisition, Tesco avoided the potential pitfall of relying on price competition and operating efficiency as its key competitive advantage in Japan, something that dogged the efforts of both

Case Study 3.1:   Tesco in Japan – *continued*

Carrefour and Wal-Mart. It now has strategic options whether to build its new Japan base through growth of existing operations at C2, acquisition of more mid-sized operations like F'rec, or expansion into more common international store formats such as hypermarkets, but almost certainly it will aim for a mix of all three formats and strategies. Wal-Mart does not have as many strategic options, being boxed into relatively inflexible strategies with Seiyu, nor does it have a business that is already profitable. While high consumer prices in Japan certainly do present an opportunity to compete on price, Tesco should also be able to compete through quality food and niche specialization. C2 and F'rec may be a modest start, but they could well provide a springboard to rapid and major growth.

The only worry for Tesco is just how much time it has and how much money the next stage will take. While a good, profitable business, C2 Network is small. It is not even a major player in its own local market around Tokyo. As the rest of the Japanese retail industry modernizes and the use of M&A begins to increase as a means to expand market share, Tesco will also be forced to act or risk the possibility of missing the boat. In addition, as with Carrefour and Wal-Mart, operations in Japan are beholden to impatient boards back at home that must consider the various merits of different international markets.

With Carrefour gone and Wal-Mart and Tesco already here, Japan now has a fairly full market of large, general merchandise retailers. There are few other firms that have the international ambitions or the stable domestic markets that these firms do. Auchan and Casino are active in other parts of Asia but, while Auchan already has a wine wholesaling operation in Japan, retail market entry is probably unlikely. Companies such as H.E. Butt in the US or J. Sainsbury in the UK have the type of formats and positioning that hypothetically would do well in Japan, but the former has no current overseas ambitions to speak of, and the latter is another company struggling at home.

So, for the time being, Japan is unlikely to see many new supermarket or general merchandise stores enter from overseas. But then again, it already has the important ones.

Summary: the revolution is over

Japanese retailing has undergone more than a decade of upheaval. Some, notably academics, more traditional firms, and some politicians, still cling to a hope that little has changed or will ever change, but reality is slowly entering even these dusty protected corners of Japan. The revolution is today almost over. As we will see in the following chapters, Japan is no longer a country where the small independent retailers are more important than large, corporate chains, and it is not a country where manufacturers dominate retailers in supply chains, although many still make the attempt. It has taken a long time to achieve, but today Japan has a distribution system that is led from the front by large, efficient, and prospering retail companies.

4
Wholesaling and *Sogo Shosha*

There are two ways to look at wholesaling in Japan. One way is to admit that the wholesale sector remains an influential and important part of distribution, far and above that in most other industrialized nations. This is true, but the importance of wholesaling increasingly varies from one merchandise category to another. In food and household products, wholesalers cling to traditional systems, but in others, such as apparel, they have become something of an irrelevance, except when firms that originated as wholesalers have moved on to become retailers in their own right.

The second way to consider wholesaling is to discuss the role and influence of General Trading Companies or *Sogo Shosha* as they are known in Japanese. Some writers have recently referred to these companies as dinosaurs (see Meyer-Ohle, 2004), but such an analogy is misleading. Yes, in terms of size the *Sogo Shosha* are Japan's largest companies, but they are far from being extinct, dormant, or in any way inactive. For good or bad, these monster-sized wholesalers have actually increased their influence within domestic distribution in Japan. Having said that, however, the role and skills of the *Sogo Shosha* remain largely traditional.

In this chapter we consider the two areas of wholesaling in general and also the role and activities of the *Sogo Shosha*.

Wholesale distribution in Japan

While Japanese distribution may no longer be the archaic, manufacturer-led and manufacturer-controlled system that it once was, independent wholesaling continues to survive as a separate and active part of the channel. Having said that, change in the wholesale system is now gathering pace and taking place. Wholesalers are increasingly less important and fewer in number, with the remaining firms consolidating into larger groups or taking on more specialist logistics based roles. This trend is still staunchly resisted by both the largest independent wholesalers and by many manufacturers (see NMJ, 2004), but the demise of traditional wholesaler firms is now close to inevitable. Even in the most traditional sectors such as food and FMCG, the *Sogo Shosha* are pushing this process along, causing the last bastions of the traditional system to come under threat of extinction.

Wholesalers have continued to be part of the distribution environment in Japan for both good and bad reasons. It is the good reasons that are now fast becoming irrelevant, while the less economically sound reasons continue to be a problem. Wholesalers remain a necessary part of the distribution channel largely because of the overall structure of retailing as well as the geographical make-up of the country. Small, independent retailers still number in the hundreds of thousands (see Chapter 3), and it is their existence that keeps the majority of Japan's 350,000 or so wholesale businesses afloat. The topography of Japan's main islands is another factor. Put simply, getting product from one part of the country to another is difficult and expensive. As a result, wholesalers provide all the traditional roles that wholesaling always has: sourcing a variety of product from a wide geographical area, breaking bulk, providing storage, and even providing some financial support in hard times.

In addition, however, wholesalers in Japan were employed by manufacturers as both a buffer and a control mechanism in their attempts to control channels. In a number of sectors, for example electronics and cosmetics, what are called wholesalers in the statistics, are in reality the wholly owned sales arms of major manufacturing firms. These are set up as exclusive wholesale subsidiaries and act as primary wholesalers. That is, their role is to conduct business with large retailers and to supply product to smaller, regional wholesalers in less accessible parts of the country. In many cases, these companies never handle product at all, simply setting up and handling sales activities and then the paperwork. Actual product supply is organized through other firms entirely. By establishing such sales companies, manufacturers ensure that they have direct control of all aspects of negotiations with the larger retailers and are in control of product movement, sales discounts, and even final retail pricing, at all times.

There have even been some extreme cases of such activity. In the 1970s, both Matsushita and Sony took objection to Daiei selling products below the prices they had laid down as "recommended". While such demands were technically unlawful, legal proceedings were not an option, probably due to the political power and importance of such manufacturers at the time. At first, both Matsushita and Sony withdrew all their products from sale in Daiei, but with Daiei growing at unprecedented rates and taking an increasing share of consumer electronics sales overall, it was a channel that few could ignore. The solution? Set up mock-independent sales firms solely to deal with Daiei. This simple but dated example illustrates the traditional nature of the market, the power of Japanese manufacturers, and, at the time, a rare case of how the growing capability of better retailers managed to overcome that power. (See Chapter 6 for further discussion.)

Unfortunately for wholesalers in general, retail store numbers are now in rapid decline as we saw in Chapter 3. As a result, many wholesalers are no longer required. The parallel growth of larger, more modern retailers places pressure on small retailers and wholesalers alike, further driving the trend to small firm decline. Equally, manufacturers are no longer able to ignore the demands and expectations of the better, larger retailers. They represent just too vast a market with too much access to consumers, causing even manufacturers to forsake the wholesaler middlemen.

Consequently, wholesalers are now going through a process of major change or simple elimination. While the largest are using their markets and influence to cling to traditional methods and practices, even at the top end, there is a shift towards more technical services such as information systems or warehouse management support. Such services are provided to larger manufacturers and retailers alike and add a second line of business to that of supplying merchandise to smaller retailers. Others have moved directly into retailing, as is the case with a number of apparel wholesale groups such as Five Foxes, Onward, and World, while companies such as CGC have turned themselves into buying groups operating at the behest of retailers rather than manufacturers.

The overall trend, however, is clear. Manufacturers have realized the need to streamline every aspect of their business and to improve direct links with increasingly powerful retailers. The influential and growing retailers are now better positioned and more competent in terms of consumer knowledge, marketing power, and market reach. A more simplified model is replacing the traditional system, and even this step is likely to prove a precursor to an inevitable and massive consolidation. Today, wholesale power varies significantly by product category, but the trends are the same: fewer, larger firms, with more emphasis on specialist logistics and supply services, and less on intermediary sourcing activities.

More so than in the retail sector, the true power in wholesaling lies in the hands of the very largest firms. Furthermore, even when we exclude the activities of the *Sogo Shosha*, in FY2003, Japan had some 62 wholesale firms with sales over ¥100 billion (see Table 4.1). Five companies now exceed ¥1 trillion, and 10 companies more than ¥500 billion. The largest companies are those selling pharmaceuticals, food and beverages, and books and other media. In other sectors, the largest apparel wholesaler, Onward Kashiyama, ranks only twentieth with total group sales under ¥300 billion, and the largest office equipment wholesaler, Uchida Yoko, or the largest sports wholesaler, Mizuno, are smaller again.

The majority of companies in the list saw sales increase in FY2003 with large companies doing relatively better. Essential efforts at restructuring and efficiency improvements meant that profitability improved for many of the largest firms, although there are still plenty which struggle and margins are very low. While categories like food, books, and medicines generate lower average gross margins of between 9.4 per cent and 11.5 per cent, these firms have the highest sales per employee of any sector and are not the poorest performers in terms of net profit per employee (see Figure 4.1). Furniture is

Table 4.1 Japan's leading 30 consumer goods wholesale companies, FY2003

Company	Main Category	HQ Prefecture	Sales ¥ mn	YonY %	Pretax Profit ¥ mn	YonY %
1 Kuraya Sanseido	Pharmaceuticals	Tokyo	1,283,925	0.7	19,312	41.5
2 Kokubu	Food	Tokyo	1,239,719	5.8	7,046	−9.2
3 Suzuken	Pharmaceuticals	Aichi	1,194,024	12.6	29,492	7.9
4 Alfresa Holdings	Pharmaceuticals	Tokyo	1,066,577	–	15,266	–
5 Ryoshoku	Food	Tokyo	1,061,408	0.5	10,039	1.7
6 Nihon Access	Food	Tokyo	772,424	1.5	2,563	12.2
7 Nihon Shuppan Hanbai	Books, CDs, Video	Tokyo	735,350	−1.5	6,593	4.7
8 Tohan	Books, CDs, Video	Tokyo	648,885	−3.0	7,181	−8.5
9 Toho Yakuhin	Pharmaceuticals	Tokyo	532,712	11.9	8,597	29.4
10 Itochu Shokuhin	Food	Osaka	505,631	2.5	5,900	−10.7
11 Mitsui Shokuhin	Food	Tokyo	493,991	4.3	1,359	–
12 Kato Sangyo	Food	Hyogo	483,535	2.8	6,324	8.9
13 Meidiya	Food	Tokyo	453,947	−1.6	−1,090	–
14 Arata	Household & cleaning	Chiba	420,576	8.2	8,008	4.8
15 Nihon Shurui Hanbai	Food	Tokyo	406,055	3.9	706	–
16 Paltac	Household & cleaning	Osaka	361,019	–	7,632	–
17 Asahi Shokuhin	Food	Kochi	344,647	1.5	2,580	5.4
18 Nishino Shoji	Food	Tokyo	306,202	2.1	2,045	−15.6
19 Astem	Pharmaceuticals	Oita	285,435	1.4	4,767	0.1
20 Onward Kashiyama	Apparel	Tokyo	267,745	1.7	25,243	15.3
21 Yamae Kuno	Food	Fukuoka	247,292	2.4	3,488	−12.6
22 Vitalnet	Pharmaceuticals	Miyagi	246,151	1.9	2,054	−20.4
23 World	Apparel	Hyogo	236,225	1.5	15,606	29.0
24 KSK	Pharmaceuticals	Osaka	234,981	4.7	2,745	28.0
25 Sutazen	Food	Tokyo	207,016	7.9	2,431	92.6
26 Sanseiya	Food	Osaka	196,742	1.9	–	–
27 San-esu	Food	Tokyo	188,534	8.2	1,723	4.7
28 Maruichi Sansho	Food	Nagano	183,737	−2.7	810	11.9
29 Atol	Pharmaceuticals	Fukuoka	177,500	−0.2	2,838	−8.1
30 Chuhoku Yakuhin	Pharmaceuticals	Aichi	164,140	1.4	969	−0.8

Notes: Some data unavailable or incompatible with previous financial years
Source: NMJ (2004b)

the one main outlier, with the third highest gross margins of 32.4 per cent, but by far the highest net profit per employee of over ¥4.5 million. Apparel and sports wholesaling generate the highest gross margins with 32.7 per cent and 33.3 per cent respectively, but also generate the worst performance for both sales and net profit per employee. These figures reflect the large number of small retailers in these sectors and the continuing wholesale business that supplies them requiring large sales forces to do so.

Overall sales rankings, as ever, are largely academic in this case and the important trends are hidden by the figures. This particular ranking would have looked very different in 1999, with Kokubu and fellow food wholesalers well ahead of all others and pharmaceutical wholesalers largely unnoticed outside their own category. The sudden rise of pharmaceutical wholesalers comes almost entirely as the result of merger and acquisition (M&A) activity in the sector. Now, M&A is becoming a trend in food, household items, and will undoubtedly spread to other categories too. The deal broker and coordinator of these mergers in almost every case was a *Sogo Shosha* (NMJ, 2004b: p. 204). With larger retailers dealing directly with manufacturers, wholesalers were forced to face up to the realities of a bleak future as independents and came to the obvious conclusion that joining forces with old competitors was the better option.

Since 2000, pharmaceutical wholesaling has set a precedent that other merchandise sectors are now keen to follow. In the drug sector, the initial motivation behind consolidation was as much to do with meeting new opportunities as it was combating threats. Several Japanese pharmaceutical manufacturers are already global players in terms of drug development, and, despite recent reforms and deregulation, most continue to enjoy regulation-enforced competitive advantages in the domestic market. Both domestic manufacturers and existing wholesalers saw an opportunity in the growth and consolidation of drugstore chains and in the deregulation of drug and medicine retailing in general. As illustrated in Chapter 10, this move was encouraged through the growth of two modern drugstore groups, the Aeon Welcia Alliance and Matsumotokiyoshi. The new ability of these mass retailers to legally sell prescription drugs was also a factor. Followed by the initial moves that brought Kuraya Sanseido into existence, other pharmaceutical firms quickly followed the trend, with both Atol and Everlth now joining Kuraya, and Aswell and Fukugami forming Alfresa.

Similar consolidation is now accepted and taking place in the household goods and the food categories. Arata is a new firm made up of five previously independent wholesalers, including a part of the Itochu organization. The move was followed by both Ogawaya and Kano Shoji joining the category leader, Paltac. Such moves may pave the way for future mergers in quick succession, with a number of analysts suggesting a rapid and far reaching fall in wholesale company numbers by the late 2000s (JapanConsuming, 2005).

Food, once the strongest and most independent wholesale category has more or less lost the battle to stay that way. In this case, however, the situation is complicated by the interest and influence of the

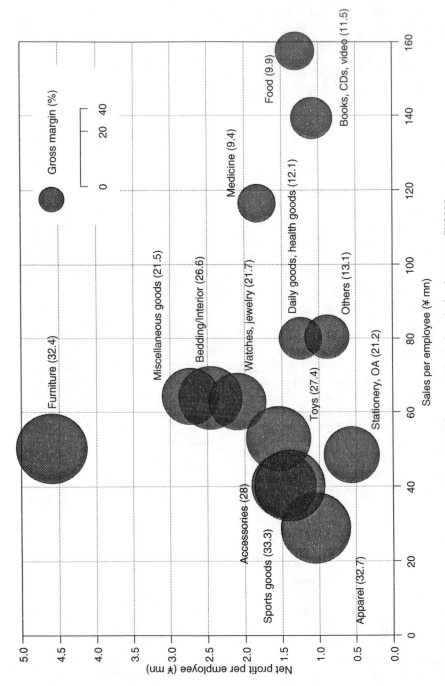

Figure 4.1 Comparison of gross margins, net profit per employee by wholesale sector, FY2003
Source: Based on data from NMJ (2004b, p. 207)

Sogo Shosha. Kokubu remains the largest food wholesaler by far, but poor profitability and a large debt burden, mean that it may be only a matter of time before it too must merge. It is the archetypical traditional retail firm. It supplies some packaged groceries on an exclusive basis, maintains huge accounts with the largest retailers, has almost monopoly positions in a number of regions, and, as a result of such power, demands that its wholesale prices are maintained and never undercut. Its current size and position are maintained largely because the firm is able to keep out many smaller competitors – a factor that was abundantly clear in its refusal to deal with overseas retailers. The development of large retailers with the power to deny Kokubu's terms has come as a major shock to the company and one that it has, so far, refused to accommodate (see NMJ, 2004b).

Kokubu's only major rival for many years has been Ryoshoku, which is part of the Mitsubishi trading house group. While not as large as Kokubu, safe under the umbrella of this exceptionally powerful parent, Ryoshoku has diversified successfully into logistics services and specialist products. As in pharmaceuticals and household goods, Ryoshoku is now leading a gradually accelerating trend towards consolidation in food wholesaling. In 2003, two firms, Saihara and RY Food Service, merged into the Ryoshoku family. In addition, Ryoshoku's parent, Mitsubishi, having become the owner of Lawson in 2001, has taken further steps to build its own wholesale empire. In 2003, it established a new subsidiary under the name Alliance Network. The Alliance Network forms shareholding links between five major food wholesalers and provides a platform for various joint business initiatives and information sharing. Meidiya, the seventh largest food wholesaler and another long-time Mitsubishi affiliate, is one of the five firms that joined the Alliance Network. This is a precursor to full integration into a Mitsubishi operated food wholesale operation, due to come into existence sometime in 2005 (NMJ, 2004b).

Mitsubishi is not the only *Sogo Shosha* active in consolidating the food wholesaling category. Itochu Shoji, Mitsui Bussan and Marubeni are also in the process of developing large wholesale groups. Itochu Shokuhin is the fourth largest wholesaler in its own right, and is also the most important of the various firms that took a share of Nihon Access, the number three company. Itochu, like Mitsubishi, has a major incentive to grow its food supply services to meet a need from the Familymart convenience store chain it acquired back in 1999. Marubeni remains the smallest of the four main *Sogo Shosha* at present, but it has direct control over Nacs Nakamura and strong links with confectionary wholesaler, Sanseiya. Marubeni is also the joint venture partner with Metro, a major shareholder in Maruetsu, the second largest supermarket chain in the country. In 2005, it became the designated rehabilitation leader to Daiei (see Chapter 3).

Mitsui Bussan is the one *Sogo Shosha* with no major retail interests apart from a loose tie-up with Ito-Yokado. This relationship is now developing and Mitsui is taking an increasing share of Ito-Yokado's business, both in terms of imports of food product and in the supply of foods to the Seven-Eleven chain. Mitsui is basically replacing Seven-Eleven's previous main supplier, Itochu Shokuhin. It is now in the process of bringing other long-term associated wholesalers into a more formal grouping. Formerly known as Sanyu Koami, itself a company formed through mergers, Mitsui's food wholesale subsidiary became Mitsui Shokuhin in 2004. Kato Sangyo, another major wholesaler that is also partially owned by Mitsubishi and Sumitomo, is another Mitsui target for acquisition (see Asano et al, 2004).

So Kokubu remains Japan's last major, independent food wholesaler. It managed to merge beverage wholesaler Hiroya into its own operations in 2004, and has a business partnership with Ryoshoku to run some logistics services around Tokyo, but so far it has resisted any move to become formally aligned with one of the *Sogo Shosha*. At the same time, it is now the exception rather than the rule. Food wholesaling, as has happened in pharmaceuticals and in apparel, is moving away from its traditional roles and practices and redefining itself into a more supply services orientated business. As well illustrated by these examples, the influence and leadership of the main *Sogo Shosha* is paramount.

Sogo Shosha

The influence of *Sogo Shosha* in the current changes taking place in wholesaling is unavoidable. *Sogo Shosha*, are a hugely important feature of distribution in Japan, and their influence is spreading over the distribution system like a blanket. It might be possible to overstate the importance of *Sogo Shosha* when talking about retail operations at the micro level, but these massive companies have overwhelming influence at numerous stages of the supply chain. They offer financing, both domestic and international logistics services, warehousing, procurement services, information systems, shipping and transport, consulting, go-between services and much more. They have an almost monopolistic control of imports and procedures, and now are developing a growing interest and influence at the retail stage. In some respects, the influence of the *Sogo Shosha* is so pervasive that it is easy to overlook, but costly to ignore.

When overseas companies come to Japan, the larger operations almost immediately attract the attention of one or more *Sogo Shosha* and most will be contacted by them. For some smaller companies, it may seem that their business is unaffected by the *Sogo Shoshas'* presence, but in truth, because of their influence over Japanese partners and suppliers, this is rarely the case. Since 1999, *Sogo Shosha* have made a number of direct investments in retailing and have been influential in the rehabilitation of all of the failed or nearly failed retail operations that have arisen in the intervening years.

While their traditional role has evolved from importers, to brand managers, to master licensees, to wholesalers, the lack of innovation within retailing during the 1990s led all of the leading *Sogo Shosha* to believe they could do much better. The future development of retailing in Japan will certainly be influenced by the strategic direction taken by large *Sogo Shosha*.

Japan's *Sogo Shosha* are some of the most famous of all Japanese companies, and some of the most difficult to unravel. Everyone knows their names: Mitsui Bussan, Mitsubishi Shoji, Sumitomo Shoji, Itochu Shoji, and Marubeni make up the big five, closely followed by Sojitz (formed by a merger between Nissho Iwai and Nichimen) and Tomen. Together, these seven companies alone had combined sales of more than ¥64.33 trillion in 2003 (see Table 4.2). On the most conservative of estimates, counting only the declared activities of main parent companies and only those directly involved in trade, these seven account for 17 per cent of total exports from Japan and no less than 25 per cent of total imports (see JapanConsuming, 2002b). Other, broader estimates claim with some validity that these same companies are involved in at least part of the procurement, shipping and handling of more than 70 per cent of Japan's imports, with the figure jumping to nearer 80% when considering bulk raw materials and foodstuffs alone (New Frontier, 2004).

Sogo Shosha are truly giants. They are also into everything. As is clear from any textbook about Japanese business, today's *Sogo Shosha* are the reincarnation of the famous pre-war zaibatsu that General MacArthur wanted to break up and disband (see Abegglen, 1987). Few people would want to suggest he failed in this aim, and the *Sogo Shosha* themselves have invested a lot of time and PR in claiming that the only link to the past is their names. It is certainly true that these companies accounted for almost all of Japan's war machine heavy industry, and, although the same companies are still the largest domestic manufacturers of weapons technology, their role in this global industry is tiny compared to US firms (New Frontier, 2004). In many ways, however, today's *Sogo Shosha* are just as powerful, albeit in a commercial rather than a military sense. They have a direct and, in many cases, overwhelming influence both on supply chains throughout Japanese distribution and, perhaps most importantly, are equally involved through financing.

At their core, the *Shosha*, as they are generally known, are principally finance and wholesale trading groups. Each group is part of one or more of the major banking concerns in Japan. Their main overseas trading businesses deal in bulk raw materials, food, industrial goods, and consulting, the last of these predominantly for Japanese firms looking to move overseas (see also Chapter 12). Each company maintains impressive transport networks, including heavy shipping, containers, warehousing, and the logistical and IT infrastructures necessary to manage them. In terms of heavy industry, they drive Japan's oil refining, satellite communications, and domestic transport industries.

Table 4.2 Leading general trading house companies, annual results, FY2003

Company	Total Assets	Sales	YonY	Pretax Profit	YonY	Employees	Consolidated subsidiaries	Non-consolidated affiliates	Total Group Companies
	¥ mn	¥ mn	%	¥ mn	%				
Mitsubishi Shoji	8,390,475	15,177,010	13.9	150,218	146.9	49,215	893	515	1,408
Mitsui Bussan	6,716,028	12,281,517	7.0	86,887	34.8	39,735	424	299	723
Itochu Shoji	4,487,282	9,516,967	−9.0	−92,046	−259.6	40,737	452	193	645
Sumitomo Shoji	5,012,465	9,197,882	−0.3	109,035	281.2	33,799	575	217	792
Marubeni	4,254,194	7,905,640	−10.1	58,900	62.1	24,417	348	154	502
Sojitz Holdings	3,077,022	5,861,737	na	48,461	na	14,600	245	168	413
Toyota Tsusho	1,032,602	2,787,793	8.2	40,572	20.5	12,630	176	na	na
Tomen	769,075	1,604,084	−23.0	21,584	57.5	5,612	125	na	na

Notes: Sojitz Holdings was formed from Nissho Iwai and Nichimen in 2003
na: not available
Source: Company Reports and websites

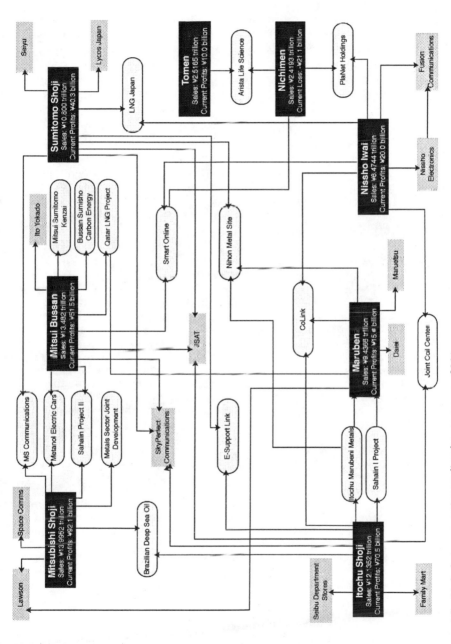

Figure 4.2 Links between major trading house groups, 2001
Source: JapanConsuming (2002a)

And so on. You get the point; these companies are seriously large and have multifarious interests. As Table 4.2 shows, each of the major houses operates literally hundreds of subsidiaries and affiliates. The number is so great that many remain rather distant affairs, veiled by their relatively small size. In addition, hundreds of the same group concerns are located, or registered, outside Japan.

Moreover, the largest *Sogo Shosha* themselves are heavily interrelated. As Figure 4.2 shows, all seven of the top *Sogo Shosha* collaborate on numerous projects and although the figure is based on slightly older data, the situation is unchanged today (see Shukan Toyo Keizai, 2004b). While the diagram provides only a limited picture, there are other and more complex links at the financial level with group banks often working together to finance projects both large and small. There is a complex cross-shareholding relationship between all the leading trading houses, their banks, and their numerous subsidiaries.

Case Study 4.1: Are the *Sogo Shosha* going to change Japanese retailing?

This snap shot of *Sogo Shosha* involvement in retailing and distribution will soon be out of date and would take several books to cover in depth. It is certain that these giant companies will continue to expand their domestic distribution interests, taking controlling stakes wherever possible. While it is true that their interest in overseas brands and retailers entering the market has helped a number of firms gain a foothold in Japan, others would say that such a large and powerful partner can be difficult to work with: you either do it their way, or not at all.

There are a number of issues still to be resolved. One is the relationship between Sumitomo Shoji and Wal-Mart. Sumitomo was instrumental in broking the deal that saw Wal-Mart take a small stake in Seiyu back in 2002, then expanding this stake to a controlling interest some months later. As part of the deal, Sumitomo remains the second largest shareholder and was heavily involved in the due diligence process prior to Wal-Mart's actual buy-in.

Sumitomo is no stranger to retailing. Back in the 1950s, it also did a deal with Safeway, the Californian supermarket chain, to jointly open stores in Tokyo. The deal was short-lived, with Safeway pulling out only a few months later, but Sumitomo stayed in the business. Today, the company still exists under the Summit name and operates some of the most efficient and profitable supermarkets in the sector (see Chapter 6). Sumitomo has never pushed the Summit chain forwards in terms of size and volume, preferring instead to build slowly, maintaining profits, and using the chain as a major supply outlet for the Sumitomo food trading and wholesale operation.

In addition to Summit, Sumitomo has a stake in Mammymart, another supermarket chain, as well as directly owning and operating Tomods, a mid-sized drugstore chain. It is also involved in joint-ventures with other overseas retailers and brands such as Otto-Sumisho, Eddie Bauer, and Coach, the luxury accessories firm. In theory, Sumitomo provides little more than real-estate services and local market and management know-how to the Wal-Mart operation, but it also has the opportunity to gain invaluable know-how and experience in distribution,

---

Case Study 4.1:   Are the *Sogo Shosha* going to change Japanese retailing? – *continued*

logistics, and information systems. If, as seems likely, Wal-Mart starts looking to buy other retail operations in Japan, Sumitomo could be yet again an invaluable go-between and facilitator.

The other *Sogo Shosha* won't be far behind. Mitsui Bussan is developing its role as supplier to Ito-Yokado in leaps and bounds, although this is the one Shosha-retailer relationship where overall mutual benefits remain unclear. Mitsui may hope to marry its Ito-Yokado links to an overseas retailer, but this time with Ito-Yokado in the driving seat. For the time being, Mitsui has become the predominant supplier for Seven-Eleven Japan, the key Ito-Yokado subsidiary and the largest retailer in Japan, which is not an insubstantial achievement in itself.

As already mentioned above, Itochu is now the owner and operator of Familymart, the third largest convenience store chain, has stakes in Loft, Parco, and in Seibu Department Stores, and is probably the most active of all the trading houses in terms of licensing overseas brands. Marubeni has clear ambitions on food retailing, with its stake in Maruetsu and in subsidiary Pororocco, and now in Daiei. Mitsubishi acquired Lawson from Daiei in 2001, and has clear and growing links with Aeon, both in terms of shopping centre development, and in developing information systems for Ministop, Aeon's convenience store chain.

Today, throughout Japanese distribution the names of the *Sogo Shosha* appear again and again. Discussion and illustration of the role of *Sogo Shosha* is overwhelming in its scope. In the 1990s, a few observers dismissed these monster companies because of their legacy as import wholesalers of raw materials, banks, and heavy industry manufacturers. This was a myopic view, however, and one that overlooked the strategic ability of the same companies to see the potential for real change within the domestic Japanese market. With the problems in the retail sector brought on by a poor economy and low consumer confidence, it was the *Sogo Shosha* that recognized the need and the opportunity in taking over from the more traditional retailers. They have been the single most effective driving force behind changes in the Japanese distribution system since 1995. By further investing directly in retailing as well as introducing new management systems into the companies they've acquired, general trading companies now have a direct interest in every aspect of distribution in the country.

Although trading houses remain the largest importers and licensors of foreign branded product and are even blamed for the demise of some potentially successful overseas retail company entries into the market, they are very important indeed. What is more, whereas retail formats will adjust and wholesale companies will decline, *Sogo Shosha* are here to stay.

Involvement in consumer goods and brand licensing

In addition to bulk trading, all the major *Sogo Shosha* have also built stables of consumer brands, including numerous famous overseas names. The services that they provide for these brands usually begin with the role of the principal or master licensee for the brand in Japan. What is less well understood by too many overseas firms, however, is that once initial contracts are signed, the *Sogo Shosha* farm out distribution and sub-licenses, often to multiple companies and in many cases without the control of the original overseas licensor, holding on to the role as facilitator and importer of any non-licensed product. At the same time, they provide their sub-licensees with supply chain management services from raw materials to production. In other words, *Sogo Shosha* benefit from both the top and the bottom of the license operation.

Many overseas companies used to talk to *Sogo Shosha* as a first point of entry into the market with the result that working with a trading company came to be seen almost as de rigueur (JETRO, 1987; JCCI, 1989). Even if it were true in the distant past, today it is certainly not the case. Many companies now know Japan well enough to realize that, given enough resources, they can do a lot better on their own in the long-term. Few large overseas companies will be totally free from the overtures of the trading houses, however. One or more of the *Sogo Shosha* have had a hand in every one of the major overseas retail entries over recent years. Marubeni has partnered with Metro, Mitsubishi Shoji with Boots, Sumitomo with Wal-Mart, Mitsui informally with Carrefour through Mitsui Real Estate.

Now, the *Sogo Shosha* also recognize that they are no longer the unquestioned option for new market entrants and have shifted their emphasis accordingly. They also know that domestic retailers, particularly larger general merchandise chains, no longer need the *Sogo Shosha* to do their importing for them. This has led to two major strategic changes. First, the major *Sogo Shosha* are all becoming directly involved in retailing themselves. Secondly, they are taking whatever steps necessary to tie-up with retail chains such as Ryohin Keikaku, Five Foxes and Fast Retailing, and are attempting to lure GMS chains back into line with various logistics and procurement services overseas.

Coming down from their lofty positions as facilitators and non-bank bankers, the *Sogo Shosha* are now involved in distribution and retailing, more often than not through strategic investments. Most of the top houses have long been involved in distribution as wholesalers (see above) or, on occasion, as owners of minor retail chains. In 1999, however, Itochu Shoji acquired a controlling stake in Familymart, the third largest convenience store chain. This was the first jump into major league retailing by a top *Sogo Shosha*. Since then all of the leading companies have followed with the exception of Mitsui. In some ways it is an obvious move. The *Sogo Shosha* excel in data acquisition and processing, logistics, and general wholesale functions. Adding direct control of retailing was inevitable. It also allows them to leverage their considerable supply networks overseas.

The weakness of domestic retailing was also a major factor. In part, many retailers have built up too much debt with banks, and so, indirectly, with the *Sogo Shosha* themselves. In addition, groups such as Daiei, Saison, Mycal and others lost their direction strategically, diversifying too far away from their core retail business, and were desperate to dispose of parts of their retail stable (see Chapter 3). The *Sogo Shosha* are more than happy to take them over. On the one hand, these are probably the only domestic companies with the resources and the influence to solve these problems; on the other, these store groups offer a simple, if somewhat expensive, entry into mature retail businesses. Top executives have even gone on record as saying that their intervention was one of the few ways they could help to save domestic retailing from eventual collapse or takeover by overseas interests. Both are major motivations and should not be underestimated.

The *Sogo Shosha* are not, traditionally, retailers, but they are aggressive strategists and they are willing to learn and learn quickly. Where better to learn about retailing than at the hands of major overseas retail chains? Once again, the *Sogo Shoshas'* interest in overseas retail entry is obvious. On recent results, however, it is questionable whether the overseas companies they have worked with and learnt from have really understood the possible consequences to themselves. The multifarious group interests of all of the leading trading houses mean that, almost invariably, they become not only partners with the overseas firm, but are also competitors. In a world of limited resources, in particular talented managers, *Sogo Shosha* often find it hard to justify keeping their best personnel in operations that benefit an overseas partner over and above their own domestic subsidiaries or affiliates. This is not to criticize *Sogo Shosha* which have the interests of their domestic market clients, wholesale customers, and retail customers at heart.

One thing to bear in mind when working out what the *Sogo Shosha* will do next is to remember their surprisingly domestic focus. Despite their global reach in terms of overall business, it would be a mistake to consider *Sogo Shosha* as truly multinational companies because all of their operations, no matter what the location, are directly aimed at serving the market in Japan or, at the very most, the interests of other Japanese companies overseas. Yes, they are some of the most international of companies in terms of reach, but their agendas are largely driven by domestic considerations. They do not show any signs of wishing to become global or even A-national. Senior executives would claim they also have the interests of the Japanese economy at heart too. Certainly they have long experience in the field of joint ventures and working these to their advantage. It is questionable whether the same can be said for the overseas companies who succumb to the significant charms of a *Sogo Shosha* partnership.

Summary: wholesale change in wholesaling

In the history of Japanese distribution, discussion of the wholesale sector has taken up as much literature as that dedicated to the overwhelmingly large number of small retailers in the country. Today, however, things are changing very rapidly indeed. As small retailers disappear, so too do small wholesalers. As larger, more powerful retailers appear, even the largest wholesalers come under pressure to offer much more than merchandise selection and bulk-breaking services. The old argument that using wholesalers is much more efficient than direct buying from manufacturers is still heard in Japan. Every overseas retailer attempting the market is still told he must work within the traditional system of wholesalers. Why, then, are Japan's own retailers bypassing the system at every opportunity? The answer is clear: the days of traditional wholesaling in Japan are numbered.

Then there are the *Sogo Shosha*. Huge, overwhelmingly powerful, working in every type of industry, with massive international reach and crushing domestic political influence, the *Sogo Shosha* are still here. In some ways they can be seen as part of the traditional system, but whereas other, category specific wholesalers have done little to change, these companies have diversified into retailing themselves. With typically astute strategic vision, they remain vitally important facilitators in the Japanese distribution system at every stage, and increasingly are powerful retailers in their own right.

Part II

Old Retailing: General Merchandisers

5
Department Stores

History and position

Traditional department stores continue to survive in Japan and even in some cases, to prosper. Whereas elsewhere the department store industry is limited to some specific examples such as Harrods, Gallerie Lafayette or Bloomingdales, there are still some 350 department stores across Japan, mostly companies operating just one store, along with a dozen or so major chains. The oldest trace their roots back to the seventeenth century when the merchant class began to emerge and intermarry with the samurai class. Today, the majority of department stores are minor players in the overall retail industry, mostly being small, regional stores operating as independent retail businesses, but the larger chains rank among Japan's largest retailers. They include the most prestigious retail outlets in Japan and are vital for apparel and cosmetics sales. They are also important outlets for premium foods.

Even though there are so many department stores operating in Japan, the sector as a whole is still relatively small. It splits between very large companies such as Takashimaya, Mitsukoshi and Millennium Retailing, and tiny regional companies with single stores that are unknown outside their local markets.

Official statistics define department stores as large format, full-service, and full-line retailers. By large format, it means that stores are at least 3,000 sqm, or more than 6,000 sqm in the six designated major cities (see Table 3.2, Chapter 3). In reality, the majority of department stores are significantly larger. There are several with sales space over 50,000 sqm and are some of the largest retail outlets in Asia. Some of the biggest of all include Sogo Yokohama (74,108 sqm), and Seibu Ikebukuro (63,470 sqm). Some stores, such as Matsuzakaya's HQ store in Nagoya at 86,747 sqm, also claim large sales space, but as with Tobu Ikebukuro (82,963 sqm) and a number of others, this store is split between several different buildings. The biggest store by sales, Mitsukoshi Nihonbashi, claims space of 124,256 sqm, but this includes four different Mitsukoshi stores operating in various parts of Tokyo, all managed centrally. There are a number of statistical anomalies like these that need to be remembered when looking at department stores. Other than being big, a department store is full-service, providing face to face, counter sales and very little self-service. They are also full-line, with no less than 10 per cent of sales, but no more than 70 per cent of sales, in any one of the three general categories of food, apparel or household. While not formally defined, most department stores are also positioned near the top end of the market.

In practical terms, the majority of department store outlets have one or more food floors (most commonly located in the basement of the store) cosmetics on the ground floor, followed by several floors of apparel, including women's, men's, and a number of age ranges down to children's and baby wear. On the whole, however, the targeting for the better stores is skewed towards slightly older, female clientele who are better able to afford department store prices. Upper floors carry toys, ceramics, furniture, sportswear and many other lines limited mainly by the size of store.

Department stores also offer a full range of services. Most stores offer a wide range of wedding services from clothing to ceremony arrangement. Other key services include gift sales at the mid-year and end of year traditional gift seasons, called *o-chugen* and *o-seibo* respectively. Approximately 12–15 per cent of annual sales are made in these two seasons alone, with stores turning over a full floor to gift item display in July and December. Recently, like Christmas in the West, stores have been bringing gift sales forward to stretch the season longer.

Finally, but very importantly, almost all department stores also offer personal accounts to their most exclusive and high spending customers. These are called *gaisho* – literally "outside sales". In the 1800s, when department stores first grew into large companies, *gaisho* accounts were used to reach customers outside the a store's sales areas, with salesmen traveling throughout the country. Today, *gaisho* staff concentrate on sales to corporate customers and wealthier private individuals.

Department stores: urban and regional

In more general terms, department stores are often classified into urban (or "city") and regional. In turn, urban stores are easily distinguished between older, traditional stores and those established by private railway companies (Figure 5.1). The most important stores are the urban department stores, many of which trace their history back 100 years or more. These stores began life as kimono retailers, mostly in Tokyo and Osaka, evolving into department stores in the late 1800s.

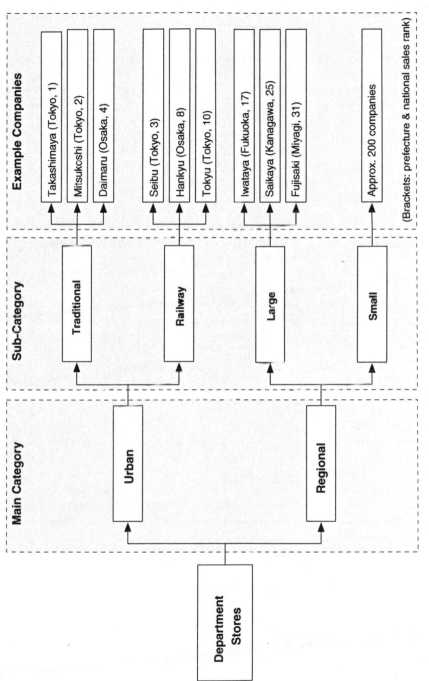

Figure 5.1 Summary of usual Japanese classification of department store types
Source: Authors

At the time, they were the most powerful retailers in Japan, wielding significant influence throughout the country. There is a famous example of this. The majority of Japanese consumers are today aware that chocolate companies introduced Valentine's Day into Japan as a marketing gimmick in the 1960s. Few consumers know that the November children's festival called *Shichigosan*, or 7-5-3 Festival, was also engineered through marketing. Until the late 1800s, 7-5-3 was limited to a small shrine in Tokyo. Through their extensive *gaisho* systems, department stores spread the festival throughout country, selling children's formal apparel, presents, and numerous other services related to the festival. Even better, as the festival's name suggests, every child at the age of 7, 5, and 3 became the market. The tradition continues even today, with consumers blissfully unaware that it was all engineered by department stores.

Railway companies began opening department stores much later, but are still more than 50 years old in many cases. Private railways realized that commuter footfall was their major competitive advantage. Coupled with large real estate holdings, additional vertical space above stations, and large cash flows generated from consistent and massive commuter traffic, all of the major railway companies entered retailing through subsidiary businesses. Today, Seibu (although, Seibu retail and railway interests split at an early stage), Tokyu, Odakyu, Keio, and Tobu in Tokyo, Hankyu, Hanshin, and Kintetsu in Osaka, and Meitetsu in Nagoya are all large examples of this phenomenon. Each of these companies is a major retailer in its own right, and several have further diversified into supermarket and specialty retail formats. More recently national railway operator JR has also diversified into retailing with successful developments at, for example, Kyoto, Nagoya and Sapporo stations.

Since 1990, many of the railway affiliated retail companies have had financial problems. Seibu was the heart of the Saison Group, a conglomerate that was one of the first major retailers to require group wide restructuring. It divested parts of its group, selling off controlling stakes in both Parco and Loft in FY2001, and selling partial stakes in Seibu to Itochu, and the controlling interest in Seiyu to Wal-Mart. It was finally merged with Sogo to form Millennium Retailing in 2003 by former Seibu president, Shigeaki Wada. Due to similar problems, Tokyu was the first major department store to close a large Tokyo outlet when it closed its Nihonbashi store in 1998. In Kansai, Kintetsu reshaped itself by amalgamating several department stores under one central administration and by changing the store positioning towards a younger consumer. Kintetsu's stores are located close to its stations and in several cases have the luxury of little local competition, but the company has still struggled to maintain any significant growth.

Railway affiliated companies have the advantage of station locations, larger chains as compared with traditional stores, and more centralized buying and management, balanced in most cases by a lower market prestige and positioning. All urban stores live by their high market status and prestige value, but, many have shifted away from direct retail management and more into real estate and floor space management, allowing suppliers to control space in their stores (see below).

For the best companies, the problems of the poor economy in the 1990s forced numerous changes and improvements in management. Among the largest chains, all but Seibu and Sogo have survived as independents. However, the format as a whole remains inefficient in nature, and there is only so much room for luxury retailing even in Japan. The ones that will survive in the long-term are those that have made the most far-reaching changes to management and retail operations.

Traditional sales methods

Until recently, department stores were traditional retailers in every sense of the word. Since the war, they have been purveyors of list price goods, sold to the precise specifications of manufacturers and wholesalers. In most cases, department stores have handed over the control of sales space to brands and manufacturers in the form of concessions or through the system of sale or return, known in Japan as *itaku hanbai*.

In the heyday of the department stores in the 1980s, this was not a problem. Consumers were prosperous and eager to spend. Conspicuous and ostentatious consumption was a means to display an individual consumer's economic success to the world – one of few ways Japanese have to make up for cramped, expensive housing, poor sanitation in regional areas, short holidays, limited scope for other leisure activities, and so on. Department stores, with their high prices and ingratiating sales styles encouraged this consumption boom and prospered from it. Consumers commonly requested the most expensive items available, and stores were happy to supply them.

Yet, by relying on suppliers for almost every aspect of the marketing mix, even down to retail pricing, most stores gave up control of the most basic aspects of their business. This type of retailing developed over many years, largely as a convenience to the stores themselves, but also due to the power and persuasion of the suppliers. The result was that department stores rarely controlled either sales space or sales staff, and by allowing suppliers to set prices, also relinquished control over their own bottom line. Having adopted this type of management, it became increasingly difficult to revert to a normal retail system with direct store control. Many stores failed to innovate in store design and marketing, and today department store buyers still rarely play more than a political role in the operation of the store, liaising between top management and suppliers on issues of sales and marketing budgets and which suppliers to favor.

The consumption boom died in the early 1990s. Department store chains spent the whole of the 1990s grappling for ways to survive, and, being a conservative and traditional business format, the majority found even small changes difficult. The over reliance on suppliers had left some companies with inadequate management. Too many senior executives were both unwilling and, arguably, unable to change their focus towards retailing. This was only exacerbated by ever tighter budgets. Since 1992, 102 stores have gone out of business or switched to different retail formats, leaving just over 350 actual department stores (Figure 5.2).

While it is surprising just how many stores survive, the reason is not particularly difficult to understand. The decline in department store retailing began much earlier in other countries and now there are only a few, usually upscale companies, scattered around the world such as Harrods, Bloomingdales, Sachs Fifth Avenue, Bon Marche. Other examples are less well known outside their own cities. The ones that have survived and, in the best cases, that have actually grown, are those that have managed to mix the better aspects of chain store operations while keeping at least some of the exclusive, upscale retail concepts that the format was founded upon. Nordstrom and Neiman Marcus in the US and John Lewis and Debenhams in the UK are four examples of companies that have followed and succeeded along precisely these lines.

Department store retailing in Japan has lasted longer because they have continued to match consumer preference and more importantly, the demand for prestige gift-giving. They are old, traditional stores that collectively breathe both high levels of trust and reassurance as well as luxury and exclusivity – with the prices to go with it. The importance of peer acceptance and of social status in Japan was such that buying from the right store, particularly when choosing gifts, was vitally important and many consumers did not consider a low priced store when there was a department store nearby. Buying gifts at the right department stores demonstrated that you had gone the extra mile, you hadn't skimped on cost, and you had made the effort to impress the recipient of the gift. As Figure 5.3 shows, the two gift-giving seasons in June and December remain a huge and vital proportion of, department store sales each year.

Department stores have long formed the establishment, are nice and pricey, and everybody knows what they are getting. Equally, high added value discretionary items such as women's apparel have also been ideally suited to this form of retail environment. Older women particularly want

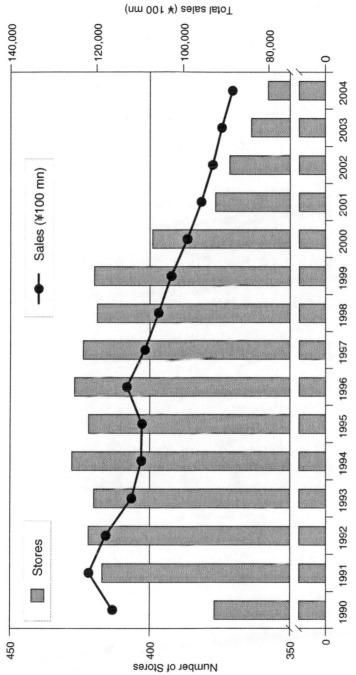

Figure 5.2 Department store sales and store numbers, 1990 to 2004 (calendar years)
Source: METI (2005)

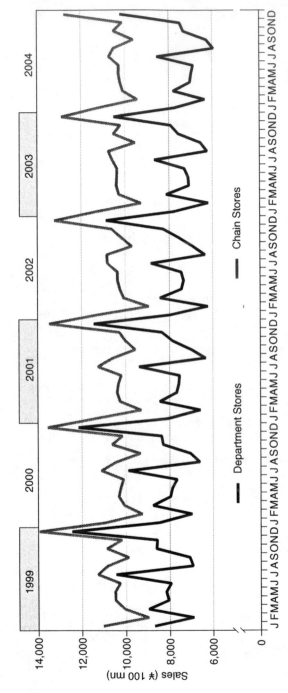

Figure 5.3 Month to month sales for department stores and chain stores, January 1999 to December 2004
Source: METI (2005)

the reassurance that they are buying the best brands and can enjoy the very best formal service while they do it.

While department stores may survive, their importance and their share of overall retail sales are declining. Sales have been in almost constant decline since the late 1980s. Figure 5.2 shows a slight improvement in 1996, but it has been all down hill since then. Furthermore, the rate of loss of stores will continue to increase. This will partly be because of closure but also because of the growing enthusiasm for merger or takeover of regional stores by the top chains as the overall fall in department store sales forces further amalgamation. And sales are very likely to continue to fall. In 2004, the department store sector saw sales fall a further 2.8 per cent to ¥7.88 trillion according to the Japan Department Stores Association. This marked the first time combined sales had been below ¥8 trillion since 1988. Although regional stores fared badly, Tokyo department stores also had a particularly rough year. Overall Tokyo department stores, consisting of 13 companies and 27 stores, saw sales fall 3.4 per cent in 2004, the eighth consecutive year of decline. Combined sales were ¥1.92 trillion, down from a peak of ¥2.94 trillion in 1991, a total loss of ¥1 trillion or 33 per cent of sales. This was despite an increase in sales space from 865,000 sqm to 953,000 sqm. Sales per square meter fell from ¥3.39 million in 1991 to ¥2.02 million, a huge fall of around 40 per cent.

Department store buying groups: the basis for merger

The latest trend in department store retailing is that of merger and acquisition. The sector is now moving rapidly towards concentration into the hands of just five groups: Takashimaya, Mitsukoshi, Isetan, Daimaru, and Millennium, and even this might be too many. The better regional stores now face the prospect of alliance with one of these companies, while the worst have few places to turn.

The only visible example of a merger has been that between Seibu and Sogo to form Millennium Retailing. More usually, however, the largest companies are looking to more formally gain affiliation from regional stores that have long been part of their buying groups. More formal affiliation now comes with the prospect of management support and movement of executives from top Tokyo companies to regional stores. This approach amounts to a takeover or merger but leaves the store name in place with a separate operation, allowing existing management to save face.

As in other distribution sectors, cooperation and joint-venture agreements between groups are common and have existed for much of the past 40 years. Even the largest department stores are cooperating on logistics and product design. Takashimaya and Mitsukoshi, the top two department store groups, are major rivals in the consumer market, but behind the scenes, they have various joint agreements on gift merchandising and product development. In another example, Keio and Hanshin agreed to formal cooperation on product development in 2002.

Japan has four major department store buying groups with almost all 350 stores nationwide belonging to at least one of these (Figure 5.4). These affiliations are fluid and subject to change. Recently not only are companies within the group exchanging more merchandise and management, but there is a growing trend towards tie-ups between competing groups. In Tokyo, for example, Matsuzakaya and Takashimaya share logistics and delivery services, while in Kansai Takashimaya does the same with Hankyu. The ties in merchandise supply both within buying groups and across groups are also strengthening. In 2001 for example, Takashimaya announced that it would provide its own retail brands for sale at other associated department stores and Isetan has been developing brands for use across its affiliates since 2000. Smaller, regional department stores are making more use of these traditional buying group connections to help their sagging sales. For the leading companies, this is an excellent way to extend their influence and, possibly, expand their chains. Mitsukoshi for example, took over operations of Fukushima based Usui Department Stores in Fall 2003. This was two years after it began providing Mitsukoshi own brand merchandise, Mitsukoshi senior managers, and joint procurement and operations procedures under the guise of buying group services.

Merging with other firms and strengthening ties with buying group members also help some of the leading chains reduce their dependence on a single key store. As Figure 5.5 shows, most of the top chains share this weakness with Hankyu particularly suffering from dependence on its Umeda store in Osaka. However since Hankyu is a partner with Isetan in the ADO buying group, it is able to off set this weakness by sharing purchasing, as to some extent is Isetan, which is dependent on its Shinjuku store.

Regional affiliates also offer the opportunity to experiment with new lines and sales techniques while at the same time increasing management influence. Isetan, for example, has rolled out its News Square sales unit of ladies apparel to many stores in its ADO buying group. In addition to sales and merchandising know-how, Isetan also provides ordering support and information technology to some members. Member stores pay a percentage of sales as a license fee, but Isetan gains far more in terms of closer control of regional ADO members and market scale. In April 2002, Isetan added Izutsuya to its list of partners, taking it away from the Mitsukoshi group. This deal helped tighten Isetan's grip on Kyushu department stores following its acquisition of a stake in Iwataya,

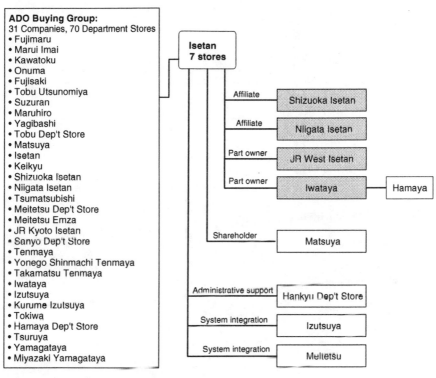

Figure 5.4 (a)   Isetan ADO buying group
Source: Company Reports

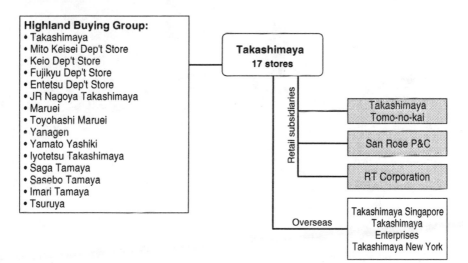

Figure 5.4 (b)   Takashimaya Highland buying group
Source: Company Reports

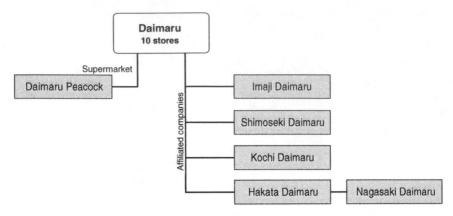

Figure 5.4 (c)   Daimaru buying group
Source: Company Reports

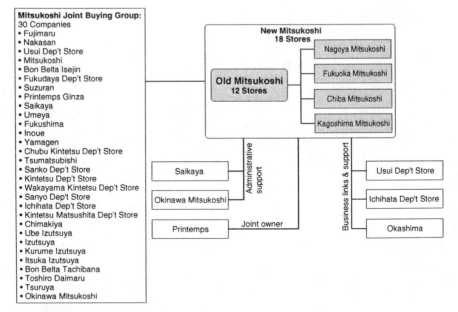

Figure 5.4 (d)   Mitsukoshi Joint buying group
Source: Company Reports

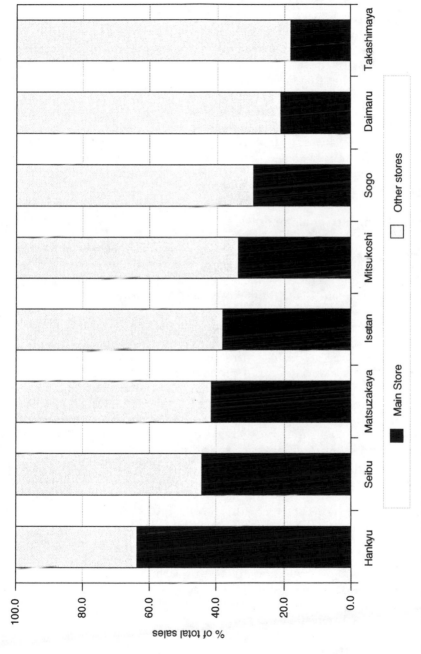

Figure 5.5 Proportion of total sales generated from main store alone for leading department stores, FY2003
Source: Company Reports

and existing ties with Yamagataya and Tsuruya. The partnership with Izutsuya included sharing of information and joint product procurement. Such consolidation is a clear response to consolidation by the other store groups.

Such close cooperation between companies is typical of Japanese business. Department stores, which are often competitors at heart, recognize the crisis that their sector as a whole is in. The next step might be actual mergers between companies, but more likely this will only happen when a large department store is able to absorb one or two of the better regional outlets. Most regional companies see such cooperation as long-term strategic alliances, with more invasive interference from top chains as a stopgap measure to see them through difficult periods. However, Japanese corporate history suggests that, once the large chains get a foot in the door, they are unlikely to back out.

Streamlining into chain operations

For the past 10 years, in addition to taking control of regional stores, the larger department stores have gone through a series of structural changes and repositioning exercises. While it is easy to observe first-hand the effects of these at the main Isetan, Mitsukoshi, and Daimaru stores, much more has gone on behind the scenes.

Takashimaya, the largest of the department store groups by sales (Table 5.1), has the most problems still to overcome, partly because it was the only large group to add retail space in the mid-1990s. It now operates 17 stores and not all of them are performing well. Many analysts still consider Takashimaya far too diversified, with the largest number of overseas outlets, including stores in Singapore and Taiwan, and various interests outside retailing. It still has three of the seven largest (over 60,000 sqm) individual stores in Japan. Recently, it has made some disposals, selling its stake in Sotetsu Rozen and Takashimaya Store, two supermarket chains, in 2003.

For many Japanese consumers, Mitsukoshi remains the epitome of high prestige retailing in Japan, but that has not helped the company's results in recent years. To its credit, however, since 2003, the company has taken a number of steps to radically improve its fortunes. First, Mitsukoshi consolidated its group, bringing a number of regional subsidiary stores firmly under senior management's control in FY2003. Then, at the end of September 2004, it took the almost unprecedented step of announcing that it would close stores in Osaka, Yokohama (including satellites) and Kurashiki outlets. This restructuring allowed it to slash its interest bearing debt from ¥350.5 billion in 1998 to around ¥245.68 billion. In addition to taking over management control at Usui Department Store, it also acquired Printemps Ginza from Daiei.

Table 5.1   Leading department store firms with sales over ¥20 billion, (non-consolidated) FY2003

Company	Sales ¥ mn	YonY %	Operating Profit ¥ mn	YonY %	Pretax Profit ¥ mn	YonY %
1 Takashimaya	935,991	-2.9	18,014	120.2	17,429	83.1
2 Mitsukoshi [1]	686,517	0.1	11,931	-8.9	9,421	-8.3
3 Seibu	522,918	-13.9	21,122	117.3	16,232	–
4 Daimaru	470,514	8.9	13,309	7.8	13,077	7.1
5 Sogo	448,211	-1.3	13,265	99.4	14,013	73.5
6 Isetan	438,431	0.9	10,112	0.7	11,236	-17.8
7 Matsuzakaya	322,308	-1.2	1,765	-23.7	1,408	-10.1
8 Kintetsu	316,319	-3.4	3,614	-6.3	3,561	-10.2
9 Hankyu	313,701	-2.7	12,516	8.7	13,109	5.7
10 Marui[2]	262,527	-0.4	16,358	–	17,222	–
11 Tokyu	225,455	-7.6	8,103	52.1	4,528	39.3
12 Odakyu	164,605	1.2	1,840	33.7	1,695	9.8
13 Hanshin	119,879	10.2	2,673	52.2	2,824	45.9
14 Marui Imai	110,990	-6.6	1,853	-9.8	1,698	-19.5
15 Iwataya	109,895	26.4	2,209	5.9	2,126	2.1
16 Izutsuya	93,779	1.2	4,174	30.0	2,806	-30.9
17 Meitetsu	84,556	-3.0	878	-7.3	987	5.5
18 JR Tokai Takashimaya	82,707	7.2	4,231	13.0	4,107	49 1
19 Daiwa	80,943	-2.7	474	7.0	668	48.1
20 Matsuya	80,653	-0.7	1,315	0.4	1,190	4.5
21 Saikaya	78,599	14.6	472	13.2	457	193.2
22 Tsuruya	74,165	-2.3	1,114	894.6	980	-64.0
23 Maruei	44,928	-3.7	599	2,203.8	462	-85.3
24 Jujiya	38,903	-6.0	938	59.8	590	-17.8
25 Sanyo	25,751	-1.2	175	-29.1	101	-25.2
26 Nagano Tokyu	23,253	-6.5	524	-29.4	468	-12.5

Notes:
[1] Mitsukoshi results are FY2002 due to significant accounting changes in FY2003
[2] Marui figures for September 2003 to March 2004 only due to accounting changes
Source: Company Reports

Finally, it opened a new annex to its headquarters store in Nihonbashi in October 2004.

Another major Tokyo store, and probably Japan's best managed store, is Isetan. Isetan's focus has been more about raising operational profitability. It has reduced interest bearing debt burden from ¥228.19 billion in 1998 to only ¥99.73 billion in 2003. It has long been well respected as a brand store and for having the strongest fashion sales in the country, but it has also been reliant on the single Shinjuku flagship store for a significant proportion of sales. This situation has been marginally alleviated, because the same Shinjuku store has been positioned so well that it is currently the most improved store in the country. In 2003, Isetan overhauled the menswear annex of the Shinjuku store, further enhancing its reputation as the leading fashion department store. The company is now targeting 25 per cent of all apparel sales in Tokyo.

Daimaru too managed significant improvements in its fortunes from 2000 on. Like Mitsukoshi, it took steps to rationalize its operations, although as a much smaller group this meant cutting out unprofitable and largely unnecessary non-retail subsidiaries. Like Isetan in Kyoto and Takashimaya in Nagoya, Daimaru was also the beneficiary of JR's desire to leverage retail sites at its main stations, and it now manages the successful JR Sapporo store that opened in March 2003. It also benefited from plans for a new building for its Tokyo Station store, and is likely to manage other JR developed stores elsewhere in the country, the next being one in Sendai, Miyagi Prefecture.

These structural changes have helped the leading department stores consolidate their positions in the main urban centers, leaving them in a strong position to compete with high end specialty stores. The major unknown in department store retailing however, is the fate of Millennium Retailing. Millennium was formed from the amalgamation of the bankrupt operations of Sogo and Seibu Department Stores. The group received major financial backing from Mizuho in 2004 and, in early 2005, announced that debt rehabilitation would be completed a year ahead of schedule in 2006. Eleven Sogo stores were retained following the company's collapse and, importantly, they now operate more as a single chain. In addition, and despite being targeted for liquidation by the group's creditors, Sogo has managed to hang on to its Shinsaibashi site in Osaka, and this is due to reopen in 2005. Seibu is the largest chain of department stores in the country with 18 separate locations, but almost all Seibu stores have seen sales fall in recent years. Having turned Sogo around, Millennium will turn its attention to Seibu operations, and particularly the Seibu Ikebukuro store. This was Japan's best selling store throughout the 1980s and 1990s, but is now in rapid decline.

The plan now is to take Millennium Retailing public by 2007. Proper management and a more consistent organization of all the stores in the group gives the potential to turn it into Japan's most effective department store chain, along the lines of Sears in the US, or John Lewis in the UK. As such, it will be the first department store to make this switch to centrally managed chain operations.

Case Study 5.1: Mitsukoshi: the next 100 years

In 2004, Mitsukoshi celebrated 100 years as a department store. It is one traditional retailer that is likely to survive, but it continues to struggle to improve performance as day-by-day new, more dynamic retailers bite further into its trade. In order to prepare itself, the company spent the early 2000s tidying up its corporate structure and reducing its debt burden. Late in August 2003, Mitsukoshi celebrated its 99th anniversary in unusual style: it delisted from the Tokyo Stock Exchange. The old company was replaced with a brand new one called, once again, Mitsukoshi. While this magic trick effectively reset all Mitsukoshi financial figures, it is probably the least significant of a series of changes finally implemented in the biggest restructuring and reformulation plan to come out of any solvent department store to date.

At the core of the "new" Mitsukoshi was a newly amalgamated group of the old parent and four large regional subsidiaries. From a retailer with 12 stores and some autonomous subsidiaries, Mitsukoshi Version 2.0 became a chain of 18 stores (Table 5.2) in a single company capitalized at ¥113.9 billion from assets of ¥563.6 billion and total debts of ¥449.7 billion. The subsidiaries in question were Fukuoka Mitsukoshi, Chiba Mitsukoshi, Kagoshima Mitsukoshi, and the very successful Nagoya Mitsukoshi operations. By using a reevaluation paper profit of ¥180 billion on land and other assets, the chain was able to wipe out accumulated consolidated losses resulting from unfunded retirement-benefit obligations and deferred tax liabilities.

In addition to its corporate housekeeping efforts, Mitsukoshi is a good example of how department stores are attempting to slowly reduce their personnel costs, particularly the imbalance of too many senior staffers. One way to do this was to make working at Mitsukoshi less remunerative. From November 2003, Mitsukoshi implemented new personnel policies, included in which was a 10–20 per cent cut in executive compensation. Other subsidiaries, which still numbered more than 20, were merged or closed down, reducing the number to 13 overall. These final measures reduced costs by around ¥7 billion a year.

Mitsukoshi introduced more practical improvements to store operations as well but sales at its stores still lag behind competitors. In addition to its main 18 stores, Mitsukoshi controls another 106 sales outlets in Japan and abroad. Of these only the Nihonbashi store has sales over ¥100 billion a year, compared to Takashimaya which has four stores of that size. Mitsukoshi also has only four stores selling more than ¥50 billion compared to six at each of Takashimaya, Millennium, and Daimaru. It was not surprising therefore that in September 2004, Mitsukoshi announced that it would close its Osaka, Yokohama (including satellites) and Kurashiki outlets. The combined loss in sales to Mitsukoshi from the three closures was only about ¥59.4 billion, or about 12 per cent of total sales in 2002. In addition to the three main outlets, Mitsukoshi also closed six smaller, satellite stores including Haneda Airport, Senzoku in Meguro, Hakodate, Azushima in Kagawa, and Makurazaki in Kagoshima. At the same time, it also converted its Shinjuku store into a shopping building with specialty store and luxury brand tenants.

Case Study 5.1:   Mitsukoshi: the next 100 years – *continued*

Table 5.2   Mitsukoshi stores in Japan, 2003

Stores	Prefecture	Sales ¥ mn
Nihonbashi [1]	Tokyo	301,650
Sakae	Aichi	86,912
Ginza	Tokyo	65,283
Sapporo	Hokkaido	58,359
Fukuoka	Fukuoka	47,502
Sendai	Miyagi	44,415
Chiba	Chiba	33,070
Ikebukuro	Tokyo	29,960
Shinjuku	Tokyo	29,438
Takamatsu	Kagawa	29,042
Osaka	Osaka	28,644
Matsuyama	Ehime	26,386
Yokohama	Kanagawa	23,975
Niigata	Niigata	22,497
Hoshigaoka	Aichi	21,586
Hiroshima	Hiroshima	19,774
Kagoshima	Kagoshima	13,753
Kurashiki	Okayama	8,868
Affiliated Stores		
Printemps Ginza	Tokyo	27,690
Affiliated Companies		
Okajima	Yamanashi	17,100
Usui Department Store	Fukushima	16,865
Ichihata Department Store	Shimane	11,822
Okinawa Mitsukoshi	Okinawa	10,981

Note:
[1] Nihonbashi store figures include stores in Ebisu, Tama, Kichijoji and Shinjuku Alta
Source: Company Reports

While closing some stores, Mitsukoshi has also invested in rebuilding its most important stores. In late 2004, Mitsukoshi opened the new annex to its flagship store in Nihonbashi with 10 stories above ground, two below and 15,000 sqm of retail space, increasing the total floor space to 66,500 sqm. The construction cost ¥16.5 billion.

Despite closing some of its own stores, Mitsukoshi still decided to take further control over the ailing Usui Department Store based in Fukushima. Mitsukoshi had been operating this family owned store since 2000, but with the intervention of the Industrial Revitalization Corporation (IRCJ) in August 2003, Mitsukoshi was officially able to step forward as the sponsor to take over

---

Case Study 5.1:   Mitsukoshi: the next 100 years – *continued*

the store's rehabilitation. Usui was one of three companies included in the first batch of firms being helped by the IRCJ. With this government financial support, the store's main lender, Akita Bank, was able to waive outstanding loans, and IRCJ purchased financial claims from minor lenders. Despite Mitsukoshi's initial stewardship, Usui continued to struggle, unable to revitalize its operations in the face of competition from new chain stores in the area. It posted sales of only ¥17.4 billion in 2002 for a loss of some ¥200 million.

Through this determined effort of restructuring, closures and investment, Mitsukoshi has come a long way towards turning itself around although it is still a far cry from returning to the glory years of the 1980s. Arguably, it is still the most prestigious nationwide operation with the strongest brand, but it lacks a certain punch in terms of scale compared to Takashimaya and Millennium, and is still yet to display the necessary dynamism to compete in Japan's new retail era. Not surprising that, despite Mitsukoshi's sidestep move, analysts recommending a Mitsukoshi merger with Takashimaya have yet to change their opinions.

Consolidation from the center by the leading chains

Although the other companies do not have Millennium's store numbers, they too are hoping to increase management centralization and move away from store-by-store operations. All of the top companies are creating a single executive management structure. The leading chains have many things in common, but perhaps more important than their high ranking in the minds of luxury and status conscious consumers, all five companies have a significant and highly visible presence in Tokyo. Tokyo locations give department stores a clear and solid sales base from which to rebuild the rest of their chains. Companies lacking this presence, or which have failed to take advantage of it, are increasingly finding themselves falling behind. The gap between Tokyo and the regions, even between Tokyo and Kansai, has grown and will be a long-term fact of department store retailing. With competition from specialty retail chains, areas outside the big conurbations are no place to be a lone, unprotected department store. Even the second tier of companies, such as Matsuzakaya, Kintetsu, and Hankyu, which have stores in Tokyo but have their main stores outside the capital, are not faring nearly as well as their larger rivals.

Department stores are still influential and make up a major share of retail sales, but they are having to work very hard to get fit after years of sloth and over-indulgence. By 2015, the department store sector will have changed even more dramatically. Some analysts believe there are likely to be fewer than 200 stores left compared to the 350 of today (Japan Consuming, 2004), and the majority that remain will be closely affiliated to, if not actually wholly-owned by, the largest five chains. There are a few single operations, such as Marui Imai in Sapporo, Fujisaki in Sendai, Fukuya in Hiroshima, and Tsuruya in Kumamoto, that may well survive as independents, but even these are more likely to see the benefits of closer ties with the bigger groups.

6
General Merchandise Retail Chains

Since the 1960s, general merchandise retailers have been the most important retailers, as well as the most innovative. From 1972 until 2000, a GMS chain called Daiei was the largest retailer in Japan by sales. Daiei has since declined, but GMS chains are still at the core of the largest retail groups.

At the same time, the fortunes of GMS chains are changing rapidly and the format is no longer the de facto industry powerhouse that it once was. General merchandise retailing is becoming less important as specialists improve and expand in almost all individual merchandise categories. Large, diversified commercial groups are outmoded and find it more difficult to target specific consumer segments. The early years of the twenty-first century represent a significant and testing period for these chains as they attempt to adjust to new distribution realities.

Japan's largest retail groups

General Merchandise Store (GMS) chains operate large retail stores, second in size only to department stores, and both of these important store formats are operated by some of the largest retail companies. There, however, the comparison ends. GMS companies are neither as numerous nor as distinct as department stores in Japan. They have, however, been far more successful in recent decades and can be rightly labeled the leaders of modern Japanese retailing.

Sitting at the top of Japanese corporate retail rankings, these firms are household names in most parts of the country: Daiei, Ito-Yokado, Aeon (or Jusco as it was until 2001 and as many of its stores are still called), Seiyu, and Uny are the leading five chains. There are smaller, regional chains, including Olympic, Fuji, Izumi, Izumiya, Heiwado, Posful, and Kyushu Jusco. All 12 companies are far from small, but the smaller regional chains, notably Fuji, Izumiya, Posful and Olympic blur the distinction between

GMS formats and the smaller, more specialist food supermarket (see Chapter 7) and home center formats. Increasingly, the home centers in particular share many of the store size and merchandising characteristics of GMS chains, and are more like non-food GMS formats than DIY stores seen in the West (see Chapter 10).

Formally defined, a general merchandise store has the following characteristics in Japan:

- Large format (at least 1,500 sqm but often much larger, exceeding 20,000 sqm in some cases)
- Self-service
- Merchandise sales are split between the three broad categories of food, apparel and household goods, and each amounts to no less than 10 per cent of total store sales, but no more than 70 per cent in any one category
- The format is organized as a multiple chain of more than 10 stores

A GMS chain is distinguished from a department store through the use of self-service, from supermarkets in that less than 70 per cent of merchandise sold is food, and from other similar formats by size. In Japan, "large" is usually defined as exceeding the regulatory size under the Large Store Location Law. This means that the majority of stores in a chain will be larger than 3,000 sqm (or 6,000 sqm in the main metropolitan areas).

Table 6.1 provides a full list of major GMS chains for FY2003. Missing from the list is the now formally defunct Mycal operation that was, until 2001, the fourth largest GMS chain. Whereas Mycal as a company is gone, its stores and operations live on under the rehabilitation guidance of Aeon and, since 2004, have been performing well enough for Aeon to include them in its main sales figures, making it by far the largest GMS chain in the country. Many of the original Mycal stores, including its brand formats Saty and Vivre, continue to operate under Aeon's guidance, along with Mycal Kyushu and Mycal Hokkaido (now called Posful: for those interested, "Posful" stands for Positive Forever Universal). Mitsui Bussan also supports Posful. As already noted in previous chapters, this type of bankruptcy followed by absorption into a competing firm is a commonplace means of rehabilitation in Japan. Daiei has now shared the same fate.

In 2004, the largest retail conglomerate was Aeon Group. Aeon overtook Ito-Yokado that year thanks to the inclusion of sales figures from Mycal stores for the first time. Ito-Yokado, while operating a GMS chain of that name as its core parent chain, is the owner and operator of Seven Eleven Japan, which alone is the single largest retail chain in the country (see Chapter 8). Seven Eleven Japan is also the most profitable retailer, and

Table 6.1 Sales, pretax profit, and store numbers for leading general merchandise store retailers, consolidated and parent only, FY2003

Company	HQ	Consolidated Accounts					Parent Only Accounts				
		Sales	YonY	Pretax Profit	YonY	Subsidiary Firms Nos [4]	Sales	YonY	Pretax Profit	YonY	Store Nos
		¥ mn	%	¥ mn	%		¥ mn	%	¥ mn	%	
1 Aeon	Chiba	3,546,215	14.9	131,354	3.1	129 (+20)	1,764,365	3.7	27,593	-18.5	364
2 Ito-Yokado	Tokyo	3,542,146	0.3	200,787	5.9	64 (+11)	1,493,962	-2.2	42,317	-14.1	177
3 Daiei	Tokyo [1]	1,993,619	-9.3	31,500	146.4	101 (-33)	1,430,256	-8.2	15,545	14.6	266
4 Uny	Aichi	1,167,568	-1.0	39,254	-16.9	25 (+7)	720,214	-4.8	13,010	-24.0	151
5 Seiyu [2]	Tokyo	1,032,000	13.6	2,925	-	29 (-8)	692,360	13.1	550	-	404
6 Izumi	Hiroshima	407,647	6.4	17,742	12.7	17 (-1)	332,264	3.4	12,965	2.5	70
7 Izumiya	Osaka	368,879	7.3	5,278	30.6	21 (+3)	328,161	1.9	3,651	13.2	85
8 Heiwado	Shiga	353,780	0.9	11,739	17.8	18 (-1)	319,258	0.5	9,696	19.2	89
9 Fuji	Ehime	308,095	8.4	3,818	14.0	4 (-1)	298,217	1.6	3,512	16.9	80
10 Olympic	Tokyo	136,296	-3.9	3,775	2.8	4 (-2)	117,008	-3.0	2,925	7.8	46
11 Posful	Hokkaido	-	-	-	-	1 (-)	126,608	-3.6	1,517	-46.9	20
12 Aeon Kyushu [3]	Fukuoka	-	-	-	-	1 (-)	162,481	24.5	1,903	-33.8	31
13 PLANT	Fukui	-	-	-	-	1 (-)	45,201	7.2	1,361	-20.2	10

Notes:
[1] Daiei HQ is officially listed as Hyogo, but its main offices are located in Tokyo
[2] Seiyu changed its accounting period in 2003. Figures shown for period ending December 2004
[3] Aeon Kyushu changed its name from Kyushu Jusco in September 2003
[4] Brackets indicate change in group subsidiary numbers since 2001–02
Source: Company reports

Case Study 6.1:   Daiei: debts bigger than some countries' GDP

As Table 6.1 showed, the top GMS chains are genuinely large companies. In 2005, both Daiei and Aeon sit at the head of conglomerates numbering more than 100 companies each, although Daiei's assets are now to be pared down in order to restructure the company. Daiei represents a classic case of a traditional Japanese retail group, although its history and problems are mirrored by Saison Group and by Mycal. After growing to be the largest retailer in the country in 1972, Daiei was the first truly powerful retail buying force ever in Japan. It was the first professional, multiple retailer, and, along with Ito-Yokado, the first multi-format retail group. Based on this success and bolstered by strong leadership from its founder Isao Nakauchi, Daiei saw huge potential for expansion during the heady days of the booming 1980s economy. The company diversified both vertically and horizontally. By 1990, it had the largest chain of GMS stores, the second largest convenience store chain, operated several of the biggest restaurant chains in the country, and had interests as diverse as hotels, resorts, golf clubs, credit cards, radio and TV stations, and one of the more successful professional baseball teams. Most of this business empire was built as a result of the ambition and financial guarantees of Nakauchi himself. Several of his acquisitions during this period were opportunistic. A quarter share in the huge Recruit publishing business was acquired when the company's survival was threatened after political scandal. The Kiss FM radio station and Sun TV broadcasting station, both companies in the founder's hometown of Kobe, were acquired in order to save the original firms from bankruptcy. The same was partially true for the Oriental Hotel chain, again in Kobe, and while the addition of the very expensive baseball team has been offset by the team's success, it too was acquired largely due to Nakauchi's love for the sport.

Unfortunately, of course, such philanthropic business empire building has its drawbacks. During the same period, and unlike its main rivals, Aeon and Ito-Yokado, Daiei made the decision to acquire the land on which it built the majority of its stores. As with many of its acquisitions, this was to prove a significant strategic error. In 1992, when Daiei founder Isao Nakauchi announced his retirement at the age of 70 to allow his eldest son, Jun Nakauchi, to succeed him, the reaction from Daiei's bankers was so negative that he was forced to reverse his decision indefinitely. Daiei continued to survive on the basis of its large cash flow, but from the late 1980s onwards, interest payments on its debt were so large that the group's profit shrank, limiting investment in retail operations.

In 2004, Daiei had total debt of some ¥2.16 trillion. Of this, more than ¥1.6 trillion was interest bearing. Aeon, now the largest GMS group, also has high debts, but they are three times lower than Daiei at its peak (see Table 6.2). In October 2004, Daiei lost its political battle to remain independent because creditors and politicians decided management had not dealt with the debt problem. While Daiei expected to reduce interest bearing debt by half to some ¥900 million, the firm's leading creditor banks decided not to provide further debt waivers to support it. As a result, Daiei was handed over to the Industrial Revitalization Corporation of Japan (IRCJ) to undergo investigation and to be packaged out to a rehabilitation sponsor. Not surprisingly, Wal-Mart, which acquired Seiyu in 2003, and Cargill, were two overseas firms that expressed an interest in sponsoring Daiei's rehabilitation, with Wal-Mart even prepared to forego public funds to do so, because of the consumer access that Daiei's better stores would provide. However political pressure meant that the IRCJ dismissed such proposals at an early stage. The IRCJ also dismissed Aeon as a potential sponsor, and the rehabilitation rights went to Marubeni, a long-time Daiei shareholder and business associate. It also has its own interests in supermarkets having taken over

Case Study 6.1: **Daiei: debts bigger than some countries' GDP –** *continued*

control of Maruetsu, another Daiei affiliate, and Pororoca, a supermarket subsidiary acquired from Mycal. By staying out of the hands of Aeon, Daiei will continue as an independent retail company, and has the stated aim of moving out of the GMS format and to focus on food supermarket operations in future. This will entail the closure of 53 of its 266 stores and the selling off of much of its non-food operations.

Table 6.2   Interest bearing debts at major retailers, 2004

	Interest Bearing Debts ¥ mn	2003 to 2004 % change	2002 to 2004 % change	Sales to Debts Ratio
Daiei	1,638,354	–0.4	–23.4	1.22
Aeon	709,999	2.0	–3.1	4.99
Seiyu	459,067	–0.3	–25.0	2.04
Ito-Yokado	267,826	–25.8	–3.9	13.23
Uny	256,888	3.9	1.9	4.55
Mitsukoshi	249,546	–4.9	–4.9	3.67
Sogo	220,814	–8.9	–	2.03
Takashimaya	214,388	1.3	–20.8	5.20
Marui	187,390	0.0	–1.4	–
Izumi	139,285	–0.4	1.1	2.93
Daimaru	119,829	–16.6	–16.6	6.83
Tokyu Department Store	110,813	–15.5	–49.4	3.36
Izumiya	107,857	–1.4	–5.5	3.42
Heiwado	104,384	–9.5	–20.1	3.39
Isetan	94,469	–21.4	–35.8	6.51
Kojima	86,870	0.5	–	5.52
Kintetsu Department Store	77,935	–29.2	–25.7	5.29
Fuji	76,678	1.5	–	4.02
Best Denki	70,049	–11.4	–19.5	5.07
Parco	67,341	–16.0	–	3.53
Posful	67,034	–	–	1.89
Yamada Denki	61,944	–11.3	–	15.16
Matsuzakaya	60,722	–7.1	–20.3	6.18
Edion	60,404	–11.3	–	7.19
Izutsuya	59,035	–12.6	–	2.15
Maruetsu	56,254	–0.3	–	6.48
Maruzen	52,909	–19.0	–	2.21
Joshin	50,430	–6.2	–	4.86
Iwataya	41,619	–6.9	–51.4	2.67
Hankyu Department Store	35,259	–30.4	–57.1	10.91
Olympic	29,811	–7.3	–	4.57

Note:
Marui sales to debt ratio not available due to accounting changes. Change on 2002 shown where available
Source: Company Reports; Yahoo! Japan (2005)

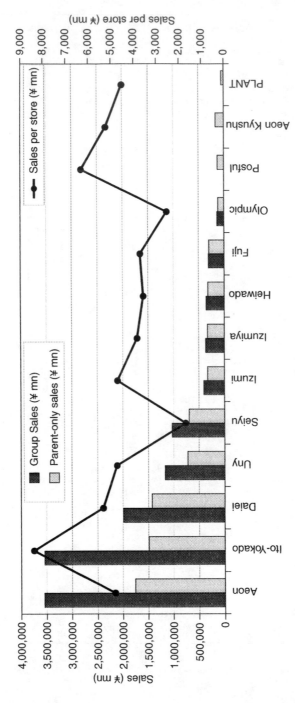

Figure 6.1 General merchandise chain total group sales, parent-only sales, and sales per GMS outlet, FY2003
Source: Company Reports

Ito-Yokado itself is the third most profitable. As Figure 6.1 shows, there are significant differences in size between the companies. By group, both Aeon and Ito-Yokado are now close to twice the size of Daiei, which, in turn is a little under twice the size of Uny and Seiyu. The sixth largest group in 2004, Izumi, was 2.5 times smaller than Seiyu, and Olympic was only half of its nearest rival Fuji.

The same pattern is repeated at parent company level. Three chains, Aeon, Ito-Yokado, and Daiei, exceeded ¥1.4 trillion in GMS sales for 2004, with Uny and Seiyu less than half this figure. Again, Izumi was less than half that of Seiyu, and there is a further drop off for Olympic, Posful, Aeon Kyushu, and PLANT. The last of these chains is a relatively new company with only 10 stores, and is included here largely because of its similar format.

Profitability varies greatly across company as does sales per store. Due to the ongoing restructuring of retailing in Japan, pretax profits remain unstable and highly variable year by year, although this is now a problem that companies like Aeon and Ito-Yokado are keen to overcome. Not only are retailers looking to operate in new ways and to actively attract customers, they are also having to contend with new accounting practices and, in several cases, with new ownership. This situation is expected to settle down over the next few years. In FY2003, only Seiyu showed a serious shortfall in profit and this was largely due to changes in accounting introduced by its new US parent, Wal-Mart. At the other end of the scale, Ito-Yokado remained highly profitable compared to other firms, but Aeon has also shifted its strategic thinking away from the traditional Japanese aim of size, cash flow, and market share by sales, and also generated a respectable profit, the highest in the firm's history.

As with profitability, Ito-Yokado also stands out in terms of sales per store (see Figure 6.1). It was the only chain to achieve ¥8 billion per store in 2004, with Posful the second highest at ¥7.3 billion per store. Both Daiei and Aeon Kyushu achieved more than ¥5 billion per store, but all the other chains were below this figure, including Aeon. Again, Seiyu's figure was reduced as stores previously operated as subsidiaries were introduced to the accounts for the first time in this financial year, many of them small-scale supermarket format stores.

When size matters

GMS companies have long led the retail sector from the front, although their actual contribution is perhaps more muted than in many industrialized nations. Since the 1960s when Daiei, Ito-Yokado, and Aeon (then Jusco) first began to be companies of genuine size, there have been a few minor scuffles with manufacturers, but on the whole, retailers have been happy to sit back and allow others to control distribution channels. For the manufacturers, the incentive to do this came largely through control of prices and supply. The argument was that by fixing prices, margins were maintained, customer service could be assured, and a continued flow of new, exciting products found their way to the market. Less successful products were quickly removed and discarded. To the benefit of retailers, manufacturers took upon themselves a significant proportion of distribution costs, and almost all marketing costs. The problem, of course was that this system led to higher prices at stores and very little differentiation between competing chains. But as Japanese consumers are the same people who work for major manufacturers and retailers, the system was allowed to survive for a surprisingly long time.

As summarized in Table 6.3, the GMS chains were the instigators of some of the most important disputes between retailers and manufacturers. GMS chains were the only retailers with size enough to take on manufacturers, and in each case in the table, the manufacturers in question are generally market leaders. Some extreme cases, such as the dispute between Daiei and the leading electrical manufacturer, Matsushita, continued for more than 20 years despite the fact that the issue was the illegal use of price fixing and non-supply of product. In reality, consumers could still find Matsushita products (mostly under the National and Panasonic brands) in Daiei stores. As noted previously, the face saving way this was done was for Matsushita to set up a separate wholesale sales company that could then supply Daiei indirectly. A similar solution was used by Sony after another contest of wills.

In this way GMS chains changed the retail landscape. By the 1980s, they were too big and had too much buying power to be ignored. Daiei, in 1990 was the largest seller of electrical goods in the country, although in the general statistics, the general merchandiser was distinguished from Best Denki, a specialist consumer electronics chain. Today, the importance of GMS retailing has shifted, but the buying and selling power of this format within the market still makes the companies that operate them the most powerful in the industry.

Today, there are five GMS chains that form the core of the industry: Aeon, Ito-Yokado, Daiei, Uny, and Seiyu. With Daiei's future now hanging in the balance, some see a two-horse race for the top spot between Aeon and Ito-Yokado. Seiyu, like Daiei and its historical parent Seibu Department Stores, also faced bankruptcy until it was acquired by Wal-Mart, and although the Wal-Mart management has achieved a major shift in strategy in a short-time, Seiyu is still relatively small in terms of overall scale. Uny has undertaken its own restructuring and is a highly respected retailer, but it remains a regional company with the vast majority of sales arising from its home base in Aichi Prefecture (see below). Furthermore, both Seiyu and Uny are not developing the same kinds of large scale GMS outlets seen in the past, with both moving towards more specialist formats. Seiyu's stores

Table 6.3 Some examples of disputes between GMS chains and manufacturers

Date	Disputing parties	Details
1964		Japan legislates against Resale Price Maintenance, except for books, CDs, newspapers
Oct. 1964	Daiei & Matsushita	Matsushita stopped supply of its products after Daiei unilaterally cut retail prices
Mar. 1965	Daiei & Kao	Kao stopped supply to Daiei after Daiei unilaterally cut retail prices
Jan. 1974	Jusco & Nisshin Shokuhin	Jusco stopped all trading with Nisshin in protest at rise in wholesale price
Sep. 1974	Daiei & Shiseido etc.	Daiei challenges cosmetics manufacturers to stop fixing retail prices
1975	Daiei & Matsushita	Manufacturer employees demonstrate against Daiei's own branded color TVs
Jul. 1993	Kawauchiya & Shiseido	Shiseido stops supply after price reductions
Mar. 1994	Daiei & Matsushita	Matsushita starts limited supplies to parts of Daiei group
Feb. 1995	Daiei & Suntory	Daiei removes all Suntory products from its shelves in protest at wholesale price levels Dispute settled in 5 days
Mar. 1996	Daiei & Matsushita	Matsushita resumes normal supply to Daiei
Feb. 2003	Aeon & Prima Ham	Aeon stops sale of all Prima Ham products after unapproved additives are found in own brand products made by Prima
Mar. 2003	Aeon & Prima Ham	Aeon reports Prima Ham to police for breaking food safety laws
Nov. 2003	Seven Eleven & Yamazaki Bread	Seven-Eleven starts sales of jointly developed products,10 years after removing all Yamazaki products from its shelves
Jun. 2004	Aeon & Sharp	Sharp demands stoppage of sale of directly imported (and very popular) Aeon own brandTFT TVs. Problem resolved in 1 week

Source: Compiled from newspapers and from NMJ (2004, p. 86)

will increasingly come under the influence of Wal-Mart's strategy and Uny has found its own niche in upscale food retailing with its Apita fascia. In this way, it is true that in GMS retailing at least, Aeon and Ito-Yokado are the companies to watch.

Aeon: Japan's new retail giant

Aeon is now Japan's largest retail group by sales, floor space, and large store numbers. It is a company that grew not through organic expansion, but by merger and acquisition (M&A). Although Aeon insists its history stretches back to the 1700s (see http://www.aeon.info), the modern day Aeon retail business began as a small Kansai based kimono store in 1926. In 1946, Takuya Okada became the seventh generation owner and new company president, and almost immediately began turning the retailer towards food. Through a series of mergers and friendly acquisitions, Jusco expanded around Kansai and soon into other areas. This company tradition of merger and absorption rather than takeover of smaller firms remains a core strategy; it continues to soak up other firms and is using the same approach to expand both its supermarket and drugstore operations (see Chapters 7 and 11).

In addition, Okada kept his company firmly focused on retailing. Although Jusco did diversify somewhat, notably into consumer credit, restaurants, some consumer entertainment, and also by opening stores overseas at an early stage, the group never moved far away from retailing in the way that caused the downfall of Daiei and Saison (see Figure 6.2). The company grew steadily under Okada's leadership, until in 1997, Motoya Okada took over from his father as Aeon's new president and the eighth generation owner. In Japan, the succession of company presidency is commonly kept within the family although this is now less popular than it once was. At Ito-Yokado, the son of founder Masatoshi Ito was groomed for the presidency, but decided on a different career and, as noted above, creditors openly rejected the idea of a family succession at Daiei. In Aeon's case, however, after an education at Babson College in the US, and having subsequently worked in Aeon since 1979, Motoya Okada's promotion to president has been a very clear success.

With the succession came a completely new strategy for Aeon. Business strategy among Japanese retailers is often difficult to read, rarely stated publicly, and often concentrates on the day-to-day issues of solving problems and making small, incremental improvements to business. Aeon changed this stance completely. Its new strategy, called Global 10, was released in 2001 and can be summarized as follows:

- To be one of the largest 10 retailers in the world by sales by 2010

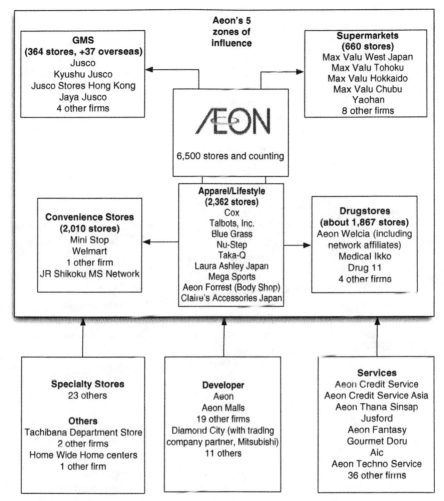

Figure 6.2 Aeon Group: major group interests, 2003
Source: Company Report

- To be the leading retailer in Japan in all of the company's main formats of general merchandise stores, supermarkets, drugstores, and home centers, by 2010
- To achieve group sales of ¥7 trillion
- To achieve economies of scale
- To drive these goals through IT and logistics developed specifically for Aeon
- To implement an EDLP merchandising strategy

In a lot of its PR, Aeon quite openly states that it sees Wal-Mart as its single most important competitive threat and was actually making this claim long before Wal-Mart entered the Japanese market in 2002. Much of what has been developed at Aeon since 2001 is also based largely on best practices found elsewhere in the world. Aeon's own branding system is being developed by US firm Daymon, and its IT systems are based on similar systems used by Wal-Mart. Aeon has no compunction about using overseas consultants and is willing to learn and apply anything that will help meet its goals. On the logistics side, Aeon is the first Japanese retailer to attempt a completely independent distribution system. It has developed a network of Aeon exclusive, but third-party owned and operated, distribution centers across the country. These are split into five levels (see Table 6.4). The really innovative part of this strategy, for Japan at least, is the National Distribution Centers (NDC) and National Cross-Docking Centers (NXD), neither of which were used by retailers in the past. Aeon's aim is to have as much of its merchandise as possible pass through its own centers. It hopes to greatly reduce costs, cutting more than ¥20 billion from its logistics budget that stood at ¥120 billion in 2002 (Suzuki, 2002: p. 186), and so create the first Japanese system that allows for Everyday Low Price (EDLP) merchandising. This is a major step towards modernization as it openly rejects the traditional manufacturer-led price promotions that were the sole method used in Japan in the past. The switch is not without problems, however, with only 40 suppliers agreeing to use Aeon's distribution centers as of November 2004 and some, such as the food industry leader Ajinomoto, openly refusing to use them (Asano et al, 2004). But, again, Aeon and its fellow GMS chains are now too large, and too important for manufacturers to entirely ignore.

Aeon has not completely forgotten how it grew, however. It still has a healthy desire to absorb other, usually willing domestic chains both as a source of growth and as a way to protect its preeminent position. Aeon took responsibility for Yaohan after that company went bankrupt in the early 1990s, and has transformed it into the solvent and viable supermarket chain now called Max Valu Tokai. In 2002 it acquired a controlling stake in Inageya in Tokyo. Inageya is a major supermarket chain, and at the time of acquisition, Aeon officials were quoted in Asahi Newspapers as saying:

> There is nothing in this stake that can directly benefit our business. But if we didn't take the shares, a foreign company or a trading house would have. Our decision was important. (Asahi Newspapers, 12 June 2002)

In truth, the Inageya stake would have held little attraction to most overseas firms, but the possibility of a trading house such as Marubeni moving to take over the company and consolidate its growing supermarket interests in Tokyo represented a threat.

Table 6.4 Aeon Distribution Centers: nationwide development in five size categories

Location/Name	Opening Date	Type/Function	Floor Size	Management Firm
Sapporo	2005 (est.)	RDC, XD, PC		
Aomori	2003	XD		
Akita	2003	XD, PC		
Morioka	2003	XD, PC		
Sendai	2001	RDC, XD, PC	39,833 sqm	Senko
Shinshu	2004	XD, PC		
Niigata	2003	XD, PC		
Hokuriku	2003	XD, PC		
Kita Kanto	2005 (est.)			
Kanto	2002	NXD, RDC, XD, PC	64,220 sqm	Fukuyama Transport
Shizuoka	2002	XD, PC	10,689 sqm	Nichirei
Chubu	2002	NXD, RDC, XD, PC	35,740 sqm	Nihon Transcity
Kyoto		PC		
Kansai	2003	NDC, NXD, RDC, XD	85,645 sqm	
Hyogo	2002	RDC,XD		Hitachi Transport
Hiroshima	2005 (est.)	RDC, XD, PC		
Shikoku	2003	XD, PC		Nichirei
Kyushu	2003	RDC, XD, PC	18,480 sqm	Hitachi Transport
Okinawa	2003	RDC, XD, PC		
Others		XD and/or PC		

Notes:
NDC: National distribution centre
NXD: National cross-docking centre
RDC: Regional distribution centre
XD: Cross-docking centre
PC: Processing centre (usually on separate site)
Source: Suzuki (2002, p. 187); Larke (2005)

This was followed in 2002 by Aeon acquiring rehabilitation rights for Kotobukiya, a major Kansai supermarket chain, and for Mycal, at the time Japan's fourth largest GMS chain. In 2004 it also acquired controlling stakes in Super Joy, a supermarket chain in Hokkaido, and Kasumi, another major supermarket in Kanto. Elsewhere, Aeon's shopping mall development firm called Diamond City, a joint-venture with Mitsubishi that began back in the 1940s, has been throwing up new, large scale shopping malls across the country at the rate of five to 10 a year.

As a result of all this activity, Aeon is by far the largest retailer by floor space with some 3.2 million square meters of shopping space in 2004. It has already achieved many of its strategic goals, although as some subsidiaries

Table 6.5 Aeon Group estimated total reach for 2004

	Companies	Stores	Sector Rank †	Sales † ¥ mn
GMS	13*	364	1	2,001,559
Supermarkets	11	579	1	632,878
Key Affiliates	4	300†		450,423
CVS	2	2,361	7	74,708
Department stores	3	3	–	127,863
Drugstores	12	1,867	1	180,000
Key Affiliates				568,200
Home centers	1	57	1	187,774
Key Affiliates	4	300†		434,581
Specialty chains	27	2,627	2	449,161
Services	64	976	–	501,962
Shopping center development	30		1	49,240
		Estimated total retail sales		5,658,349

Notes:
*: three GMS companies outside Japan
†: estimated figure
Key affiliates are firms with confirmed relations to Aeon
Source: Compiled from press reports; Company Reports

remain outside the consolidated accounts, it is difficult to pinpoint certain figures. Table 6.5 summarizes where Aeon stood in 2004. If unconsolidated affiliated companies are included, notably the Aeon Welcia Drugstore Alliance and the newly formed group of home centers (see Chapter 10), then Aeon is already the leading retailer in the GMS, supermarket, drugstore, and home center sectors. Although the table makes assumptions that largely ignore Aeon's own accounting principles, it offers a reasonable summary due to the close relationships between companies as formed both through share-holding and management tie-ups. The power of Aeon's reach in supermarkets and home centers is overlooked by many, and with some justification as both are highly regionalized markets, but the structure for a future nation-wide buying system is clearly there, and Aeon has already implemented such a system for its drugstores.

Aeon's only major problem is profit and where to find it. Sales densities at its GMS chain are some of the poorest of all the leading firms because space has been expanded rapidly without similar boosts in sales. In addition, part of the Aeon legacy of expansion by merger means that shopping malls and other shopping buildings are the mainstay of its store portfolio. As a result, much of the company's income comes not from retailing per se, but actually from tenant rents – i.e. from the success of other, mostly specialty, retailers. In 2004, Aeon grossed ¥62.5 billion from tenant rents, which if deducted from total income would actually have meant an operating loss of ¥38.5 billion rather than the ¥24 billion profit that was actually posted (Shibata and Tsumoto, 2004).

Having said that, Aeon is currently a Japanese retailing hero, at least for politicians, consumers, and its tenant retailers. Having such a clear goal and actually working towards that goal makes the company unique among its peers. Aeon is already at a size unprecedented in Japanese retail history. It is active in China, Malaysia, and Thailand where it has a combined set of 37 GMS outlets, and is seen by many as the key challenger to Wal-Mart even back at home. Problems with shifting from a supplier-led strategy based on market share and tenant rents will not be solved overnight, but at least the company is moving in the right direction and meeting these problems head on. Presenting a challenge to the traditional aspects of the distribution system is probably the single most worrying issue that Aeon faces, but, based on sound retail economics, the trickle of suppliers that understand what Aeon is trying to do and how they can benefit from it, may well become an avalanche very soon.

Aeon and Ito-Yokado go head-to-head

Ito-Yokado is currently the only GMS chain that has the size and ability to challenge Aeon and the Aeon versus Ito-Yokado debate is one that has raged in Japan since the turn of the century. In reality, of course, Aeon and Ito-Yokado are not in direct competition. True, they are the two most advanced and currently the most economically healthy of all the big retail groups, but there is no reason why both companies cannot share the Japanese market. Careful planning, along with large store development restrictions, mean that individual stores rarely come into competition. On the other hand, competition in terms of their dealings with suppliers will become a growing issue. Beyond that, Aeon and Ito-Yokado are very different entities with the only common factor being that both operate large-format general merchandise stores.

What is important, however, is that these are the only two firms with a clear opportunity and financial mandate to actually change the industry as a whole. Despite the exit of Carrefour in 2005, Wal-Mart and Tesco remain unknown entities in terms of their influence on Japanese retailing, although their presence gives credence to the potential of the market. So it is up to domestic retailers, specifically Aeon and Ito-Yokado, to make the necessary changes in attitude and channel control. What gets observers excited is that they are both looking at this period of change in very different ways.

Aeon's push for sheer size has been dubbed "un-Japanese" in the press because of the openly competitive pressures it places on the market. By contrast, the quieter, less abrasive expansion of Ito-Yokado has been labeled as more gentlemanly, and ipso facto, more Japanese. It could equally be argued, however, that Aeon's strategy is one pursued by retailers almost universally in Japan – the aim of high market share and sales capacity over and above profit. In the past, few retailers have managed to acquire significant market share, even in narrow merchandise categories or small regional areas, but almost all retailers emphasize physical size, buying power, merchandise volume, and cash flow well before profitability or, related to that, operational efficiency. Until recently, Ito-Yokado was without question the only exception. It has always considered profit to be paramount within its business goals, and this strategy is now being emulated by specialists like Yamada Denki, Fast Retailing, and Shimamura.

Ito-Yokado's obsession with the bottom line has led to a strategy of gradual, conservative group development, but one that has, so far, worked well, albeit in an environment of low competition. Ito-Yokado not only operates Japan's highest selling and most profitable retail chain, Seven-Eleven Japan, but the core Ito-Yokado GMS chain is also Japan's second most profitable retail operation. In addition, the group includes Denny's Japan restaurants, York Benimaru supermarkets, and, most recently, IY Bank. All are run with similar aims. Like Aeon, Ito-Yokado is also expanding rapidly into China with plans for some 300 convenience stores and a dozen GMS outlets around Beijing by 2008. At home, however, the two companies are clearly very different, both in philosophy and actual operations. They are also different in what they've achieved in the domestic market.

Table 6.6 shows a breakdown of store locations by prefecture for each of the main chains. Including Aeon's two main subsidiaries in the south of Japan, Aeon Kyushu and Ryukyu Jusco, shows just how close Aeon is to national store coverage. In 2004, Yamanashi and Kagoshima were the only prefectures with no Aeon GMS outlet. Daiei was present in 39 of the 47 prefectures, but will reduce this number as stores are closed down in 2005 and 2006. Seiyu store numbers are incomplete based on this data source (Nihon Keizai Shinbun, 2004), but even if they included all of Seiyu's major subsidiaries, the chain only covers around two thirds of the 47 prefectures. Ito-Yokado had

Table 6.6   Locations of general merchandise stores for leading chains, February 2004

Prefecture	Aeon	Ito-Yokado	Daiei	Seiyu	Uny	Total Stores
Hokkaido	4	15	10	10		39
Aomori	6	4	1			11
Iwate	8	1	1			10
Miyagi	17	3	2	1		23
Akita	10	1				11
Yamagata	7		2			9
Fukushima	5	4	1	2		12
Ibaragi	15	6	1	2	5	29
Tochigi	8	4	1		2	15

Table 6.6 Locations of general merchandise stores for leading chains, February 2004
– *continued*

Prefecture	Aeon	Ito-Yokado	Daiei	Seiyu	Uny	Total Stores
Gunma	3	3		3	5	14
Saitama	7	20	14	31	6	78
Chiba	22	21	13	16	4	76
Tokyo	4	32	31	76	1	144
Kanagawa	8	29	28	24	12	101
Niigata	17	2	2		2	23
Toyama	6				8	14
Ishikawa	6		1		4	11
Fukui	1			1	5	7
Yamanashi		3	2		1	6
Nagano	26	5	2	2	5	40
Gifu	12	2			14	28
Shizuoka	16	6	2	10	13	47
Aichi	23	8	6	9	56	102
Mie	23				6	29
Shiga	4		2	7		13
Kyoto	5	1	2	7		15
Osaka	21	2	32	12		67
Hyogo	26	2	45	5		78
Nara	9		3			12
Wakayama	3		1			4
Tottori	4		1			5
Shimane	5					5
Okayama	10	1	2			13
Hiroshima	4	1	3			8
Yamaguchi	4		1	1		6
Tokushima	6		1			7
Kagawa	6		1			7
Ehime	4		1			5
Kochi	1		1			2
Fukuoka	14		27	7		48
Saga	9			2		11
Nagasaki	7		6	3		16
Kumamoto	11		3			14
Oita	34		3			37
Miyazaki	14		2			16
Kagoshima			4			4
Okinawa	28		2			30
No. of Prefectures	45	24	39	21	17	47
Totals	483	176	263	231	149	1,302

Notes:
Aeon numbers include Aeon Kyushu and Ryukyu Jusco
Seiyu numbers omit regional subsidiaries
Daiei numbers to February 2004
Source: Compiled from Nihon Keizai Shinbun (2004)

stores in only 24 prefectures, with only seven stores south of Nagoya, and Uny was present in only 17 prefectures. In Uny's case 38 per cent of its total chain was located in its home prefecture of Aichi alone. Ito-Yokado had a similar proportion of stores in Tokyo and Kanagawa, and Seiyu had almost 30 per cent of stores in Tokyo.

The contrast between Aeon and Ito-Yokado is again the most marked despite the two companies leading the sector. Ito-Yokado is concentrated in the northern half of Japan and particularly in Tokyo. Tokyo, Saitama, Chiba, and Kanagawa prefectures accounted for 67.3 per cent of sales in FY2003. In the same area, Aeon had only 41 stores in total, accounting for only 15 per cent of total sales, but this is an increase of eight stores since 2002.

While Aeon has added stores extensively in the 1990s, Ito-Yokado has maintained a steady, conservative expansion in store numbers and store space, safe in the confidence of its long tried and tested formula. Aeon, as with many Japanese chains that have relied on rapid store expansion as the cornerstone of their growth strategy, has seen profitability and store efficiency fall. However, it has pulled well ahead of all other chains in terms of size, and is arguably fast approaching a critical mass that suppliers and consumers alike cannot ignore. In addition to stores, Aeon has invested heavily in both IT and logistics infrastructure and is moving towards a retail system of profitability through cost control. This is in contrast to Ito-Yokado, which relies on high quality stores and merchandise and the higher gross margins that they command.

Not only is Aeon looking to be large, it is also investing more in general retail facilities with less emphasis on a single core GMS format, while pursuing specialty retailing through separate operations. Again, the very different strategies of space and shopping center style retail diversity at Aeon, and core format, efficient direct operation at Ito-Yokado set the two chains well apart. Also, deflationary pressure on prices and, as a result, retail margins, means that Aeon has followed the common path of generating income from marketing sources such as rents and supplier rebates. Ito-Yokado, with its greater cost efficiency, has managed to avoid this route, providing a much more stable business platform. Deflation has hit Ito-Yokado too, and the company has been working to adjust to lower retail prices for the past three years, but the trend has not hurt it as much as others.

Ito-Yokado continues to be its own boss within its stores. The chain is famous for giving high levels of autonomy to individual outlets in terms of merchandise ordering and control, even training part-time workers to order for their own, small merchandise sections. The company aims to offer clearly targeted product to well defined local markets. At the same time, Ito-Yokado works with suppliers to keep distribution costs well down, and coordinates with supplier marketing campaigns and pricing. It was one of the first chains to actively and publicly reduce the number of wholesale suppliers working with any one region or even one store. In many cases a single key supplier is designated and other wholesalers are required to work through that distributor if they want their product in Ito-Yokado stores. Coupled with perhaps the most advanced information collection and management system for any retailer, the company is able to control supply chain costs relatively well.

For Aeon, as mentioned already, rather than look at internal considerations, shopping center formats were seen as able to generate the extra income. Of the stores opened in the later half of the 1990s, most were shopping centers. These serve a much wider customer area than a typical Ito-Yokado outlet and cater to a much broader target of customers. While this may in some cases generate a higher traffic flow, it also means that Aeon has given up a large amount of direct control within its stores. A lot of the sales area is operated by tenants with their own problems, costs, and limitations. Equally, among suppliers Aeon has a reputation for following market trends and only reacting after a competitor achieves a hit. This reactionary behavior is, again, a model followed by most retailers, with Ito-Yokado being one of those companies leading the way.

Another comparison is the two companies' different approach to pricing – something that is increasingly important as deflation continues in Japan. For Ito-Yokado, low prices are not a major consideration. It aims more to generate a regular, more targeted and constant customer flow throughout the week with, what it calls "fair pricing". In the spirit of EDLP, it believes that significant price reductions would not generate that much greater customer footfall as stores are designed and located to cater for particular defined markets. The chain consistently emphasizes quality to the extent that customers do not expect it to be the cheapest place to buy. Aeon, however, claims to aim for the US standard of EDLP, although there is still little evidence that it has achieved it. Aeon's past and present presidents have said they hope to offer a consistent, internationally standardized price, based on the assumption that Japan's prices will continue to fall for some time. It is also the reason for Aeon's continued search for ever more floor space, giving it ever greater buying power and buying reach, and allowing it to manipulate prices even further.

So which of these two companies are likely to win out? Interestingly enough, in November 2001, Ito-Yokado and Aeon opened their first jointly developed shopping mall in Yamato city, Kanagawa Prefecture. Shortly afterwards a study of consumers showed that there was a marked differences between the two chains. Overall, 45 per cent of customers used Ito-Yokado, while only 32 per cent used Aeon's Jusco store. Almost twice as many people chose Ito-Yokado for most of their shopping as those who chose Aeon. In line with Ito-Yokado's aim to attract customers back often, 51.3 per cent of respondents using the center more than twice a week favored the company over Aeon. But equally, those customers coming only once a week or less also preferred Ito-Yokado over Aeon to a ratio of 40.6 per cent versus 32.7 per cent. Both stores suggested a first year sales target of ¥12 billion, with Aeon's specialty store tenants adding a further ¥8 billion. Ito-Yokado exceeded its target by at least 30 per cent, but Aeon only just made it.

Summary: Only Acon and Ito-Yokado

In many ways, GMS retailing in Japan is indeed now a two-horse race at the national level, but there is no reason why both cannot be winners. Aeon and Ito-Yokado have the top slots more or less to themselves, although Wal-Mart and Tesco will hope to have something to say about that over coming years. The two big Japanese chains will play a major role in shaping the retail landscape over the next 10 years, and a significant part of this change will be in how they both react to overseas entry and manage to convince suppliers to bend to their will. Aeon clearly believes it can outsize all other companies and aims to be the biggest in whatever it does. Ito-Yokado remains much more market focused, aiming to bring customers into their stores on a regular and consistent basis.

Both strategies could work, but not in the same place. Aeon will likely consolidate its physical presence with better retailing operations and greater efficiency over coming years, but how and when it will gain the support of suppliers and finally begin to generate significant returns is still unclear. Where it comes into direct market competition with stores that are in some ways better in the eyes of consumers, it could well find itself in trouble. Hopefully for Aeon, such cases will only occur in a few local markets rather than throughout the country.

Aeon's management frequently cites overseas companies as its key competitors, perhaps rightly, but perhaps not. It appears to have taken its eye off domestic firms, perhaps in the belief that they are nothing to worry about. Ito-Yokado would disagree. While the end of the last decade was as hard for Ito-Yokado as it was for anyone else, the company's customer orientation continues to pay off. Ito-Yokado is unlikely to change its strategy in any radical way over the next few years. It really does not have to. It too will watch the developments surrounding Wal-Mart closely, but with perhaps less concern than many of its domestic competitors.

7
Food Supermarkets

The Japanese food supermarket format is one of the most complex and difficult to unravel. Fresh food is one sector that even the largest chains have almost unanimously failed to modernize or come to terms with. The standards of some stores in even the largest chains would disappoint both retail experts and any holidaying health inspectors from overseas, but, in recent years, a small but growing number of chains have improved to be as good as any food retailer anywhere in the world. There are several reasons for this:

- The supermarket sector remains highly fragmented with no national chains, but many regional players
- It is the last major retail sector yet to take the step towards modern retail management systems. Within the sector there are some examples of excellent, modernized retailers mixed with many old fashioned and inefficient chains
- The sector competes across formats, both with general merchandise stores and department stores, which invariably sell food on one or more of their floors, and convenience stores and fast-food chains fulfilling the role that supermarkets often fulfill in other nations
- Official and formal definitions of supermarkets are misleading and complicated by terminology

In this chapter, we take a detailed look at the supermarket sector as a whole. Because of its fragmented development, supermarkets are one area of retailing that will modernize in leaps and bounds over coming years. As food is such an important category, on a cursory consideration it is surprising that such developments have not occurred earlier. Arguably, food retailers have been held back by all the most resistant vested interests of traditional Japanese distribution systems:

- Strong manufacturer control of channels
- Large, powerful food wholesalers

- Archaic and regionalized perishable food wholesale system
- The powerful political influence of traditional farmers

Low margins in this sector have probably caused the largest retailers to place a low priority on food retailing among their many problems and restructuring strategies. This is now about to change. More importantly, there are significant opportunities for overseas retailers in this sector.

The problem of definition

The tendency to borrow and adapt words from other countries is one of the most endearing and confusing aspects of the Japanese language. In Japanese, a supermarket is almost universally known as a *super* (technically, "sûpâ"). Unfortunately, the word *super* is used by official statistics to refer to any form of retail format deriving more than 70 per cent of sales from a single merchandise type, employing self-service, and having a floor space exceeding 250 square meters. As a result, a large Aoyama Shoji menswear store is also counted as a *super*, i.e. an apparel supermarket.

In this chapter, we are naturally referring to a retail format employing self-service and predominantly selling food. In addition, because of the complication of other formats overlapping into the food sector, we differentiate from GMS chains, where stores sell a wide range of merchandise; from department stores, where self-service is not the main sales technique; and convenience stores, which are defined by their smaller size, longer opening hours, and predominantly franchise based organization system. A supermarket is therefore a store deriving at least 90 per cent of sales from food in a self-service environment.

The food supermarket sector overview

Based on the above definition, there were some 466,590 food retailers in Japan, of which 17,692 were self-service food supermarkets (see METI, 2003: Table 7.1). Because of the small, non-incorporated nature of most retail enterprises in Japan, the Census measures the size of business by number of employees per store. Even using this imprecise method, however, it is clear that the majority of food supermarkets are incorporated businesses, employing a relatively large number of people. The size of supermarkets is also increasing both in terms of average floor space, which increased 5.3 per cent from 1999 to 2002, and average employee numbers per store, which grew 11.4 per cent in the same period. The vast majority of employees are, however, part-time, with full-time employees accounting for only 20.7 per cent of the total and averaging fewer than 10 per store.

Between the previous two Census reports, store numbers and sales were both down around 5 per cent, although total sales space grew by 5.3 per cent.

Table 7.1   Japan's food supermarket sector according to 2002 Census of Commerce

	Unit	Value	Ratio %	2002/99 %
Total Store numbers	Stores	17,692	100.0	–5.4
Outlets by number of employees				
2 or less	Stores	120	0.7	–4.0
3 to 4	Stores	359	2.0	–12.2
5 to 9	Stores	1,439	8.1	–7.0
10 to 19	Stores	2,957	16.7	–16.2
20 to 29	Stores	2,636	14.9	–18.8
30 to 49	Stores	4,190	23.7	–9.9
50 to 99	Stores	4,599	26.0	9.9
100 or more	Stores	1,392	7.9	36.6
Employees	People	782,817	100.0	5.4
Unpaid family employees	People	1,104	0.1	
Salaried employees	People	8,147	1.0	
Permanent, full-time	People	162,092	20.7	
Part-time, temporary	People	611,474	78.1	
Other Employees	People	14,185	100.0	
Seasonal	People	10,581	74.6	
Seconded employees	People	3,604	25.4	
Sales	¥ mn	15,903,155	100.0	–5.0
Sales floor space	sqm	16,396,603	100.0	5.3
Averages				
Employees per outlet	People	44.25		11.4
Full-time employees per outlet	People	9.16		
Part-time employees per outlet	People	34.56		
Sales per outlet	¥ mn	898.89		0.4
Sales space per outlet	sqm	926.78		11.4

Source: METI (2003)

Nevertheless, using the same Census figures alone, supermarkets now account for 38.5 per cent of total food sales of all retailers, even though, by store numbers, they represent less than 4 per cent of retailers that specialize in food.

Major food supermarket chains and their role

A key factor for the supermarket sector compared to all of the other major retail formats is its regional nature. Ignoring the food operations that are covered in our section on GMS chains, there is currently not one nation-wide chain of food supermarkets. Having said that, Aeon, in one of the group's most farsighted and rapid expansion moves, is the first major retailer to make the attempt to rectify this gap (see below). There are no others.

There are two types of food supermarket chains: major regional and sub-regional. The majority of consumers will only know their local supermarket chain and no more. The majority of food shopping is done locally from home either by bicycle or on foot, a practice that is also encouraged by con-sumers' preference to shop every day for fresh food. In the major metropoli-tan areas, there are a handful of larger chains, some of which appear in the normal retail sales rankings, but none of which are even close to the largest GMS and department store chains by sales volume. Most chains are consider-ably smaller and remain virtually unknown outside their limited geographi-cal coverage. Here, however, lies their interest because some of these smaller chains are now showing remarkable signs of innovation and ability. As a result some have, or are, attracting attention as possible takeover targets from larger chains such as Aeon or even overseas concerns.

Japan's largest food supermarket chains, those with annual sales in excess of ¥100 billion for FY2003 are shown in Table 7.2. A number of the compa-nies in this list are somewhat secretive about their results due to their private share holdings and, in some cases, because they are unlisted sub-sidiaries of larger concerns. Many of the largest supermarket chains are now part of much bigger retail groupings. Life Corporation is currently the largest chain in terms of sales and remains aloof from other groups, but the company's charismatic chairman is said to maintain close personal links to several of the largest retail groups. The chain's less than impressive profit figures over the last few years have led to speculation that it would join with either Aeon or Seiyu. Numerous press rumors suggest the possibility of merger with other, similar chains such as Yaoko and Eco's although such a development would be advantageous to Life alone. The company posted a modest increase in pretax profits for FY2003. Life was boosted by the bankruptcy of Kotobukiya, its main local rival in southern Kansai, in 2002, and from the demise of some Daiei stores.

Maruetsu is currently the second largest supermarket chain, but for many years led the rankings. After its poor performance in the 1980s, Daiei took a controlling stake in Maruetsu, only for Daiei's own problems to rebound and further hurt the company. In 2000, Marubeni acquired the controlling share in Maruetsu and has since been attempting to restructure the company with mixed success. This has included the addition of other, much smaller Tokyo based supermarket chains, and the acquisition of Pororoca from bankrupt Mycal Group. Maruetsu has the store locations and food experience to become a serious supermarket chain under Marubeni's tutelage and with the added advantage of the trading house's considerable fresh food supply chain links. It is also growing its own FoodEx chain of upscale, small format stores in central Tokyo. The addition of Daiei to

Table 7.2 Leading food supermarket companies in Japan with sales volume over ¥100 billion, FY2003

		Notes	Operating Base Prefecture	Sales ¥ mn	YonY %	Pretax Profit ¥ mn	YonY %	Stores	Sales per Store ¥ mn
1	Life Corporation	1	Osaka	376,138	−0.1	3,166	−23.8	189	1,990
2	Maruetsu	2,3	Tokyo	364,446	−1.7	5,197	−4.3	207	1,761
3	York Benimaru	4	Fukushima	284,058	4.9	13,367	11.3	104	2,731
4	Tokyu Store	5,6	Tokyo	266,910	−2.8	5,254	41.3	89	2,999
5	Okuwa	1	Wakayama	229,702	−0.7	6,724	10.1	125	1,838
6	Kasumi	7	Ibaragi	228,859	−6.1	5,788	−7.2	119	1,923
7	Inageya	1,7	Tokyo	221,564	−2.0	5,007	−3.4	127	1,745
8	Arcs	13	Hokkaido	187,393	21.1	5,891	24.7	140	1,339
9	Valor		Gifu	186,736	11.5	7,359	7.1	116	1,610
10	Summit	10,11	Tokyo	177,810	9.9	3,690	1.8	78	2,280
11	Mandai		Osaka	176,801	2.4	4,808	5.5	–	–
12	SunLive	8	Fukuoka	175,528	−2.5	1,518	12.4	208	–
13	Max Valu West Japan	7	Hyogo	170,146	0.9	3,003	−33.0	126	1,350
14	Marunaka	8	Kagawa	167,819	2.2	7,055	−11.6	–	–
15	U-Store	9	Aichi	153,630	3.3	3,626	−23.5	71	2,164
16	Yaoko		Saitama	151,832	11.4	5,688	12.7	73	2,080
17	Taiyo		Kagoshima	133,643	0.1	4,855	0.9	86	1,554
18	Yamanaka		Aichi	112,620	−1.4	397	−19.6	70	1,609
19	San-ei		Okinawa	111,598	10.3	7,181	17.1	56	1,993
20	Kansai Supermarket	10	Hyogo	109,528	−3.8	1,375	−48.6	53	2,067
21	Sanwa	13	Tokyo	108,500	4.0	2,168	−20.3	–	–
22	Marushoku	8	Oita	107,293	−2.9	1,649	−2.6	–	–
23	Daimaru Peacock	12	Tokyo	106,016	–	–	–	–	–
24	Sanyo Marunaka		Okayama	101,559	10.5	2,473	7.8	–	–
25	Sotetsu Rozen	5,14	Kanagawa	101,435	−4.6	549	−21.2	67	1,514
26	Eco-s	15	Tokyo	101,338	10.6	1,999	20.3	66	1,535

Notes:
1, Nichiryu buying group; 2, Partly owned by Marubeni; 3, Partly owned by Daiei; 4, Ito-Yokado subsidiary; 5, Hasshakai buying group; 6, Tokyu Railways Group subsidiary; 7, Partly owned by Aeon Group; 8, Part of Marushoku Group; 9, Uny subsidiary; 10, AJS buying group; 11, Partly owned by Sumitomo (Summit: wholly owned); 12, Daimaru subsidiary; 13, CGC buying group; 14, Sotetsu Railways Group subsidiary; 15, Selco group
Sources: Company Reports; NMJ (2004.6.24, pp. 1–6; Asano et al (2004); Otsuka and Kaneko (2004)

Marubeni's portfolio should, in theory, create even greater opportunity, although Marubeni still lacks a record of successful supermarket operation.

The third largest chain is York Benimaru, one of the up and coming food retailers in Japan. York Benimaru is a major subsidiary of Ito-Yokado and is run with the same efficiency and eye to profit as the rest of the group. The company has been growing strongly in recent years and was the only one of the leading seven chains that increased sales in FY2003. More importantly, York Benimaru is by far the most profitable supermarket chain in Japan and the only one to break ¥10 billion in pretax profit. York Benimaru is squarely based in the Fukushima area north of Tokyo, but its success has led to greater things. Rather than expand nationwide, however, Ito-Yokado is introducing the chain into China as part of its three format strategy around Beijing. York Benimaru will operate supermarkets alongside the Ito-Yokado GMS format and Seven-Eleven convenience stores with plans for several dozen stores by 2008.

The fourth largest chain is Tokyu Store, subsidiary of the Tokyu Railway Company and related to Tokyu Department Store. As with Maruetsu, Tokyu is a solely Tokyo based chain, but with a more upscale positioning at many of its stores, recently shifting some of its more central locations over to its Precce fascia and closing a number of older, less prestigious stores. Despite this, Tokyu's profitability was poor for many years and has only just begun to recover. It has slipped down the sales rankings and is currently struggling to keep up with developments in the Tokyo market and in the industry as a whole. It remains the second largest of the six big companies currently attempting to carve up the Tokyo market, but compared to its rivals, is arguably related to the weakest of the groups. Maruetsu, Inageya, and Summit are all affiliated to more powerful and more food orientated parents, whereas Tokyu suffers from the debt problems at its railway parent and at Tokyu Department Stores.

While Japanese observers make little of the fact, grouping and affiliation are becoming vitally important as the supermarket sector restructures. Of the leading 26 firms with sales over ¥100 billion in FY2003, only seven have no formal links to larger parents or buying groups. Even so, these companies are actually related to buying groups by the need to use large, nationally powerful food wholesalers for supply. Increasingly, the parents in question are amalgamating, with Aeon, CGC, and the railway buying groups notably prominent among the leading firms. Aeon operates a group of seven subsidiary chains of food supermarkets under the Max Valu name. In addition, Aeon has added controlling stakes in both Inageya and Kasumi in recent months, and this is just among the leading companies. Aeon is open about its desire to continue to add more volume through similar acquisitions. At the same time, while the scope of its supermarket operations are by no means hidden or private, Aeon is careful not to openly publish consolidated figures. Already, four Max Valu chains, West Japan, Tohoku, Chubu, and Hokkaido have sales of ¥50 billion and over, and Max Valu Tokai, a company which has arisen from the ashes of bankrupt Yaohan, is not far behind. In total, the complete Max Valu operation accounted for estimated food sales alone of more than ¥610 billion in FY2003, making it by far the largest food supermarket in the country (see Figure 7.1). Overall it lies sixth, beaten only by the three leading convenience stores (see Chapter 8) and the

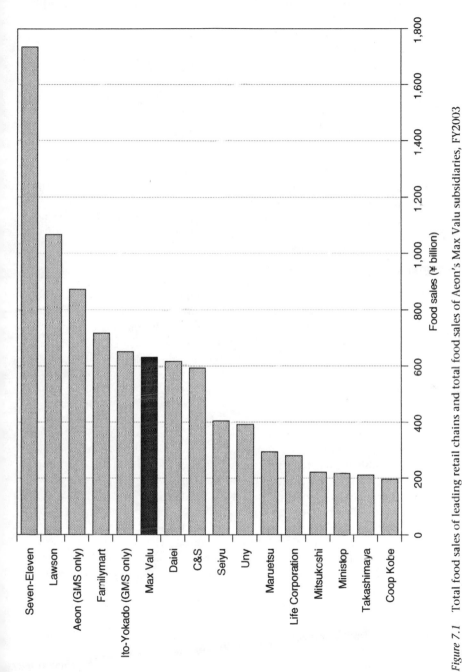

Figure 7.1 Total food sales of leading retail chains and total food sales of Aeon's Max Valu subsidiaries, FY2003
Note: Max Valu estimated for all Aeon controlled supermarket chains
Source: JapanConsuming (2004)

two main GMS chains, including its own parent Aeon. But it has already surpassed Daiei in terms of food sales and is more than twice as large as the next nearest supermarket chain, Maruetsu which ranks only eleventh overall.

Furthermore, Max Valu benefits both from investment money and new stores donated from its parent. Rather than close down smaller, older Jusco GMS outlets, Aeon is passing them on to one of its Max Valu subsidiaries for refurbishment and revitalizing. The switch from a small, inefficient GMS operation to a food store has been a highly successful strategy. Max Valu also sells the same Top Valu retail brands that are found throughout the Aeon Group. The only problem Max Valu faces at present is, as with its parent, profitability. Rapid expansion and older store conversions mean that Max Valu as a whole lags behind some of its rivals. In FY2003, the largest of the Max Valu subsidiaries made only ¥3.003 billion in pretax profits (see Table 7.2), the lowest figure of the leading 11 chains. This, again, is something Aeon will be looking to fix in the near future.

Regional and sub-regional differences

The other key characteristic of note is the geographical spread of the leading food supermarket chains. Only 10 have their home bases in Tokyo, and only two, including Life Corporation, in Osaka. Even including prefectures adjoining these main urban areas, that is Saitama, Chiba and Kanagawa around Tokyo, and Kyoto and Hyogo around Osaka, 12 of the top 26 chains and 35 of the leading 55 chains are based elsewhere in the country. Some, such as Okuwa in Wakayama, which by sales alone is the fifth largest chain in the country, and SunLive in Kyushu, remain rather obscure operations because of private ownership and aversion to press coverage, but they are in fact major operations with 125 and 208 stores respectively.

Other chains, such as Mandai in Osaka, Marunaka and affiliate Sanyo Marunaka in Kagawa and Okayama, Valor in Gifu, Yaoko in Saitama, Mammymart, and Belk in Saitama, are all companies that have managed to beat the general malaise in the retail sector and record respectable sales growth for most of the 1990s. Yaoko, Valor and Belk especially have been impressive performers.

The reason for this regional split is largely due to the historical development of food distribution. Perishable food is still available to most chains solely through local wholesale markets where produce is auctioned on a daily basis. Supplied through a complex system of national and local farming cooperatives, often with government control and support, the food wholesale distribution system is one of the most multi-layered and has the longest supply chains of all. By the time perishable items reach the store, they are often already quite old, resulting in a high spoilage rate and the need to buy frequently in small lots. Of course, today the larger chains are taking every step possible to bypass this system and secure stable, high volume supplies, but direct dealing with producers is still limited to the very largest chains. GMS chains organize perishable food imports themselves with the support of *Sogo Shosha* (general trading companies), and some of the larger supermarket chains can access similar mechanisms (see Supermarket buying groups below). In addition, supermarkets and other retailers continue to emphasize strong local consumer tastes, although with packaged groceries now supplied nationwide, it is doubtful that such regional differences are as significant as they once were.

Consequently, food supermarkets in particular have maintained a certain regional independence. This complex wholesale supply system is also one reason why Aeon chose to develop a set of seven Max Valu subsidiaries rather than immediately rolling out a single supermarket chain nationwide. It is also a system that is difficult to break or bypass, but with its relative inefficiency and the poor quality of food in some areas, it is also a system that will gradually make way for supply chains organized and controlled by the larger retail chains.

A number of small supermarket chains hold strong positions in their respective, limited regional areas. Many of these may rapidly become takeover targets as bigger chains expand. There are a lot of small but capable chains that are ideal for acquisition by larger companies and the bigger retail groups are well aware of them. For some, merger with a large Japanese group will be seen as preferable to competing with the same group. On the other hand, private ownership of most of these chains, along with the rarity of hostile takeover bids in Japan, means that such a trend is likely to remain gradual for the time being. Even if merger and acquisition activity should increase, the majority of cases will be of regional chains joining together in order to compete with the larger, nationwide operations of Aeon and Seiyu. There is also unwillingness among Japanese supermarkets to be owned by a non-Japanese company. Where poor performance dictates a need to consider takeover by a larger concern, most will look to their domestic competitors rather than allow an easy takeover from overseas. Aeon is well aware of this pressure and, as with the cases of both Inageya and Kasumi, is more than willing to take ailing supermarket chains under its wing.

Cooperative society retail chains

In addition to its large number of regional supermarket chains, Japan also has a surviving network of cooperative societies that sell food and household merchandise direct to consumers (see Table 7.3). Under Japanese law, each cooperative is restricted to operate within a single prefecture. This limits their activities significantly despite the support of a central coordinating body based in Tokyo, the Japanese Consumer Cooperative Union (JCCU).

Table 7.3 Leading retail cooperative societies with sales over ¥50 billion, FY2003

		Operating Base Prefecture	Sales ¥ mn	YonY %	Pretax Profit ¥ mn	YonY %
1	Coop Kobe	Hyogo	284,731	–2.0	–	–
2	Coop Sapporo	Hokkaido	167,272	8.0	3,063	23.4
3	Coop Tokyo	Tokyo	151,607	3.3	2,678	–1.9
4	Coop Kanagawa	Kanagawa	143,459	2.2	107	–88.2
5	Saitama Coop	Saitama	108,382	2.8	1,454	–29.9
6	Miyagi Coop	Miyagi	95,991	0.1	727	–38.3
7	Chiba Coop	Chiba	86,590	–1.9	2,153	–22.3
8	Kyoto Seikyo	Kyoto	65,209	0.4	1,123	–6.3
9	Toyota Seikyo	Aichi	63,477	–0.5	379	1.1
10	Coop Shizuoka	Shizuoka	58,893	2.5	746	–8.0
11	F-Coop	Fukuoka	54,154	–0.9	734	–4.8
12	Tokyo MyCoop	Tokyo	53,359	7.0	1,018	–21.8
13	Okayama Coop	Okayama	50,364	1.4	354	–20.8

Source: NMJ (2004a)

As in many other countries, cooperative societies are finding it increasingly difficult to compete with large, chain store retailers that do not suffer any restriction in operating area. This does not mean that all Coops are minor concerns, however. One, Coop Kobe, is one of the most successful retail cooperative societies in the world. Coop Kobe has also struggled in recent years, but was still the third largest supermarket chain in the country and the thirty-first largest retailer overall. It claims membership rates of around 80 per cent in its home city of Kobe, a town with a population of around 1.5 million. Indeed, the chain commands striking loyalty among city residents, and one that developed despite Kobe also being the hometown of Daiei.

All Coops place strong and seemingly sincere emphasis on consumer issues such as food safety and product quality. This manifests itself in the high proportion of food retail brands, competitive pricing, and high quality perishable food, and results in high consumer loyalty.

There are only a handful of surviving consumer cooperative retailers of any significant size and most are now actively moving towards business models similar to that of normal retailers. In the past, they employed a unique system of direct sales rather than retail stores. Local housewives would organize themselves into small ordering groups called *han*. Each week, members of the group would order food products that would be delivered to a central distribution point, often the lobby of a local housing estate. Such a system worked well in Japan's group orientated society. Not only did ordering and picking up orders form a popular social event for housewives, but there was also considerable peer pressure on members to maintain sales.

With the widespread penetration of major GMS and supermarket chains, along with the growing proportion of wives who work, the *han* system soon became too expensive for both consumers and operating societies alike. It still exists in many areas and some of the smaller, rural cooperatives continue to rely on the system for most of their sales. It is only a minor part of the business of larger societies, however, with Coop Kobe for example, having extended the service to full door-to-door delivery to individual households rather than buying groups.

In FY2003 there were still five cooperative societies with sales above ¥100 billion, and in their particular areas they have a significant impact on consumer purchasing patterns and mindset. On the whole, however, consumer cooperative retailing is now in steady decline and is unable to compete with capitalist orientated retailers.

Supermarkets: the top of the market

As with the apparel sector, food retailing is not immune to the Japanese concern with prestige and quality. Competing directly with food supermarkets in major cities, leading department stores also sell a high volume of food including fresh produce. Every major department store has a food basement, called *depa chika* (literally department underground) and these prove a major consumer draw every evening. In addition to gift items such as cakes, rice crackers, and wines, a lot of the food on sale is delicatessen style, ready to eat items such as salads and sushi, but *depa chika* also do a roaring trade in hotel chef branded curries, organic vegetables, bakeries, and even high quality rice balls. As Figure 7.1 showed, Mitsukoshi is the thirteenth largest food retailer in its own right, with Takashimaya just a little behind.

It is not just the department stores that cater to consumers' love of exclusive, high profile food retailing. Spread around high income and traditionally more affluent enclaves, there are a significant number of exclusive and frankly expensive supermarket chains, or *kokyu super* in Japanese. None of these chains are particularly large in scale or sales, but the quality of service and merchandising they offer makes them stand out.

In addition, a few of them have shown remarkable resilience during the harder trading conditions of the 1990s. Notable examples include Isetan's subsidiary Queens Isetan, Kinokuniya in Aoyama, and Itochu owned Shell Garden. The continuing expansion and success of these chains despite poor consumer confidence reflects the continuing demand for luxury that juxtaposes an increasing concern for finding better value. These exclusive supermarkets have long offered the quality of merchandise and service reflected in their higher selling price. It is true that prices at exclusive markets have also declined, but by a smaller degree than in general, and there have even been some new developments in recent years such as Tokyu Store's Precce format and the introduction of the Dean & Deluca chain by Itochu. While a small part of the supermarket sector as a whole, these chains are so common in certain high income areas that they should be noted. In addition, they are one of the few formats that have actually stayed profitable.

Supermarket buying groups

Although the supermarket sector is one of the most fragmented of all, with only two super-regional chains (three if we count Aeon's Max Valu Group) and few large companies, it is not as disorganized as it often seems on the surface. Largely behind the scenes, and in a style similar to that employed by department stores and electrical retailers, a large proportion of supermarket chains are organized into buying groups.

There are four major and four minor buying groups currently in operation. Again, in addition to the eight independent groups, Aeon's Max Valu Group could soon be considered a ninth example. In many respects, particularly in buying operations, it is these nine groups that are in direct competition, much more so than is the case for individual supermarket chains. In some areas, particularly in Tokyo, Saitama and around Osaka, the concentration of medium and small supermarket chains means there is a lot of direct competition between retailers, but there is actually much more behind the scenes in the supply chain.

The four main buying groups are Nichiryu, CGC Japan, National Supermarket Association, and Nihon Supermarket Association (see Table 7.4). The second four groups operate less as buying groups and far more as education and information diffusion bodies. These are the All Japan Supermarket Association, Hashakai, Nihon Self-Service Association, and Selco Chain. All eight groups act as powerful political lobby groups too.

Membership of the different groups varies, and includes a certain amount of overlap. The two largest, CGC and Nichiryu, are active in importing bulk volume product, including food and non-food, particularly from China and the rest of Asia. They are also active in the development of retail brands that are sold by group member stores. The CGC brand is especially successful. Most are organized around key members. For example, in CGC, Arcs in Hokkaido, Maruwa in Kyushu, and Santoku in Tokyo are leading retail members with direct links to CGC head office.

The future of supermarkets will depend greatly on the actions of these largest groups. Together, they have the capacity to form nationwide food based retail chains and are actively encouraging mergers between some members. Arcs was formed in 2003 by the merger of major supermarket chain Ralse with several other Hokkaido chains for example. The problem is that most operate largely as wholesale operations and, although CGC is

Table 7.4 Key members of Japan's leading supermarket buying groups and associations, 2002

Group Name	Nichiryu	CGC Japan	National Supermarket Association	Nihon Super- market Association
Member Companies	19	220	485	100
Key Members	Life Corporation Okuwa Heiwado Sanei Izumi Kasumi SunnyMart Inageya	Daimaru Peacock Universe Maruwa Santoku Olympic Ralse Belk Mammy Mart	Life Corporation (As CGC)	Yaoko Ecos Maruyo Ralse
Group Name	Selco Chain	AJS (All Japan Supermarket Ass.)	Nihon Self- Service Association	Hashakai
Member Companies	19	71	210	15
Key Members	Ecos Sunshine Chain Saeki Hinoya	Summit Kansai Supermarket Queens Isetan Maruhisa Otani	Shell Garden Super Daiei Hayashi Shimizu Shoji Kinokuniya	Tokyu Store Odakyu Shoji Keisei Store Keikyu Store Meitetsu Pare Sotetsu Rozen Tobu Store Keio Store

Source: Japan Consuming (2002a)

directly involved in management and influence at the retail level, the conservative nature of these organizations so far has meant little action has been taken. In addition, buying groups are considered as wholesalers and are reluctant to openly compete with member chains in the retail sector.

The future of supermarket retailing

Supermarket retailing is set to change rapidly in the immediate future. It currently remains one of the most fragmented and underdeveloped of all the different sectors and is ripe for change. Aeon has already taken the bull by the horns and through a group of subsidiaries is now the leader overall. It is unlikely that Aeon's initiative will go unchallenged. There are more than a few domestic regional chains with the ability to compete. In Tokyo alone, Maruetsu, Summit, and Tokyu are all vying for the capital's ¥1 trillion food market. There is also the strong possibility that a *Sogo Shosha* will attempt to become increasing influential. Already Sumitomo owns and operates Summit along with major stakes in Mammymart and Seiyu, Itochu owns Shell Garden as well as, along with Mitsubishi, developing large food wholesaling concerns, and Marubeni has effective control of both Maruetsu and Daiei. Both Mitsubishi and Itochu are also active in the convenience store sector (see Chapter 8). Only Mitsui Bussan has no directly owned retail operations in food, although is has acquired a small stake in Posful in Hokkaido and is another trading house actively pursuing market share in food wholesaling.

All in all, supermarket retailing will become an increasingly interesting and important sector to watch. The modernization and consolidation of the sector will mark a real leap into the present for Japan's retail system as a whole. It will take time for the level of fragmentation to fall and for the leading national companies to emerge, but once they do, retailing as a whole will be transformed. Supermarkets in some ways represent the final frontier of traditional distribution, and one that is well overdue for exploration.

8

Convenience Stores

Convenience stores make up the most modern and innovative of all retail formats in Japan. It is safe to say that the leading players within the sector qualify as some of the best retailers in the world, both in terms of operations and retail control. This success is based on a number of key factors, most of which are unique to convenience store retailing or which originated in the sector, and have now been diffused to other formats:

• Supply chains built from the ground up
• Advanced, high-speed information technology infrastructures
• Applied merchandising integration

Each of these factors is introduced below.

All of the major convenience store chains began life as part of one of the larger groups of companies: Seven-Eleven Japan with Ito-Yokado, Lawson with Daiei, Ministop with Aeon and Familymart with Saison (Seiyu). In recent years, however, the sector has seen a significant level of restructuring with only Seven-Eleven and Ministop remaining in their original groups. In several cases, the convenience store operations have been sold as some of the few valuable assets held by struggling retail groups.

The format as a whole remains highly dynamic and innovative, and continues to lead the industry in terms of profitability and state-of-the-art facilities and techniques. As we describe in this chapter, convenience store retailing has become the only format where larger retailers have been able to implement their very best ideas, free from the problems of traditional thinking and outdated supply chains.

Definition and history of convenience store retailing in Japan

The whole point of convenience store retailing is that it should be easy to spot, always available, and, well, convenient. Japan did not invent the format, but over the past 30 years, it has made its own style of convenience store. It has been so successful that it is one of the only retail sections to have grown consistently for most of the past three decades. Today, the sector is in a state of over saturation both in terms of stores and companies, but it continues to grow where other, larger retail formats flounder.

By definition, the convenience store format has the following characteristics:

• It sells predominantly food and beverages (although precise proportions of sales are not usually defined)
• It is a small format, between 30 sqm and 250 sqm
• It operates long hours, more than 14 hours of operation a day, with a large proportion of the sector operating stores a full 24 hours a day, 365 days a year

Other characteristics that are normal in the sector include:

• Chain organization through franchising
• Heavy implementation and reliance on information technology
• Proprietary logistics systems developed specifically for the chain in question
• Advanced merchandise and inventory management systems

The convenience store (CVS: we use the Japanese abbreviation throughout this chapter) sector is relatively new to retailing in Japan. The first chains appeared in the early 1970s as large retail groups desperately sought ways around the restrictions of the Large Store Law. CVS retailing provided the obvious answer with a standardized format of only 100 sqm, well below the 500 sqm level from which the Large Store Law was applied. Although a small number of prefectures, notably Shizuoka, attempted to legislate against stores of even this small size in order to protect local independent stores, the sector grew rapidly to the mid-1980s, and continues to be the most buoyant sector overall even today.

CVS retailing proved to be far more than just a way to avoid large store development restrictions, however. Most of the largest chains grew as subsidiaries of the biggest retail groups. The main alliances are shown in Table 8.1. These retailers have employed their CVS chains as a means to break various barriers to retail development within their groups. CVS retailing involves such non-traditional operations including:

• Direct dealing with manufacturers
• Streamlined logistics, usually involving cross-docking distribution centers
• Information driven merchandising
• Merchandise development by retailers
• Price control by retailers

Table 8.1 Ownership of major convenience store chains, changes and current conditions, 2005

Convenience Store Chain	Founding Parent Company	Changes in ownership and notes
Seven-Eleven Japan	Ito-Yokado	Seven-Eleven remains within the Ito-Yokado group, but Ito-Yokado now owns Seven-Eleven operations worldwide, having acquired Southland, Inc. in 1989
Lawson	Daiei	Controlling stake acquired by Mitsubishi Shoji in 2001. Part owned by Marubeni
Familymart	Seiyu	Acquired by Itochu Shoji in 1999
Ministop	Aeon	
Circle K Japan	Uny	Merged with Sunkus 2000–01
Daily Yamazaki	Yamazaki Bread	
am/pm	Japan Energy	Acquired by Reins International in 2004
Kokubu Grocers Chain	Kokubu	
Save On	Beisia	
Chico Mart	Itochu Shoji	
Seicomart	Seicomart	Small shares acquired by Mitsubishi Shoji and by Itochu Shoji, 2004

Source: Compiled by JapanConsuming (2002a)

While such practices are normal in other industrial countries, applying them has been difficult in Japan because of the strong control over distribution channels by manufacturers, particularly in the food sector. Now, however, convenience stores account for such a large proportion of sales in several food sectors, notably soft drinks, prepared lunch boxes, and rice balls, that no manufacturer can afford to ignore them. CVS chains also sell more magazines and alcohol than any other single retail format. CVS retailing has become indistinguishable from retailing in many Western countries, with high levels of concentration, retailer controlled supply channels, and information based merchandising.

Convenience Store sector: size and scope

In calendar year 2004, combined convenience store sales amounted to some ¥7,289.2 billion. This represents around 5.7 per cent of total retail sales. This looks like a small share of retailing as a whole until it is realized that this is achieved from only 38,621 convenience stores – just 2.5 per cent of all retail outlets. In addition, as convenience stores are by definition a small format, this level of performance is quite impressive. Equally, while overall retail sales fell by 1.9 per cent in 2003 and by 0.6 per cent in 2004, and both the department store and the chain store sectors saw sales fall, the CVS sector grew by 1.7 and 2.7 per cent respectively.

The story does not end there, however. Whereas the bulk of retailing is highly fragmented with corporate retailing accounting for a significant but limited part of any particular store sector, this is not the case for convenience stores. This sector shows an unusual and surprisingly high level of concentration (see Figure 8.1) and is dominated by huge, corporate chains. Moreover, these are some of the largest retailers in Japan – period.

Seven-Eleven Japan is the largest retail company in Japan by sales and has a total sector market share of more than 33 per cent. It also sells more food products than any other retail chain (see Chapter 7, Figure 7.1) and is the leading retailer of magazines and soft drinks. In FY2003, in terms of food sales alone, Seven-Eleven sold more than twice the value of food items as Aeon's GMS chain, the largest non-convenience store retailer. Food sales at Seven-Eleven were more than five times higher than for the largest supermarket chain. Equally, Lawson was the second highest food seller, and Familymart, Circle K, Sunkus, and Ministop all appear among the leading companies. While the likes of Seven-Eleven, Lawson and Familymart battle it out on a national scale, a few smaller chains are maintaining steady, conspicuous growth in the regions. Four of them, Circle K, Three F, Poplar and CVS Bay Area are listed companies. Seicomart in Hokkaido is also significant as the largest and most dominant chain in its local market, even outperforming the national chains.

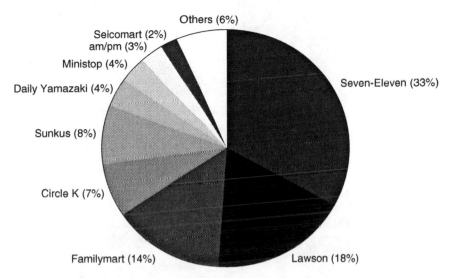

Figure 8.1   Share of total convenience store sales by leading nine chains, 2003–04
Notes: Company sales for FY2003
Sector sales for calendar year 2004
All company sales include area franchisees
Source: Calculated using Company Annual Reports and METI (2005)

Seven-Eleven dwarfs its competitors, with sales close to double that of nearest rival Lawson. It also continues to expand at a much more rapid rate and achieves a much higher sales per store ratio compared to any other chain in the sector (see Table 8.2). With this kind of selling power, Seven-Eleven is able to dictate many of its own buying terms, particularly to canned beverage, dessert, and confectionary manufacturers. Omitting Seven-Eleven from the launch of a new product is tantamount to immediate product failure. Seven-Eleven has long recognized this buying power and has openly employed it to its own advantage. This is to be expected but is seriously at odds to the image of gentlemanly relations and supplier dominance with which Japanese supply chains are usually associated. The most obvious example of such activity is in its logistics system. Unlike similar situations in the West and even at leading rival chains in Japan which generally develop and operate their own centers, Seven-Eleven requires that groups of suppliers provide the investment to build and operate the cross-docking distribution centers which are central to its operations. Although individual centers are relatively small in comparison with some modern logistics facilities, with individual centers supplying around 100 to 150 outlets and employing fleets of 20–30 two-ton trucks it means that multiple, competing suppliers are involved in center development and management. This they do willingly in order to gain access to the lucrative

Table 8.2 Japan's leading convenience store chains by sales volume, FY2003

	Note	Group	Operating HQ	Sales ¥ mn	YonY %	Pretax Profit ¥ mn	YonY %	Stores	Sales per store ¥ mn
Seven Eleven Japan		Ito-Yokado	Tokyo	2,343,177	5.9	168,899	5.8	10,303	227.4
Lawson		Mitsubishi	Tokyo	1,285,018	-0.5	38,039	13.3	7,821	164.3
Familymart		Itochu	Tokyo	954,445	2.4	27,266	1.9	5,770	165.4
Circle K Japan		Uny	Aichi	480,453	-1.1	14,030	-8.3	2,651	181.2
Sunkus & Associates		Uny	Tokyo	403,441	-0.7	10,305	-15.0	2,200	183.4
Daily Yamazaki	1	Yamazaki Bread	Chiba	251,987	-14.4	–	–	2048	123.0
Ministop		Aeon	Tokyo	245,730	2.7	7,318	-13.8	1,505	163.3
am/pm	1	Reins	Tokyo	173,159	-0.5	–	–	1420	121.9
Seicomart	1	Independent	Hokkaido	149,770	-0.9	–	–	1016	147.4
Popular		Independent	Hiroshima	129,173	-2.3	3,107	-3.8	864	149.5
Three–F		Independent	Kanagawa	111,569	-3.8	1,412	-1.5	627	177.9
Kokubu Grocery Chain	1	Kokubu	Tokyo	104,242	-3.3	–	–	609	171.2
Save On	1	Beisia	Gunma	58,816	-2.0	–	–	547	107.5
East Japan Kiosk	1	JR East	Tokyo	57,227	5.4	–	–	303	188.9
Monmart Store Systems	1	none	Tokyo	45,759	-7.0	–	–	417	109.7
Coco Store	1	Izumikku	Aichi	40,394	14.5	–	–	340	118.8
South Kyushu Familymart	1	Independent	Kagoshima	38,306	1.7	–	–	268	142.9
Everyone	1	Coco Store	Kumamoto	29,000	23.9	–	–	164	176.8
am/pm Kinki	1	am/pm	Osaka	28,346	7.6	–	–	197	143.9
Okinawa Familymart	1	Familymart	Okinawa	25,593	7.6	–	–	161	159.0

Note:
[1] Privately owned
Source: Company Reports; NMJ (2004); Otsuka and Kaneko (2004); Asano et al (2004)

Seven-Eleven market, yet it is at odds with the traditional system of whole-sale distribution in Japan as a whole. Similar requirements have been introduced for the logistics centers of parts of the Ito-Yokado GMS chain as well.

Through such cost avoidance measures along with considerable retail skill, Seven-Eleven is by far the most profitable retailer in Japan. In FY2003, it made more than ¥168 billion in pretax profits, the only retailer to break ¥50 billion for the year. In addition, profitability continues to improve, up 5.8 per cent on 2002. It is also by far the largest chain in the entire retail industry in terms of store numbers, with 10,303 stores at the end of the same financial year, 500 more than nearest rival Lawson.

Seven-Eleven is currently sustaining its parent Ito-Yokado as the latter struggles with its floundering GMS chain. Most recently Ito-Yokado has added its own banking subsidiary, IY Bank, which cleverly leverages the Seven-Eleven chain further. IY Bank is entirely cash machine (ATM) based and operates from within Seven-Eleven stores (see below for details). This is just one more example of how Ito-Yokado has put its Seven-Eleven chain to use.

Franchise system

Since soon after the opening of the first CVS in Japan by Seven-Eleven in May 1974, convenience stores have employed a franchise system. It is a commonly known secret that all chains maintain a small number of directly operated stores for training and experimental purposes, but about 98 per cent of all CVS outlets are franchises.

This type of organization fits perfectly with Japanese retail culture and has allowed CVS chains to tap into struggling mom and pop stores that were looking for a way to revitalize their businesses. Small store, independent retailing has been in decline since 1982 mostly due to natural attrition (see Chapter 3). For many independent retailers, the opportunity to join a large, successful franchise operation provides a new lease of life. Without the CVS chains, some 40,000 more retail stores would probably have closed.

Franchise agreements vary greatly from chain to chain, but are very strictly applied and involve a high degree of control by the franchisor (see Table 8.3). New franchisees can expect to work very hard for their profits, although given the right locations, profit there certainly is. Franchisors maintain armies of field supervisors, and most franchisee stores are visited at least three or four times each week. In the leading chains, franchisees have very little decision-making authority at all. All merchandising, inventory control, promotion, and customer service techniques and requirements are laid down by the franchisor and tightly enforced in most cases. Apart from paying annual sales royalties, the franchisee's main responsibility is providing staff for the store. These are

Table 8.3 Franchise conditions for leading convenience store chains, FY2002

Convenience Store Chain	Seven-Eleven	Lawson	Familymart	Circle K	Ministop	am/pm
Contract Period	15 years	10 years	10 years	15 years	7 years	10 years
Guaranteed Income	¥19 million†	yes	yes	yes	yes	yes
Royalties	43%*	34%	35%*	-	30%	30%*
Contract fee	-	¥1.5 million	¥500,000	¥3 million	¥3 million	¥3 million
Deposit	-	¥0	-	¥4 million	¥1.5 million†	¥5 million
Opening Inventory fee	-	-	-	-	¥3.8 million	yes
Accounts disclosure	-	yes	yes	yes	yes	yes
Fee for fittings	-	¥2 million	¥2.5 million	¥500,000	¥1.2 million	¥17 million
Other fees	¥3 million	-	¥3 million	-	¥580,000	¥100,000
Total	-	-	-	¥7.5 million	¥8.58 million	-
Notes for each company	†: Annual gross profits *: % gross profit		*: % gross profit		†: included in contract fee	*: % gross profit

Notes:

Figures as disclosed by companies themselves. '–' indicates non-disclosure or case by case. Contract conditions change fairly regularly.

Source: Compiled from JapanConsuming (2002a)

usually part-time students, part-time housewives, or, in some cases, the franchisee's own family. With the largest chains expecting 24–7 operation throughout the year, becoming a CVS franchise is by no means an easy option.

The power of the CVS franchise over its franchisee members has been compared to the way large car, electrical, and drug manufacturers maintained their groups of seemingly independent retail chains, called *keiretsu*. Manufacturer *keiretsu* still exist, but have now been surpassed by the larger, more efficient retail chains. It is true, however, that new convenience store franchisees have almost as little independence and self-determination as did these more traditional retail organizations. The two key differences are that, first they are no longer called *keiretsu*, and second, they are retailer developed and operated.

With this small quirk of the franchise system, CVS is still the one retail sector that is largely independent of manufacturer domination. In no other sector do retailers, large or small, maintain such control on supply and their own operations. Such independence of operations has clearly been a major contributor to their success.

Information systems

The use of information systems for ordering, inventory control and merchandise development is fundamental to CVS operations in Japan, and instrumental in allowing the chains to keep their independence from suppliers. Once again, led by Seven-Eleven with its efficient and profit driven organization and systems, the CVS format was introduced as the only clear alternative for growth while large formats were so heavily restricted by regulatory obstacles. In general, what Seven-Eleven has introduced, other chains have attempted to emulate and this has included information systems and merchandising policies.

By the end of the 1980s all of Seven-Eleven's stores, which at the time numbered 2,964 outlets, were connected to the Ito-Yokado headquarters in Tokyo by dedicated ISDN lines (see Figure 8.2). The company could and did check sales data on a minute-by-minute basis. Not only did it know what was being sold and, very precisely when it was being sold, but also who it was being sold to. Seven-Eleven instigated the recording of each customer's sex and, estimated approximately, age for each and every purchase. To record these items, shop assistants are still required to punch special keys on the cash register with every purchase. Surprisingly, however, loyalty cards have only recently been introduced and the largest chains are still reluctant to use them (see Seicomart Case Study below).

CVS chains not only collect data, they use it to improve distribution, inventory control and, to the surprise of traditional manufacturers which consider it their exclusive province, even merchandising. IT became

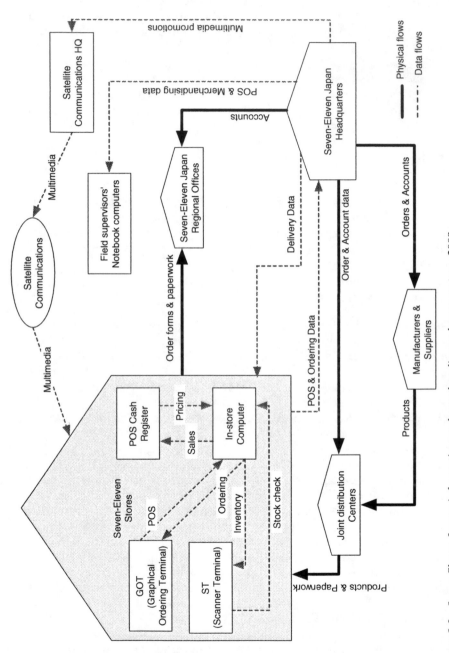

Figure 8.2 Seven-Eleven Japan: information and merchandise exchange system, 2003
Adapted from: JapanConsuming (2002a); Company Report

the backbone of CVS retailing and all the leading chains look for new ways to collect and use data. In the case of Seven-Eleven, the company employed a number of external consultants to build its system, notably Nomura to develop the software systems and Fujitsu to develop the dedicated hardware. Most other companies, as Japanese retailers prefer, built the majority of their systems in-house, recruiting whatever personnel were seen necessary for the task.

Today, the power of these information networks is being expanded further. Almost all of the large chains are increasing their provision of e-commerce services that link with existing retail store chains. This means adding multimedia access points in each of their stores where customers can order products, check information, and so on. Chief among the services offered include paying of utility bills and buying concert and travel tickets. The way this works is that customers make the order at the in-store terminal before receiving a printed barcode slip which they can take to the cash register in order to pay for their purchase. The unusually Japanese advantage of this system is that people are also able to order products on the Internet, and then pay for them in cash at their local CVS, avoiding the use of credit cards altogether. The same systems also allow most cash registers to become multimedia terminals, with advertising pumped directly from company headquarters down to the store cash terminals for customers to view while they're waiting to pay for their purchases. As mentioned above, IY Bank and similar ATM introductions at other CVS chains are the latest in a series of similar innovations.

Case Study 8.1: Seicomart: a regional CVS chain leads the introduction of loyalty cards

It is not just European chains that are leveraging frequent shopper programs (FCP) in Japan. CVS chains are well on the way to having some of the most sophisticated loyalty programs in the country, and the trend is being led by Seicomart, the largest chain in Hokkaido. Japanese CVS chains collect a myriad of consumer data and the best of them have grown at least partly due to their in-depth knowledge of customer shopping habits store by store and area by area, but also minute by minute and person by person. All of the top chains maintain high-speed data links from each and every one of their franchise outlets back to headquarters and track product sales continually, using this information to adjust inventory and supply requirements. Each one also keeps a rough check of the age and sex of each customer by having clerks punch record keys at the till during each purchase.

Case Study 8.1:   Seicomart: a regional CVS chain leads the introduction of loyalty cards – *continued*

But this simply isn't enough. Almost all convenience store employees are part-time and many are students. While student employees in Japan have a loyalty and willingness to work that would amaze managers from overseas, it is not always easy to accurately guess a customer's age, and, being students it's sometimes easier to punch the nearest button rather than even guess the correct sex. Managers at Lawson once said that the key punching method of data collection was so suspect that it had even thrown doubt on the long accepted claim that most CVS shoppers were men.

Now, CVS chains offer in-store multimedia terminals where customers can purchase a huge range of electronic items from show tickets, to insurance, to mobile phone top-ups, to utility bills, to simply paying for things they ordered previously online. It is a unique system, allowing people to avoid paying by credit card on the Internet because they can so easily do so at any of their local CVS outlets. By linking these systems with loyalty card FCP programs, chains are able to collect an even greater volume of, and even more accurate, customer data.

The idea has been pioneered not by Seven-Eleven, but by Hokkaido based chain, Seicomart. In operation since June 2000, the Seicomart Club Card now has a reported 2.4 million members – an amazing one in three people in Hokkaido alone are members. Loyalty cards are common in the UK, and Seicomart quite openly admits it learned a great deal from Tesco. It even calls its FCP the "Club Card" just like its British counterpart. Unlike Tesco's cards, however, Seicomart's Club Card is IC chip imbedded and, from October 2004, customers have also been able to use them as credit cards even outside Seicomart stores.

Other chains are now catching up fast. Lawson started its Lawson Pass program in 2002, soon after Mitsubishi took over from Daiei as company owners. It now has 1.5 million members, although by early 2005 the card was still only used to track purchases and to offer members a rather limited range of services and direct mail advertising. Familymart and Circle K Sunkus (CKS) both started their programs in 2004 and have 320,000 and 23,000 members respectively. Familymart, which has historical ties to Credit Saison, also introduced an IC chip and credit card version and has a members' day every Tuesday and Saturday when card holders get a 5 per cent discount on all purchases. CKS calls its program the Karawaza Club, but operates the card exclusively in Hokkaido and in central Japan around its Nagoya base. It is the first card to come with Edy electronic payment functionality, although there's no report of any other customer benefits.

Seven-Eleven, unusually for Japan's number one retailer, is a little behind. Its own card only started life in September 2003 and was introduced purely as a direct reaction to Seicomart. In 2005, the Seven-Eleven card was also only available in Hokkaido, had no credit function, and the company claimed to have no plans to introduce it elsewhere in the country. The cost of running FCPs is high in many cases, and as Tesco has shown in the UK, it takes a significant market share and some commitment to really make it work. Seicomart, again, studied a lot before it set out, sending employees to the UK for extended periods before introducing the scheme. The effort seems to be paying off. Some 40 per cent of purchases are made by card members, paying on average ¥880 per basket, some 20 per cent higher than the overall average. The card also helped Seicomart with

---

Case Study 8.1: Seicomart: a regional CVS chain leads the introduction of loyalty cards – *continued*

a typically CVS merchandising problem. Japanese chains have such a fast product turnaround that some categories are replenished three times a day. More than 50 per cent of the product range is replaced annually, and it is vitally important that products not only sell very quickly, but also sell long-term. Now, Seicomart can use card data to distinguish when a product is selling generally well and when it is being bought by just a handful of customers.

So far, FCPs are of interest but not a major concern for most retailers in Japan. In addition to electrical chains, department stores have run very simple programs for a long time and cooperative retailers have truly astounding membership rates, but convenience stores are the first to implement fully integrated systems linked directly to marketing and merchandising activities. It perhaps will not be too long before infant programs at supermarkets and elsewhere begin to copy their lead.

Distribution and supply systems

Second only to their love of information, supply chain management is of vital importance to all CVS chains. In the early days, CVS chains were supplied in much the same way that larger stores were. For each store, deliveries arrived constantly over the course of the day, with each product or product category being supplied through local distribution facilities, and mostly directly from manufacturers or intermediary wholesalers. At one point, Lawson was seeing an average of 70 deliveries per day per store, a ridiculous number for stores that are themselves only 100 sqm in size. Consequently, store employees' main concern was stock receipt, checking, and shelf filling, leaving them little time for customers or other duties.

Those days are now long past. Today, a typical CVS will still see from five to seven deliveries a day, but these are organized precisely to a set schedule and arranged to avoid disruption to store operations. As already mentioned, in addition to closely controlling inventory and ordering through dedicated information networks, the largest chains now employ their own systems of cross-docking distribution centers. Each center supplies 100 or more stores in its immediate area. In many cases, the distribution center will also include a separate production facility, often on the second level, which will manufacture CVS staples such as rice balls and *o-bento* lunch boxes.

In order to supply product to CVS chains, manufacturers and their wholesale companies are required to deliver product to the cross-docking centers. This merchandise is then picked by store for immediate re-shipment to individual store delivery routes. A single truck, often no bigger than two tons due to Japan's narrow inner city roads, will cover 10

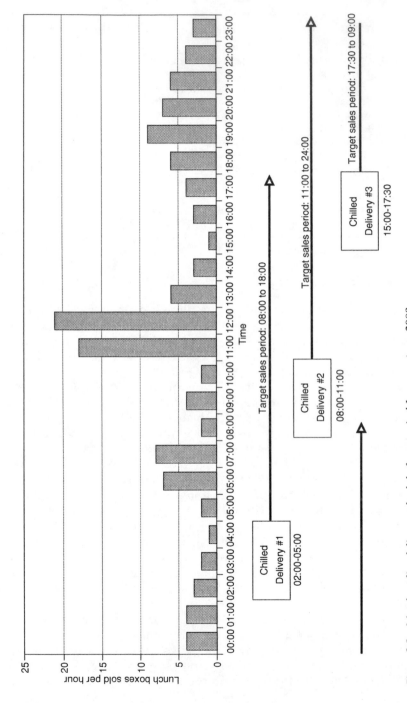

Figure 8.3   Merchandise delivery schedule for a typical Lawson store, 2003
Source: Compiled from Lawson presentation by authors

to 25 stores in a single route. Product is supplied through custom developed roll pallets and collapsible boxes, and most trucks are multi-temperature so they can carry chilled and ambient product together. A typical delivery consists of little more than rolling off one full pallet, replacing the previous, now empty, collapsed pallet, and receiving the store's stamp of receipt once product has been quickly counted and tallied with order quantities.

Major chains such as Lawson, Seven-Eleven and Familymart make three main deliveries per day to each store. These supply stores with *o-bento* and other highly perishable items that are expected to sell out within a few hours of delivery. Indeed, the leading chains expect a product turnover of two to three times a day for these items. In addition, other less perishable items will be included on the same pallet where necessary and where space allows. Each delivery is timed to correspond to peak sales times, roughly breakfast, lunch and dinner (see Figure 8.3), and is expected to sell out by, or soon after, the next delivery. At other times, stores will take up to three more deliveries of non-perishable and non-food items, some of which will still not pass through central cross-docking centers, but be delivered by local wholesale suppliers.

It is this detailed, bulk-breaking system of logistics that has helped CVS chains achieve the level of operational sophistication that they have. In addition to the basic supply of merchandise, the system allows integration of other services including mail order catalog supply and home delivery systems (see below).

Merchandising systems

Following on from the application of state of the art information and distribution systems, major CVS chains have taken one more significant and, for a retailer in Japan, highly unusual step: they plan, monitor, control, and implement much of their product development and merchandising. In all but a few cases, this does not go as far as widespread retail branding, although, once more, Seven-Eleven leads the way claiming around 50 per cent own brand merchandise by sales. In general, the chains use their sales data to cooperate with suppliers in developing merchandise suitable for the CVS channel.

There are numerous famous examples of this activity. Rice balls or *o-nigiri* in Japanese, are an ancient snack dish equivalent to a Western sandwich. In the hands of CVS chains, however, these now come with a multitude of savory fillings from tuna and mayonnaise to ground beef and kimchi. Through quite ingenious packaging techniques, the retailers have also solved the age-old problem of how to keep the rice ball's wrapping of seaweed separate and crisp until the point of being eaten. Other examples abound, particularly in the soft drink and chilled dessert categories. Many are short-lived, such as Indian lassi or Taiwanese tapioca drinks, while others become long-term hits like jelly sports drinks and Calorie Mate diet supplements. Japan already had a thriving vending machine market for canned drinks, but CVS chains have pushed this further, allowing manufacturers great scope for the development of new drinks and packaging, often with very narrow target markets, many of which then filter back into the vending channel. Not only that, convenience store products are often equally suited to supermarkets in general, allowing major retail groups which operate both formats to offer even greater opportunity to suppliers.

The key to CVS food merchandise is its ready-to-eat nature. Stores offer everything in instant form. The majority of chains also provide hot water and microwave ovens in-store, although thanks to Japan's constant worry about safety issues, most are for employee operation only. In addition to *o-bento* lunches, of which the variety and, it must be said, quality varies incredibly, chains offer instant salads, instant desserts, instant spaghetti, instant soups, and all manner of other foodstuffs.

Bread products too have changed remarkably as a result of the CVS channel. Most chains boast a large selection, marketing their products as "fresh from the factory". Bread in Japan is quite different from what would be expected in Europe or the USA, however. It is invariably flavored, often with some kind of filling or topping, and is mostly sweet. The range and variety of bread products has grown significantly over the past decade, mostly to supply the CVS channel. Westerners may be surprised by the standardized factory production quality of this particular category because bread, too, has become simply another form of fast food.

The CVS sector will continue to drive merchandise innovation, and we are likely to see a gradual but steady increase in the number of retail brands appearing within merchandise ranges. In the late 1980s, top chains such as Seven-Eleven offered franchisees a merchandise selection of up to 6,000 separate items. The majority of stores would choose and sell some 4,000 of these. In the continual search for greater efficiency and rapid stock turnover, all the large chains have now reduced this selection to around 4,000 items in total, with each store stocking only 2,500.

Services

In addition to merchandise innovations, services are a key sales point for all CVS chains. The most important of these are the ability to pay household bills, make photocopies, have photographs developed, and send parcels. As mentioned earlier, the ability to pay for Internet online purchases at your local convenience store is a very popular recent addition (see below also).

Again, CVS chains introduced these services to fill a glaring gap in the Japanese market. With banks and post offices operating short trading hours and not at all at weekends, customers are more than happy to pay bills at CVS chains. Chains benefit from holding the quite considerable sums of money in their own accounts for short periods and thus gaining interest before passing the payment on to the utility companies themselves. In recent years, major utilities and other regular bill issuers such as insurance companies have begun issuing bills which have CVS-ready barcodes already printed on them. This allows shop assistants to simply scan in the bill, which links directly with the payee's own database, displaying the correct amount on the in-store cash register.

Now the number and variety of services is expanding rapidly. In some chains, particularly those in the suburbs of Tokyo, ladies-only dry cleaning services are being offered for example. A high incidence of underwear theft is a constant problem in Japan, particularly from the washing lines of young women living alone. Several chains have set up lockers outside their stores where women can deposit laundry anonymously in the locker, returning to claim the clean items several days later and to pay for the service within the store.

Other services will undoubtedly be added to the typical CVS chain's portfolio over coming years. The most recent and one of the most important is the full integration of postal services at most chains. Japan has a number of highly efficient parcel delivery companies such as Yamato and Nittsu, and consumers can send packages by taking them to their local CVS. These services were a little more expensive, but usually much quicker than that offered by the Post Office, and had the added benefit of such things as refrigerated delivery of foodstuffs, and delivery of large items such as golf bags or suitcases. Today, however, Lawson has led the introduction of actual postal services, selling stamps and taking collection of Post Office mail.

Japanese lifestyles and convenience stores

It is debatable whether CVS chains have really developed in order to meet the needs of modern, urban lifestyles, or, in actuality, that urban lifestyles have shifted to utilize the convenience that these chains offer. It is certainly true that CVS chains are now a significant part of Japan's urban landscape and are set to become even more important in future years. When house hunting, realtors commonly note not just the distance to the nearest station but usually include the whereabouts and number of local convenience stores, for example.

In some other industrial nations, supermarkets are gradually moving towards longer and longer opening hours, with some open 24 hours. With the abolition of regulations in 2000, a number of supermarkets, notably Aeon's Max Valu stores and Okuwa, have attempted to do the same, but the role of 24-hour retailing has long been taken on by CVS chains. Their mix of merchandise and service convenience makes them ideal top up and last minute shopping venues, and because of their small size, there are few restrictions on where they can operate.

Most convenience store shoppers continue to be younger males. Chains make efforts to attract more female shoppers, and, again, their attraction as a 24-hour top up location is strong. At the same time as supermarkets are opening longer hours, CVS chains like Plus 99 are diversifying into more fresh produce, taking on the supermarkets directly while opening longer hours and in better locations.

In recent years, most food retailers have finally admitted that Japan will never be the automobile society that they once hoped. Only Aeon is continuing to develop large, out of town shopping centers accessible only by car, but generally poor roads, coupled with the sheer number of convenience stores available, mean that mundane shopping for essential items still takes place close to home and at the most convenient times. This is a perfect situation for convenience stores.

While many retail sectors struggle to reinvent themselves and rush to modernize their business practices, CVS chains are already as modern as any available in the Japanese market today. This particular format has a bright future ahead of it, with only the ambiguous problem of ever increasing competition to worry about.

Entry of major Sogo Shosha

CVS chains were the jewels in the crowns of Japan's largest, highly diversified retail groups. Not surprising therefore that these were the obvious companies to sell as times became hard. Two of the largest three chains, Lawson and Familymart, have changed majority shareholder in recent years. More interesting, and highly significant, however, is the fact that the new owners in both cases are leading *sogo shosha* (general trading houses, see Chapter 4).

In 1999, Itochu Shoji, at the time the strongest single trading house in terms of food wholesaling and supply, acquired Familymart from Seiyu. Seiyu sold its stake in the number three CVS chain in order to reduce debts. As the third ranking chain, Seiyu was struggling badly to progress its CVS operations and disposal of the chain to another party was a logical choice. For Itochu it marked the beginning of a direct involvement in food retailing, and confirmed the interest of these huge industrial groups in direct retail ownership for the first time since Sumitomo acquired Summit in the 1960s.

Since then, all the major trading houses, Itochu, Mitsubishi, Marubeni, Sumitomo, and Mitsui, have been seeking to grow their interest in retailing. Throughout their postwar history, all of these companies have acted as primary licensees for major overseas apparel brands, but had little direct involvement in retailing. Since Itochu's initial move, however, Mitsubishi has taken control of Lawson, and has taken small stakes in both am/pm and Seicomart. Outside of the CVS sector, Marubeni now controls the Maruetsu supermarket chain and has a 20 per cent share in Metro Japan, the German cash and carry wholesale operation. It has also gained control of Daiei with government backing, but as yet it is too early to know how this will develop. In addition to Summit and two drugstore chains, Sumitomo remains the second largest shareholder in its partnership with Wal-Mart in the takeover and turnaround of Seiyu Group. Mitsui is yet to acquire its own retail operations, but is the only major *shosha* not to have done so. It has taken some tentative steps into retailing however, primarily by tying with Ito-Yokado as a supply chain and procurement partner serving both the GMS chain and Seven-Eleven. It has since added an 8.58 per cent share in Posful, the reincarnation of Mycal Hokkaido.

The *sogo shosha* are involved in most business sectors in Japan and there is little surprise that they have now turned their attentions to retailing and food retailing in particular. Throughout the 1990s, food retailers failed to impress, showing a distinct lack of flexibility or innovation. It is equally not surprising, therefore, that the *shosha* believe they can do better.

Itochu had the advantage of entering the CVS sector two years earlier than other *shosha*, albeit with a company in poor financial straits. Even in 2005, Familymart's share price remained around ¥3,300, well below the price of ¥4,700 Itochu paid for the company. Faced with such problems, Itochu quite rightly took the drastic step of cutting out 500 underperforming stores in 2000, becoming the first chain to implement such major restructuring. Other chains have since followed suit, closing an increasing number of less effective stores instead of simply adding increasing capacity every year (see below).

Following on from Itochu's takeover of Familymart, Mitsubishi acquired a controlling share in Lawson from Daiei in 2002. Despite its number two position, Lawson was never managed as effectively as Seven-Eleven and this is a major reason why Daiei did not take the company public until debt reduction measures forced its hand. It took Mitsubishi a year to bring Lawson back on track, but in FY2003 achieved an increase in pretax profit of 19 per cent to ¥36.5 billion, despite a fall in sales of 0.5 per cent for the same period. The company added several sets of stores bought from other chains around the country in its attempt to increase the speed at which it moves to catch up with Seven-Eleven's leadership.

The huge procurement networks controlled by the *sogo shosha* are being gradually ramped up to supply their CVS chains. This will help in restructuring and consolidation within the major chains, and is likely to provide significant boosts in efficiency and profits. What remains to be seen, however, is just how imaginative and consumer orientated these new CVS operators can be. With the exception of Sumitomo, none of the trading houses are experienced in offering detailed, consumer orientated solutions at the retail level. Company structures and management are conservative by nature, relying on business integration and long-term financial support at the group level through in-house banking. In order to compete with each other and with the power of Seven-Eleven, Mitsubishi and Itochu are going to have to show unusual imagination and speed.

Trends in convenience store chain strategy

As mentioned in the previous section, the trend to close franchises is a new and significant one. As with many retail sectors in Japan, CVS chains have pursued the same fundamental strategy of adding ever increasing numbers of stores annually and closing as few as possible. Itochu put a stop to this, closing 500 stores in 2000, and opening the way for other chains to also increase the number of stores closing down.

Figure 8.4 indicates store numbers and changes in FY2003. Clearly the number of stores being closed down or leaving the franchise has increased with all of the leading five chains closing more than 200 stores in the year. Lawson closed a total of 429 in this year alone as Mitsubishi looked to drastically restructure the business. At the same time, the larger chains are also adding more stores. Seven-Eleven opened no fewer than 904 stores in FY2003 alone, the highest number of any of the chains and this pushed it even further ahead of Lawson, which added 625, the second highest number. In FY2004, Seven-Eleven planned to open another 950 new stores, showing that although overall store numbers are at saturation point, there is still room for restructuring in the CVS sector with franchises moving between the leading chains as well as new outlets being opened. Lawson already operates stores in all 47 prefectures, and Familymart also has nationwide coverage when its main area franchise operations are included, but Seven-Eleven is still absent from 15 prefectures leaving it considerable room to grow.

On the marketing side, CVS chains have made two important changes over the past couple of years. First, with the increase in store numbers overall and the wide range of choice available to consumers, competitive pressures have forced some chains to reduce their prices. The majority of large chains have done this by introducing cheaper retail brands on some staples such as milk and cut-breads, but the overall cost of shopping at CVS has fallen. Circle K has added a ¥100 set price stationery range, and even Seven-Eleven has cut beer prices by 9 per cent on average since 1999. It is likely that, overall, chains will continue to reduce prices, but, wherever possible, introduce other marketing initiatives which help to maintain margins as well as increasing sales volume.

Secondly and most recently, convenience store food is getting healthier. While some chains have been accused of making McDonalds look like a

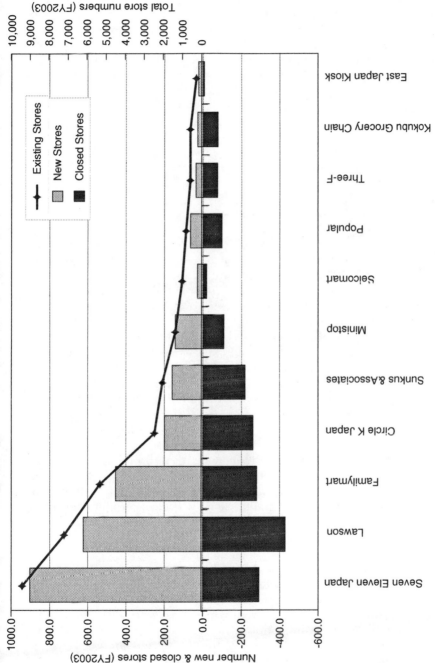

Figure 8.4 CVS chains by store numbers, number of new stores and closed stores FY2003, and planned new stores for FY2004 (where known)

Source: Compiled from NMJ (2004, pp. 264–5)

health food restaurant in the past, neither the companies nor their customers appeared worried about this issue. Now, again led by Seven-Eleven, the top chains are making some effort to change. Seven-Eleven announced in November 2001 that they would introduce a wide range of preservative and additive free fresh food products – at the time receiving noticeable public criticism from major food suppliers and preservative manufacturers such as Ajinomoto, which make money from those additives. Lawson too has begun to take this issue seriously and is gradually increasing its range of organic ingredients in many of its food products. Ties with Mitsubishi have further increased the chain's access to Chinese produce grown with at least pretensions to organic quality, although Japanese regulations on organics remain loose and genuine quality is not something consumers can take for granted.

E-commerce: clicks and mortar

Arguably, integration of convenience store services with e-commerce is the biggest and potentially most far reaching development of all. As Japan continues to lag behind many industrial nations and even some poorer Asian nations in terms of e-commerce development, the participation of CVS chains is a major exception to the rule. Again it shows the higher level of innovation at convenience chains.

Today, all of the major chains operate their own online stores in conjunction with physical stores. Some, notably Seven-Eleven and Lawson also offer in-store terminals through which consumers can access a range of the same online services. These e-commerce options are linked to physical store operations by the payment system. In almost all cases, customers are required to make final payment at their local convenience store.

Having established this system, along with the similar bill paying services, convenience stores have extended payment services to other online e-commerce sites as well. Most online payment solution providers include convenience store payment as one of their options. It is unclear just how popular this service is with customers, but as credit card use still remains comparatively limited and personal privacy a major concern for consumers, it is likely that CVS chains have again seen a significant opportunity.

ATM banking systems

As already noted, the latest addition to payment and finance services offered by CVS IT networks is direct banking itself. With the deregulation of Japan's banking system, a few companies have entered the market for the first time and, significantly, one of those is Ito-Yokado with its IY Bank venture. IY Bank is a new subsidiary of the Ito-Yokado Group, and set to become a significant one. The whole system is squarely based on the Seven-

Eleven network of stores. In the initial stage, beginning Fall 2001, ATM terminals were installed in about 3,000 Seven-Eleven outlets, and today they are found in almost all Seven-Elevens across Japan.

IY Bank services are offered entirely through the ATM. This has caused considerable consternation to traditional banks for a number of reasons. First, Japan's retail banking market is relatively uncompetitive and archaic. Customer charges are not high, but they are uncompetitive, being uniform and equal across banks. The types of services offered by different banks are also similar between competing institutions. Not only that, ATM cash services are limited with all but a couple of chains closing down all cash services from 7pm in the evenings to 8.45am next morning, and charging customers for using ATMs during the limited opening hours at weekends.

Through Seven-Eleven outlets, as with their normal retail services, IY Bank offers cash and bill payment transactions through the IY Bank ATMs 24 hours a day, 7 days a week. Not only that, but Seven-Eleven charges banks when customers use their ATM cards in machines. Naturally, most of these charges will be passed to the customer, but while banks keep their costs down through the balance of one chain's customers using their cards in another's ATMs and then vice versa, few customers will actually hold accounts with IY Bank. So while other banks will pay IY Bank for services rendered, almost no customers will use IY Bank cards in other ATM machines.

Although traditional banks insisted that IY Bank services are expensive and therefore unpopular after the first year of operation, in the field there was little evidence that consumers were put off. Such is the problem with obtaining cash out of banking hours in Japan, that most consumers are delighted with the new service, even if it means paying a slightly higher charge. Ito-Yokado claimed the venture was profitable by FY2003 and plans to take the subsidiary public by 2007.

As a result, all of the major CVS chains have followed the Seven-Eleven example and introduced ATMs in many of their stores. Estimates for 2004 put the number of CVS located ATMs at around 18,000, roughly half the total number of outlets. Unlike Seven-Eleven, however, other chains have had to make do with establishing business partnerships with traditional banks in order to do this. Ironically, this means that many stores cannot offer 24 hour operation as IT systems at the banks themselves remain woefully inadequate and require the network to be closed for several hours a day. In the meantime, Seven-Eleven's IY Bank continues to build its reputation as the option of choice.

Immediate future

CVS chains face an interesting future. The sector is at saturation in terms of store numbers, but leading chains still maintain flexibility and imagination in their operations, something that cannot be said for some other retail sectors. Competition will remain fierce, and focus on the following factors:

- Competition to convert independent retail stores with good locations into new franchisees
- Competition in new ideas for services and merchandise, particularly related to multimedia and other non-store sales routes
- Competition for geographical spread with Seven-Eleven rapidly moving out of its main areas around Tokyo and in the north of Japan
- Competition for new ideas and services, for example laundry lockers for women only, locally branded merchandise, banking services and many others

In the medium term, the sector is more than likely to see massive restructuring with smaller, regional chains becoming clear takeover targets. With the intervention of the trading houses, this is already taking place. All three leading chains are likely to consider the merger and acquisition option over coming years.

Part III

New Retailing: Specialists

Introduction to specialty merchandise retailing in Japan

For many years, large, general merchandise retailers described in Part 2 of this book have dominated Japanese retailing. These large format retailers seemed to offset Japan's large numbers of small, independent retail stores. Since the early 1990s, small retail stores have been disappearing in ever increasing numbers and are no longer of a major importance in terms of sales. Then, after a decade of low consumer confidence, general merchandise retailers are also struggling. As noted in Part 2, one or two have come through and developed strategies designed to stop their decline. These companies, such as Aeon and Ito-Yokado, are the exception, however.

Now, in the stead of both small independent stores and general merchandise retailers, Japan has seen a massive growth in specialty chain retailing. Although specialty retailers have been largely overlooked in past literature relating to Japanese distribution, they are now an important force. In every merchandise category there are specialty retailers that have grown and continue to grow despite many years of poor economic conditions and consumer confidence.

In Part 3, we consider specialty retailing in detail. We have split this part into three chapters considering apparel retailing; the new, rapidly growing specialty sectors of drugstores, consumer electronics and home centers; and then, briefly, other important specialty categories.

In Chapter 9 we consider apparel retailing in great detail. Apparel retailing alone is a huge sector and one that has not been studied in any detail in the English language literature. Yet this is strange because it is the one sector where so many international retailers have found success in Japan and one that still provides significant opportunities. But it is a very large, and very complex sector. There are numerous business models already operating in the market and apparel retailing by its very nature is the most dynamic sector of all warranting considerable attention.

In Chapter 10, we take a look at three more product sectors characterized by particular retail formats: drugstores, consumer electronics, and home centers. These three sectors appear at first glance to be unrelated, but in Japan they have a number of things in common: all have developed very quickly into modern retail formats and are continuing to lead the industry in terms of growth. For both drugstores and consumer electronics retailing, this development has meant retailers have taken control of the channel where before manufacturers were the dominant elements. For home centers, as recently as 1990, there were no retail companies of any size or significance, but today they represent some of the largest companies around and, again, one of the fastest growing of all sectors. Consolidation and high levels of concentration are also rapidly increasing with the largest companies taking a significant share of their respective markets. Moreover, as in the supermarket and GMS sectors, Aeon Group is conspicuous as being an important catalyst in this process, being involved with the largest groups of stores in both the drugstore and home center formats.

Finally, we look at the remaining specialty retail sectors. There are many of these, so in Chapter 11 we consider how specialty retailing is key to the development of shopping malls and other retail facilities.

Japan still has its fair share of general merchandise retailers. Department stores, while declining, do still survive in numbers not seen anywhere else in the world, and Aeon, Ito-Yokado, and Seiyu are three companies that continue to develop general merchandise stores. This, however, is now it. The fate of Daiei is still unknown, but both its new rehabilitation coordinators, Marubeni, along with the IRCJ, which is responsible for the process as a whole, have already stated that they plan to concentrate on the specialist food supermarket format while turning over additional store space to other specialist retail tenants. This is unsurprising as it is the excitement generated by the multitude of specialist formats that is now drawing consumers. Where general merchandise retailers flounder, achieving growth purely through additional space and organic growth, specialty retailing has at last given consumers a glimpse of something new and interesting. It is not surprising then that this is where the real action is today.

9

Apparel Specialty Store Retailing

The changes in apparel retailing since 1990 have been some of the most momentous in the entire retail industry. It is the one retail sector where international retailers have played a major role, especially in the luxury brand category. This sector is now driven by the top global brands. In addition, in many cases the brand owners themselves now control their own distribution channels, a dramatic change from 1994 when licensees and distributors controlled most of the supply. In sportswear too, brands like adidas, Nike, and Puma have grown significantly with retail stores of their own.

Compared to most other forms of retailing, there has even been relatively more success for international firms in non-luxury apparel too. Gap and Zara are two firms that show the real potential of this market. Gap entered the market independently and has grown to be a brand found in every major urban market, while Zara operator, Inditex, bought out much of the stake of its original joint venture partner Bigi in 2004 and now plans to develop a similar chain of stores.

As early as 1994, the success overseas of specialty apparel retailers like Gap, H&M, and Zara, and the entry of Gap into the Japanese market, brought a new mantra for Japanese apparel firms and retailers alike:

European design, American supply (chain management), Asian production. (EDASAP)

The diligence and perseverance with which manufacturers and retailers have applied the EDASAP mantra to their businesses is the story of apparel retailing in the last decade and it has influenced every major format including department stores and GMS chains.

The leading apparel retailers

Apparel retailing is big business. According to the METI Census of Commerce for 2002, the total apparel market, even excluding apparel sold by general merchandise retailers such as department stores and GMS chains was ¥10.980 trillion. Based on METI's monthly retail sales estimates, apparel accounts for roughly a third of total sales at department stores and GMS chains combined, so the total apparel market for 2002 can be estimated at around ¥16.69 trillion.

In terms of store numbers, Japan had 185,939 retailers selling apparel in 2002. Of these, however, 72,810 were small, non-incorporated independent stores employing two or fewer people. On the other hand, 92,724 stores were part of incorporated businesses, although as apparel retailing tends to be small format by nature, 20,971 of these still employed two or fewer people.

Table 9.1 shows the summary statistics for apparel retailers taken from the Census of Commerce for 2002. While the figures omit apparel sales

Table 9.1 Apparel retailing sector according to Census of Commerce, 1999 and 2002

	Unit	Census Year 1999	Ratio %	Census Year 2002	Ratio %	Change 1999 to 2002 %
Stores	Stores	201,762	100.0	185,939	100.0	–7.8
Incorporated stores	Stores	97,434	48.3	92,724	49.9	–4.8
Non-incorporated stores	Stores	104,328	51.7	93,215	50.1	–10.7
Sales	¥ mn	13,001,898	100.0	10,980,231	100.0	–15.5
Incorporated stores only	¥ mn	11,318,570	87.1	9,663,328	88.0	–14.6
Employees	People	747,552	100.0	719,847	100.0	–3.7
Incorporated stores only	People	542,841	72.6	529,357	73.5	–2.5
Sales space	sqm	20,032,594	100.0	19,456,403	100.0	–2.9
Averages						
Sales per store	¥ mn	64.44		59.05		–8.4
Sales per incorporated store	¥ mn	116.17		104.22		–10.3
Employees per store	People	3.71		3.87		4.5
Sales area per store	sqm	99.29		104.64		5.4

Source: METI (2003)

at GMS chains and department stores, they suggest a sector in decline. Overall sales were down 15.5 per cent, and it was one of the few categories where sales space also declined. There were marked differences between stores operating within incorporated and non-incorporated businesses. Incorporated businesses made up only 49.9 per cent of total stores in 2002, but accounted for 88 per cent of sales and 73.5 per cent of employees.

To get a complete picture of the apparel market overall, it is necessary to estimate sales at general merchandise retailers also. The problem here is that while monthly and annual statistics are available for large formats, including department stores and general merchandise stores, the Census, which is taken every three years, is the only source for specialty formats. As mentioned above, based on ratios for apparel sales for general merchandise and specialty formats in the 2002 Census, the market for apparel retailing in FY2003 can be estimated at around ¥16.64 trillion. Figure 9.1 provides an estimated breakdown of the market by the four main formats of department stores, GMS chains, specialty chains, and independent stores.

In total we estimate that while department stores account for 27.8 per cent of total apparel sales, specialty retail chains of all sizes and types now account for more than half. Independent retailers, while most numerous by store numbers, have only a 7 per cent share of the total market and this is now declining.

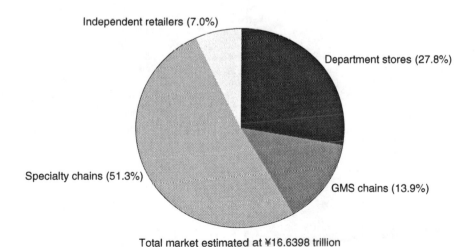

Independent retailers (7.0%)

Department stores (27.8%)

Specialty chains (51.3%)

GMS chains (13.9%)

Total market estimated at ¥16.6398 trillion

Figure 9.1   Market share of apparel total retail market by retail format, FY2003
Source: METI (2003, 2005); Authors' estimates

Table 9.2   Retailers with apparel sales above ¥50 billion, FY2003

Rank	Company	Type	Apparel Sales ¥ mn	YonY %
1	Takashimaya	DpS	494,329	–3.0
2	Aeon	GMS	490,815	–1.1
3	Millennium Retailing [3]	DpS	470,015	–
4	Ito-Yokado	GMS	342,364	–5.8
5	Fast Retailing	Casual	301,751	–11.7
6	Daiei	GMS	287,013	–3.7
7	Shimamura	Casual	275,283	6.6
8	Dalmaru	DpS	270,857	9.5
9	Isetan	DpS	253,077	0.9
10	Marui [1]	DpS	237,622	–0.6
11	Mistukoshi [1]	DpS	226,520	–2.1
12	Onward Kashiyama	Mixed	191,246	1.1
13	World	Mixed	175,065	5.1
14	Five Foxes	Mixed	175,023	–
15	Hankyu	DpS	174,702	–1.1
16	Matsuzakaya	DpS	163,073	–0.5
17	Aoyama Shoji	Men	152,124	3.3
19	Uny	GMS	148,817	–7.6
20	Kintetsu	DpS	126,089	–4.5
21	Seiyu [2]	GMS	104,072	–
22	Akachan Honpo	Kids	103,155	–4.3
23	Tokyu	DpS	99,976	–7.8
24	Xebio	Sports	91,718	4.0
25	Nishimatsuya Chain	Children	77,853	22.1
26	Sanei	Mixed	71,820	12.3
27	Aoki International	Men	68,359	0.5
28	Tobu	DpS	66,284	0.2
29	Iwataya	DpS	66,048	28.5
30	Akachan Honpo	Children	62,990	–2.6
31	Nissen	DM	62,908	19.4
32	Heiwado	GMS	62,832	–0.6
33	Leilian	Women	62,725	–3.5
34	Izumi	GMS	62,612	1.9
35	Leilian	Women	62,286	–3.2
36	Izumiya	GMS	62,255	–1.0
38	Right On	Casual	61,381	16.7
39	Aoki International	Men	61,139	–0.4
40	Odakyu	DpS	57,535	–4.2
41	Aeon Kyushu	GMS	56,105	6.2
42	Cecile	DM	55,390	–10.7
43	Haruyama Shoji	Men	53,425	–6.6
45	Sagami	Women	52,422	–3.7
46	Izutsuya	DpS	51,668	19.4

Notes:
[1] Figures for FY2002 due to accounting changes
[2] Seiyu figures for Mar to Dec 2003 due to accounting changes
[3] Millennium figures estimated for Sogo and Seibu
Key:
DpS: Department Store; GMS: general merchandise store
SM: supermarket; DM: direct mail
Men, Women, Children, Casual, Mixed: Specialty apparel
Source: Company Reports

Because of the size of the sector and the number of stores involved, the Census provides a rather unhelpful picture. Another alternative is to consider just the leading retailers of apparel by sales volume. Table 9.2 lists all 46 retailers for FY2003 that sold ¥50 billion or more in apparel. For completeness, the major manufacturing-to-retailing groups such as Onward Kashiyama, World, and Sanei, all of which are increasingly involved in retailing, were also included. Taken together, these 46 chains accounted for ¥6.592 trillion in apparel sales for the year, or around 39.6 per cent of total apparel retail sales. The leading chains were made up of 14 department stores, nine GMS chains, and two direct mail retailers, with the remainder being specialty chains of various types.

Takashimaya was the largest single apparel retailer for FY2003, closely followed by Aeon's GMS chain. If Aeon's apparel subsidiaries such as Cox, Blue Grass, Talbots, and Laura Ashley were included, Aeon would exceed Takashimaya. Millennium Retailing is the combination of Sogo and Seibu Department Stores (see Chapter 5), and despite undergoing industrial rehabilitation following bankruptcy, was still the number three apparel retailer overall. Half of the leading 16 apparel retailers were department stores and two were GMS chains, but the leading group includes five firms operating specialty formats: Fast Retailing, Shimamura, Onward Kashiyama, World, and Five Foxes. It is clear from the table that, generally speaking, specialty retailers recorded sales increases in FY2003 while almost all the general merchandise formats saw sales of apparel decline. Even in the cases of Iwataya and Izutsuya department stores, relatively strong sales growth was due to major refurbishment and the addition of new floor space rather than due to company growth and is not expected to be sustained. Department stores still have a role at the very top end of the apparel market while GMS chains also fill in at the lower end for casual and daily apparel, but growth is clearly in specialty retailing.

The rise of specialty apparel chains

Since 1990, specialty apparel retailing has increased its share of the market while that of department stores and GMS chains has steadily declined. By focusing on a particular merchandise niche, and without the stultifying overheads built up by the general merchandise retailers during the 1980s, the better specialty retailers have been able to improve and grow. At the same time, there has been a certain amount of sectoral restructuring. A number of chains that had largely made their business in the old, traditional style, allowing suppliers to dictate their merchandise and pricing, collapsed. Suzutan, for example, reduced its chain by more than 300 stores in a decade, while Cabin too slashed its chain in half. Others simply went bankrupt. Chains such as these have now been replaced by new, highly focused, and dynamic retailers that seek to control their own operations at all levels.

Table 9.3 lists the leading apparel specialty chains with sales above ¥10 billion in FY2003. What is remarkable about the table is the level of growth in the sector overall. Out of the 60 firms listed, 37 recorded sales growth for the year, and 32 recorded increases in pretax profit levels, performance that makes a notable contrast with most other retail formats. Moreover, a number of companies recorded exceptionally high levels of growth. Admittedly, many of these firms are still very small, but even in terms of pretax profits per employee, five of the top 10 retailers were apparel retailers, another, Xebio, a sports apparel chain, and yet one more, FDC Products, was a mixed fashion and jewelry chain (see Table 9.4).

The increasing incursion by specialty retailers on department store and GMS apparel sales does not mean the end of apparel retailing by these formats. A handful of department stores continue to innovate in order to survive, and the leading two GMS chains continue to add space. Within specialty apparel retailing, there are also plenty of examples of intransigence and a failure to adapt. The contrast between the leaders in innovation in this sector and the rest is more dramatic than for either department stores or GMS chains. While overcapacity is still an issue, particularly in GMS and department stores, companies like Point, United Arrows, World, Onward, Sanei, Shimamura, Honeys, and Fast Retailing, are proving just

Table 9.3   Specialty apparel retailers above ¥10 billion in sales (parent only), FY2003

Rank	Company	Type	Sales	YonY	Pretax Profits	YonY
			¥ mn	%	¥ mn	%
1	Fast Retailing	Casual	301,751	–11.7	46,968	–14.3
2	Shimamura	Casual	275,283	6.6	19,873	9.5
3	Aoyama Shoji	Casual	152,124	3.3	14,391	29.6
4	Akachan Honpo	Children	103,155	–4.3	552	–37.2
5	Xebio	Sports	91,718	4.0	8,373	33.3
6	Nishimatsuya Chain	Children	77,853	22.1	7,049	26.2
7	Aoki Int'nal	Men	68,359	0.5	5,122	27.4
8	Leilian	Women	62,725	–3.5	1,895	25.3
9	Right On	Casual	61,381	16.7	5,193	141.0
10	Haruyama Shoji	Men	53,425	–6.6	3,810	–27.1
11	Sazaby	Mixed	52,760	5.7	6,182	0.0
12	Sagami	Women	52,422	–3.7	1,018	–36.5
13	Konaka	Men	47,914	–4.3	2,864	2.1
14	Mac House	Casual	43,420	3.9	3,529	41.6
15	United Arrows	Select	42,903	21.6	5,270	10.1
16	Takeuchi Group	Women	41,750	22.3	3,090	14.1
17	Blue Grass	Women	40,662	–1.4	2,058	64.4
18	Ryohin Keikaku [1]	Casual	38,936	3.7	8,667	22.2
19	Suzunoya	Women	34,998	–4.0	584	0.0
20	Yamato	Women	34,064	0.5	1,091	108.2
21	San-ai Group	Women	32,324	–6.1	3,186	16.5
22	Sanki	Mixed	31,656	–4.5	1,273	–23.5

Table 9.3 Specialty apparel retailers above ¥10 billion in sales (parent only), FY2003
– continued

Rank	Company	Type	Sales	YonY	Pretax Profits	YonY
			¥ mn	%	¥ mn	%
23	Beams	Select	30,760	2.4	2,170	18.6
24	Miki House	Children	29,470	−6.3	1,021	−42.6
25	Workman	Casual	28,640	5.6	3,114	10.5
26	Palemo	Women	28,502	7.9	1,506	50.6
27	Rio Chain	Women	28,247	4.1	2,656	−2.9
28	Point	Casual	27,860	34.7	4,256	51.6
29	Baycrews	Select	27,075	8.3	2,280	20.0
30	Suzutan	Women	24,980	−11.3	176	−55.7
31	Pal	Mixed	24,114	28.2	1,937	32.9
32	Jeansmate	Casual	23,887	3.6	1,948	−1.1
33	Fujikyu	Accessories	23,269	8.3	3,279	−0.2
34	Avail	Casual	22,147	36.7	903	–
35	Honey's	Women	21,601	39.6	2,884	46.2
36	Cox	Casual	20,928	−8.5	526	42.2
37	Cabin	Women	20,197	−6.7	706	–
38	Sanmatsu	Women	19,517	−2.5	249	72.9
39	Shisendo	Women	19,110	1.5	–	–
40	Taka Q	Men	19,090	1.6	255	140.6
41	Delica	Women	18,719	–	3,316	–
42	Ginza Maggy	Women	18,500	−2.6	–	–
43	Ships	Select	17,713	−4.2	1,176	−31.1
44	Gotoh	Men	16,764	4.2	578	−15.7
45	Kyoto Kimono	Women	15,465	4.4	2,655	4.9
46	Lobelia	Women	14,827	−9.7	76	–
47	Oya	Women	14,730	5.4	1,150	458.3
48	Hateiya	Women	13,616	3.3	663	21.2
49	Tatsumiya	Women	13,114	−5.2	–	–
50	Eddie Bauer Japan	Casual	12,321	2.2	491	−1.0
51	Leo	Casual	12,095	1.6	802	16.4
52	Brooks Brothers Jpn	Men	11,664	–	–	–
53	Futata	Men	11,506	−2.2	150	–
54	Torii	Men	10,665	0.9	446	–
55	Mitsumine	Men	10,644	−1.6	–	–
56	Mokumoku	Women	10,584	5.8	37	23.3
57	Sakiya Create	Women	10,582	13.2	–	–
58	Lobelt	Men	10,580	−9.4	–	–
59	Barney's Japan	Select	10,334	2.1	−314	–
60	Suzuya	Women	10,243	−7.5	144.0	−40.0

Note:
[1] Ryohin Keikaku apparel sales only. Pretax profits for parent company in full
Key:
Casual, mixed, men, women, children: type of apparel sold
Select: store format employed (see below)
'–' indicates unavailable data
Source: Company data

Table 9.4   Increase in pretax profits per employee, FY2003

Company	Type	Pretax Profits YonY %
Pal	Apparel	245.0
Right On	Apparel	106.9
Honey's	Apparel	68.2
Komehama	Discount	54.1
Liquor Mountain	Liquor	49.9
Japan	Discount	48.2
Mac House	Apparel	37.7
FDC Products	Jewelry	37.7
Xebio	Sports	30.3
Aoki International	Apparel	27.3

Source: NMJ (2004)

how quickly a retail chain can grow with the right product mix, supply chain and targeted marketing.

The picture remains the same as for the retail industry as a whole. Despite improvements by some department stores at the very top end of the market, and continued volume expansion by GMS chains, the future growth of sales, and particularly profits, is firmly in the hands of specialty chains. More importantly, there is a growing polarization between those specialists that have modernized their management systems and that are in control of their own businesses, and those that still work on a day-to-day basis, relying on suppliers to dictate their merchandising and pricing.

The poorer firms are now being further pressurized by the development of retail operations by major manufacturers. These able, highly dynamic companies all have a number of things in common. They all take an active role in all aspects of the supply chain if not actually controlling it outright; they are fast moving, adapting to and shaping the fashion market; and they are clearly, and increasingly, profit orientated.

As recently as 1990, there were few apparel firms that displayed such characteristics. Now they are a powerful and growing minority. The market is segmenting into clear retail functions depending on market level, with the surviving department stores moving further upmarket, and GMS chains along with a tiny number of discount apparel retailers working to maintain share at the bottom. The interest though, is between these two extremes where fashion-focused specialty retailers will continue to challenge for share at both ends.

Specialty apparel retailing

The apparel sector is highly dynamic and extremely complex in structure. There are many types of store format, chain organization, and merchandise subcategory to consider, and the highly dynamic nature of the sector means that these are shifting and adjusting constantly. In addition, in recent years, there has been a significant amount of vertical integration within the sector, with both manufacturers taking an interest in retailing and retailers taking on greater control of their own supply chains right up to and including manufacturing. In each case, the business model becomes slightly different.

In order to create a clearer map of specialty apparel retailing, we have split the sector into the following sections:

1. SPAs (Specialty Private (Label) Apparel) Groups:
   These are vertically integrated, single brand retail chains. In order to highlight the common trends across this important category we have included non-apparel but fashion related chains such as interiors under this commonly used term.
2. Select shop chains:
   A retail format that utilizes a merchandise mix of store brands alongside a range of international fashion labels with an approximate ratio of 60:40.
3. Traditional specialty retailers:
   Any specialty chain characterized by multiple brands, and mass market targeting, is supplied primarily from wholesalers, and whose primary merchandise is apparel, including accessories and footwear.

In the following sections we consider each of these main retail formats in turn.

1. Specialty Private Apparel Groups (SPAs)

SPA stands for Specialty Private (Label) Apparel and is yet another English acronym adopted and adapted by the Japanese. It is used to denote any vertically integrated apparel group, whether retailer or manufacturer, encompassing the complete distribution channel from manufacturing to retailing of apparel. In Japan, manufacturers control most SPAs, although retailing is now becoming a dominant part of these companies' activities. SPAs include companies that are directly involved in all aspects of their retail supply chain similar to Gap and H&M. Japan currently has 19 SPA groups of any major importance (see Table 9.5) although a few other companies are now attempting to emulate the same model. These include six chains that originated overseas.

As shown in the table, SPAs can be further categorized into three types depending on the company origins:

- Manufacturer based SPAs
- Wholesale based SPAs
- Retailer based SPAs

Table 9.5 Leading SPA chain operators in Japan, FY2003

SPA Leader	Original business	Main Category	Key Retail Fascias
World	Manufacturer	Apparel	Untitled, Cordier
Onward Kashiyama	Manufacturer	Apparel	23-ku, Gotairiku, Jiyu-ku, Kumikyoku, ICB
Itokin	Manufacturer	Apparel	OfuOn, a.v.v.
Sanei International	Wholesaler	Apparel	Vivayou, Pearly Gates, Natural Beauty
Five Foxes	Wholesaler/Designer	Apparel	Comme Ca, Comme Ca Ism
Flandre	Wholesaler/Designer	Apparel	Flandre
Fast Retailing	Retailer	Apparel	Uniqlo, Theory
Ryohin Keikaku	Retailer	Mixed	Mujirushi Ryohin, Muji
Dan	Manufacturer	Socks	Kutsushitaya
Bigi	Wholesaler/Designer	Apparel	Bigi, Adieu Tristesse, Moga
Mokumoku	Retailer	Apparel	Olive des Olive
Sazaby	Wholesaler/Designer	Accessories/Apparel	Sazaby, Agnes B Voyage, Agete, Anayi
Bals	Retailer	Interiors/Household	Franc Franc, J-Period
Gap	Overseas	Apparel	Gap
Laura Ashley	Overseas	Apparel/Home	Laura Ashley
Zara Japan	Overseas	Apparel	Zara
Mango	Overseas	Apparel	Mango
Benetton	Overseas	Apparel	Benetton
Eddie Bauer	Overseas	Apparel	Eddie Bauer

Source: Compiled by the authors

Again, we will consider each of these in turn.

Manufacturer based SPAs

Manufacturer SPAs include World, Onward Kashiyama, Itokin, and Dan. These companies are all manufacturers in their primary form although World originated in the textile business. Since 2000, these companies have had a major influence on apparel retailing overall due to their determination to rationalize distribution of apparel and implement brand marketing, as well as to compete as apparel retailers in their own right. In the mid 1990s, conglomerates like Onward and World determined that their wholesale operations were under increasing threat from vertically integrated retailers. In response, they have shifted from being manufacture-led distributors to retail-led SPAs and now see a growing proportion of sales and profits coming from retail operations. These companies do not distinguish clearly between retail and non-retail activity in their accounts, but it is possible to make estimates based on the sales of their core brands.

Onward Kashiyama had sales of ¥267.7 billion in FY2003, up 1.7 per cent on the year before. Extracting the core SPA operations suggests that retailing accounted for around ¥190 billion of this total, or around 70 per cent. Its two largest SPA brands, 23-ku and Kumikyoku, accounted for ¥100 billion alone (see Onward Kashiyama Case Study below). World, the second largest firm, posted sales of ¥236.2 billion, of which around ¥175 billion, some 75 per cent, is estimated to be derived from retail operations. Itokin has taken yet a different route and is expanding directly into retailing in China.

Although Japanese business classifications still consider these companies as manufacturers, clearly retailing is now their core business. The reason is that retail operations provide the easiest path to growth in both sales and profits. Onward Kashiyama's overall sales may have only increased by 1.7 per cent in FY2003 but its core retail operations have fared much better. For example, concession sales within department stores were up 4.3 per cent in the same year and sales at shopping center tenants surged 39.6 per cent (see Company Reports). For this reason, Onward and its competitors are focused on investment in suburban shopping centers and station buildings for future growth. With department store footfall withering in the regions and growth in shopping center developments at an all time high, the opportunities for capturing share outside department stores are significant.

Wholesaler based SPAs

Wholesale based SPAs include Five Foxes, Sanei International, Bigi, Itokin and Flandre. Most of the companies in this group would have been considered design houses in the 1970s and 1980s, designing apparel, arranging manufacture through third parties and then placing product in fairly narrowly targeted brand concessions. They were commonly known as DC

Table 9.6   Top apparel conglomerates (consolidated), FY2003

Rank	Company	Sales ¥ mn	YonY %	Pretax Profit ¥ mn	YonY %
1	Onward Kashiyama	267,745	1.7	25,243	15.3
2	World	236,225	1.5	15,606	29.0
3	Five Foxes	175,023	-2.7	16,575	-27.6
4	Itokin	144,973	5.1	5,514	-35.1
5	Sanyo Shokai	142,086	0.3	13,155	0.9
6	Renown	99,949	-6.8	-560	-
7	Takihyo	83,419	0.1	3,242	32.0
8	Sanei International	91,473	10.7	7,280	32.7
9	Java Group	70,430	-6.1	9,450	13.7
10	Cross Plus	68,990	-4.0	2,499	-
10	Tokyo Style	52,715	-6.2	8,133	102.1
11	Naigai	51,901	-11.9	-2,600	-
12	Jun [1]	47,326	29.0	-	-
13	Look	43,530	-10.9	-553	-
14	Narumiya International [1]	35,319	16.2	4,242	-
15	Kosugi Sangyo	32,553	-14.1	-783	-

Note:
[1] Non-Consolidated accounts
Source: Company Reports

(Designer Character) brands based on this narrow targeting. The most famous was Bigi, a privately owned firm that reached its peak in the late 1980s, and it is this group that originated the SPA system in Japan in response to falling wholesale sales. In most cases, these companies can be distinguished from retail SPAs as they maintain at least a small wholesale function with some product being distributed to stores outside their own core retail chains. For some, such as Five Foxes, however, wholesaling has been largely eliminated from its business model.

Although most large apparel wholesalers have some small direct retail involvement, a true SPA is strategically positioned to control all aspects of supply and is heavily involved in retailing. Seeing the success of their contemporaries, major apparel wholesalers such as Naigai, Renown, Xebio, Tokyo Style and D'Urban (a subsidiary of Renown) are also trying to develop SPA business models, either by importing them (for example Xebio importing Next from the UK), licensing them (Renown licensing J. Crew through Itochu) or making their own (Naigai with Victoire).

Retailer based SPAs

Finally, the retail based SPAs include Fast Retailing, Mokumoku and Ryohin Keikaku. These companies have taken vertical control over wholesale supply and closely monitor product back to point of manufacturer. While original retailer SPAs are rare, the model is based on overseas firms such as Benetton and Gap. As already mentioned, Five Foxes is now almost entirely retailing in orientation, and the same can be said of Flandre and Sazaby. Other retailers are quickly also moving to emulate the SPA model, with Shimamura and Honeys being two prominent examples.

The key characteristic of retail SPAs is their branding. Unlike manufacturer and wholesale SPAs, they have taken a total retail branding approach, usually selling only one brand within any particular fascia and position. In Fast Retailing's case, the brand is Uniqlo, although it is now expanding through its acquisition of Theory. For Ryohin Keikaku the brand is Mujirushi Ryohin, and this brand has been taken overseas under the abbreviated name of Muji.

Overseas SPAs in Japan

Several of the major overseas SPA brands, Benetton, Laura Ashley, Eddie Bauer, Gap, Zara, Mango, and Giordano are all active in Japan. The only genuinely successful entrant has been Gap, although Benetton has been in Japan for the longest period and Zara is now expanding. In 2004, Inditex, the owners of the Zara brand, acquired half the stake in Zara Japan from its joint venture partner, Bigi. This gave it 85 per cent ownership. Benetton is seeing a revival through expansion of large format stores across Japan. The Hong Kong based SPAs have made several attempts at the Japanese market and are only just beginning to make a real impact; Giordano failed once in Japan in a joint venture agreement, but is now trying again in a second attempt, this time by maintaining more direct control.

Trading companies behind the success of SPAs

SPAs originated in the Benetton and Gap system of design, manufacture and retailing. It has become a very successful business model in Japan because it is so well suited to the existing business structure. For manufacturers and wholesalers, vertically integrated supply chains have long been normal practice and were the fundamental thinking behind the traditional Japanese *keiretsu* (see Chapter 10). Whereas the *keiretsu* model was one of fairly simple product supply, SPAs are much more centered upon marketing and branding, and the growth of retailer led SPAs such as Fast Retailing and Ryohin Keikaku is a complete reversal of the power balance of the past.

Having said that, even the new retail SPAs grew with more than a little help. All SPAs rely heavily on partners, affiliates and especially the *Sogo Shosha* as vital components of their supply channels. "Just in time" delivery, as pioneered by Toyota, is just one efficiency to hit the apparel market in recent years, and this requires significant control and support in the supply chain. In order to compete, SPAs must focus more on the business of retailing, particularly store location, branding and merchandising, meaning that they have become increasingly dependent on outsourcing for the management of supply of fabrics and production of final garments. This is particularly so for the wholesale and retail SPAs.

As traditional suppliers of yarn and fabric to apparel manufacturers, and more recently, as managers and licensees of apparel brands, the *Sogo Shosha* (see Chapter 4) are the obvious choice as partners in supply chain management. Their textile import and overseas manufacturing links are first rate, and within the same industrial grouping, they are able to organize and offer complete logistics and transportation solutions. All of the largest trading houses are highly active in organizing and driving the SPA business as a result.

Take the case of Ryohin Keikaku, the operators of Mujirushi Ryohin. Originally part of the Saison Group, the company first preferred to control its own supply chain, but it is precisely in this area where it was least competitive. When it was forced to lower prices in response to competition from chains such as Uniqlo, inefficient supply chain management meant it was impossible to maintain margins. Since 2000, however, the company has cut core suppliers from 70 to around 10. It has done this by subcontracting management of smaller suppliers to Mitsubishi Shoji. While many smaller suppliers still sell to Ryohin Keikaku, they must now do so through Mitsubishi. The sheer size and scope of Mitsubishi's international operations means it is able to streamline supply through its networks. Crucially, it can also offer Ryohin Keikaku lines of credit that can help reduce the overall cost of supply. This is one of the traditional roles of trading companies and one of the reasons they have so much influence. To seal the deal, Mitsubishi also took a 3.8 per cent stake in Ryohin Keikaku in 2002, another commonly used method of relationship building in Japan.

The rise of the SPA business model in Japan

Since 1995, SPAs have come to dominate the specialty apparel market in Japan. While other individual companies within the specialty sector have also done well, SPAs have shown consistent growth. Outside Japan, department stores such as Isetan, Mitsukoshi and Takashimaya are well known as key apparel retailers, but today SPAs like Onward, World, Itokin and Sanei International are also vital. The control they exert over all aspects of supply, along with careful selection of store locations and store size, have been fundamental to this success. The SPA model focuses on what Japanese companies are good at: efficient, low cost manufacturing, and integrated supply chains, with marketing taking a back seat. To this mix, apparel firms have added design flair and branding, but, with a few exceptions, such SPAs are only now beginning to develop such creative aspects of their business, particularly following the success of SPA retail brands like Muji, Uniqlo, and Comme Ca. SPAs have implemented the EDASAP mantra mentioned at the beginning of this chapter by first focusing on supply chains and merchandising. It is only recently that design has become important.

Case Study 9.1: Sanei International: expansion of brands and diversification through the SPA business model

The rapid growth of the SPA business model created intense competition in apparel distribution. As a result, SPA groups are increasingly looking to develop brands that clearly define niche targets. In addition, having achieved a stable market presence in one area, well-financed firms are branching out into new markets. A good example of this is Sanei International.

Until recently, Sanei International was just another mid-sized womenswear wholesale operation. It had grown steadily by developing its own retail chains under names like Natural Beauty Basic and Jill Stuart, offering broadly similar mainstream fashion for women in their 20s and early 30s. In the year to August 2004, Sanei International's existing operations produced consolidated sales of ¥91.4 billion, up ¥10 billion on the year before. Pretax profits were also strong, at ¥7.28 billion, up 32 per cent. Taking a longer view, the firm's turnover rose from ¥55 billion to ¥91 billion between 1998 and 2002, boosting it into the top five womenswear firms. Sanei International continues to expand rapidly, both through acquisition and expansion of its existing brands, boosted by access to funding following its public listing in 2003. In the short term, it will easily achieve its target of ¥100 billion in sales by 2006. Longer term, new brands will be added, greater penetration outside its core womenswear market will be progressed and expansion overseas will be extended to Europe. For example, Sanei International acquired Anglobal in September 2004, bringing with it ¥6.1 billion in turnover, 60 stores and the Margaret Howell business in Japan and worldwide. The Mitake family, who founded the business, also made it clear in a press statement in 2004 that they were working on further acquisitions to help grow the business at home and internationally (see Senken Shinbun, 2004.09.10).

During 2004, as has happened with other SPA firms, Sanei International began to make a serious attempt to diversify outside its key market. It launched its first childrenswear brand, Barbie Kids, and a sportswear brand, Double Wrap. In Spring 2005 it launched Jill Stuart New York, Baby Jane Cacharel, a brand for toddlers based on its Jill Stuart license, Charlotte Ronson, a brand for late teenagers, as well as a number of others. For Jill Stuart New York alone the company expects sales of ¥2.5 billion a year, growing to double that figure within three years.

What is different about the brands being launched recently is the diversity of their target markets. Sanei International is emerging from its comfort zone of young womenswear and moving into childrenswear, teenage fashions, sports for women in their 30s, and apparel for men and women in their late 30s and 40s, the last of these through Margaret Howell. The shift makes sense as it already has a healthy share of the young womenswear market in Japan, a market that is one of the most crowded and competitive. But it is also a gamble. If it pays off, Sanei International will probably launch new brands within each of these segments and develop into an apparel conglomerate covering all the major consumer categories similar to that already developed by Onward Kashiyama.

The significance of the new brands in terms of distribution is also worth pointing out. Almost all are targeted at shopping centers and fashion buildings, helping Sanei International further shift its distribution away from the faltering department store channel. All the major apparel groups are working hard to grab share in the shopping center and fashion building market as they have all seen the depressing future for apparel sales in all but the best department stores.

Case Study 9.1:   Sanei International: expansion of brands and diversification through the SPA business model – *continued*

Similar efforts to diversify are being made by Sanei International's competitors. For many years, World was the largest apparel conglomerate in Japan, but it lost the title in 2000 to Onward Kashiyama, which was able to pull ahead because of the diversity of its brand portfolio that covers men's, women's, and children's apparel across every positioning from mass market to luxury brands. World has been attempting to fight back. In 2004, World signed a menswear license for the Harrods brand with Mitsubishi Shoji, the master licensee in Japan. World used this to introduce an upscale menswear range in line with the brand's position as one of the UK's premier department stores.

Case Study 9.2:   Honeys: supply chain shift

The increasing variety of formats, store numbers and merchandise types in the apparel sector requires ever better control and management. Yet operational costs continue to fall and, for many SPAs, operating margins have risen steadily. This is being achieved through focus on production control, lowest cost supply and tailored information systems from factory to shop floor. Despite overall deflation in the apparel market, this has been achieved by a more ruthless approach to supply chain control than used to be the case.

An excellent example of this is Honeys. Until about 2000, Honeys was a small, little known womenswear retailer from Fukushima Prefecture, but it has since become one of the best-performing apparel chains in Japan. It operates a range of fascias, all offering reasonably priced womenswear, mostly in shopping center locations. The largest fascia is Honeys itself, but others include Cinema Club, Honey Club and She's Labo, and the portfolio is now expanding more rapidly following a listing on JASDAQ in December 2003. By FY2003 there were 250 stores with relatively modest sales of ¥15 billion, but growth rates were high. Turnover climbed 50 per cent in the five years to 2003 and pretax profits rose ten-fold from ¥200 million to ¥2 billion. Sales for the year ending May 2003 were up from ¥11.9 billion to ¥15.4 billion. In 2004, 130 stores were added.

Like Beams, United Arrows, and Point, Honeys began life in the late 1970s. Unlike its larger counterparts, however, Honeys was just a regional player, often anonymously located in the bland shopping centers of Mycal, Aeon and Ito-Yokado. Offering a mixed bag of product from the standard group of Japanese apparel manufacturers, the company was never going to excite customers in terms of innovation. Then, under the pressure of Chinese imports, Honeys changed. Forced to cut prices to compete, it shifted much of its own production to China in the late 1990s. By 2003, 60 per cent of production was under direct contract with Chinese factories and much of the rest was being produced there through third parties.

With its new Chinese production in place, Honeys cut the cost of merchandise dramatically, loosened connections with local apparel firms, improved merchandise planning, and most importantly, dramatically cut its delivery lead times. Gross margins rose to 53 per cent. To cope with the higher merchandise volumes,

---

Case Study 9.2: Honeys: supply chain shift – *continued*

the company installed an IT system to show real-time data between Chinese factory, distribution center and stores, and in January 2004 moved its warehousing to a new 15,000 sqm center, providing a theoretical capacity for up to 1,000 stores.

The company has continued to outperform the apparel sector as a whole by tweaking supply chains. It posted a 40 per cent rise in consolidated pretax profits for the first half of 2004 ended November to ¥1.6 billion, despite a fall in like for like sales. Improved profits were the result of a further cut in domestic apparel production and a shift to affiliated sources in China. Chinese imports rose 10.4 per cent, comprising just under 70 per cent of sales by value. Total sales for the half grew 41 per cent to ¥13.33 billion on the back of 71 new stores, but like for like sales fell 2 per cent. For the full year ending May 2005, Honeys was forecasting sales of ¥30.6 billion, up 42 per cent on 2003, and the China dividend was expected to further boost pretax profits by 46 per cent to ¥4.22 billion.

Despite gradual development in the past, Honeys is a new chain that seems to have the foundations for rapid growth. If it manages this growth well enough, it will be one of the 10 leading women's apparel retailers by 2006, and positioned to overtake companies like Leilian and Suzutan within two years. It is a strong example of a company using supply chain rationalizations to boost profitability as well as improve merchandise through better turnaround on best sellers and better links with factories. It is also an example of the key advantages SPA retailers have over multi-brand specialty chains that rely on independent suppliers, and it explains their much faster growth and higher returns.

So successful has this model been that it is now moving overseas, particularly into Asia. To date only Fast Retailing and Ryohin Keikaku have expanded into Europe, although Sanei International now has a European operation through ownership of Margaret Howell, a British fashion brand. Such is the power of the supply chain model developed by SPA groups that this is probably just the beginning.

In the immediate future, prospects look good for the SPA business model. It will be one that is increasingly copied, particularly by retailers looking to expand their businesses overseas. A number of trends that bode well for the sector in the domestic market:

- Concentration of market share
- Proliferation of new formats to target niche markets
- Declining influence of older, more traditional fashion retailers

Combined with the significant potential for many SPAs and their brands in Asia and other overseas markets (see Chapter 12), these companies will continue to grow for the foreseeable future.

2.   Select shop chains

Within the specialty apparel retail sector is a group of highly regarded chains catering to the middle and upper ends of the market. The format that they use is commonly termed *select shops* in both Japanese and English. The leading companies in this group are Beams, United Arrows, Ships, Baycrews, Adam & Rope, and Tomorrowland (see Table 9.7).

Select shop chains have a number of common features. They stock a full range of apparel and accessories varying only by chain, and generally include both own-brand products and a proportion of other brands, mostly imported from overseas. Although select shops are a type of specialty apparel format, their categorization as a separate group is useful given their distinct characteristics, target market, and merchandise policy. The definition of a select shop as used in Japan and in this book, is as follows:

- A specialty apparel store having 50 per cent or more of own-brand merchandise, but at least 20 per cent of product in non-store brands, often overseas apparel labels
- Price positioning for select shops is as mid- to high-end in both casual apparel and formal apparel, offering branded and designer collections

Table 9.7   Select shop chains ranked by number of stores, 2002 and 2005

Chain	Ownership	Sales ¥ mn	YonY %	Pretax Profit ¥ mn	YonY %	Store Nos 2002	2005	2005 to 2002 Change
Tomorrowland	Independent	25,374	11.9	–	–	131	132	1
Baycrews	Independent	26,000	0.0	370	–31.7	75	98	23
Beams	Independent	31,048	0.0	1,498	–1.2	65	73	8
United Arrows	World	42,903	21.6	5,271	10.1	37	73	36
Ships	Independent	17,737	–4.1	–	–	51	54	3
Aquagirl	World	–	–	–	–	10	30	20
Adam & Rope	Jun	–	–	–	–	22	27	5
Via Bus Stop	Onward Kashiyama	–	–	–	–	20	20	0
Free's	Sanei International	–	–	–	–	22	17	(5)
Barney's New York	Isetan	–	–	–	–	2	3	1

Source: Company Data

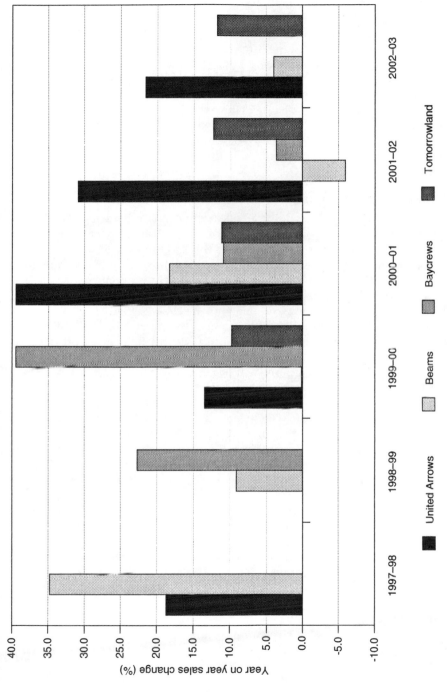

Figure 9.2 Sales growth at major select shop chain apparel retailers, 1997 to 2003
Source: Company Reports

- The reputation of the chain's buyer is one of the selling points of a store
- Buying of non-store brands (and sub contracting of own-brand manufacturing overseas) is usually undertaken directly by chain buyers, and although buying is also done through distributors or subsidiaries, where none exist, these chains prefer to buy direct

Another key aspect of the select shop sector is consistently high levels of growth during the last decade. Sales for most of the companies have increased for the past 10 years, and as much as 30 per cent in some cases (see Figure 9.2). They have proved one of the better channels for imported apparel, particularly from Europe and the US, but also increasingly for apparel labels from Asia.

The evolution of select shops

Beams used to be Japan's leading select shop chain and founded this growing retail sector. It opened its first store in the late 1970s and set off a transformation in apparel retailing. For the first time, overseas designer brands other than the very expensive luxury brands, became available in Japan, and, although not exactly cheap, at relatively reasonable prices. The kind of consumer who wanted to buy overseas apparel labels tended to be less price sensitive, so Beams grew quickly. The chain's original concept featured imported labels almost exclusively, but over the years, Beams acquired a name for its buying capabilities within the fashion press and among fashion conscious consumers. As a result, rather than just the products stocked in the stores, Beams itself began to carry serious brand value as a fashion credible retailer.

The natural consequence of this was the development of a Beams branded apparel collection. The merits of own brands in terms of both gross margins and supply chain management, along with their popularity with consumers, led to a gradual erosion in the sales share of imported brands. Today all of the main select shop chains carry more than 50 per cent own label product. Much of the remainder of select shop merchandise is still imported.

In effect, select shop chains today operate largely as SPA chains: that is, designing and selling their own product, with imported brands more as wrapping and window dressing. The imported products are used to encourage customers through the door and to create a high quality and fashionable image for the chain through fashion magazine PR. But it is this quota of overseas branded merchandise that distinguishes select shops from SPAs.

Select shop ownership

Table 9.7 shows the main select shop companies. Tomorrowland leads in terms of store numbers, but its formats are much smaller than competitors, often located within shopping buildings and department stores, and include some new SPA style mini chains. Of the others, only Beams, United Arrows, Ships, and Baycrews are independent, although United Arrows is 22.4 per cent owned by World. Via Bus Stop is a subsidiary of Japan's largest apparel company, Onward Kashiyama. Adam & Rope is part of Jun, the SPA firm, Aquagirl is part of World, Sanei International owns Free's, and Barney's New York Japan is owned by Isetan.

Their market position tends to reflect the type of ownership (see Figure 9.4). Beams, as well as being the original select shop chain, is much more eclectic thanks to its independent ownership. It often chooses brands and designers based on whim rather than sales potential (JapanConsuming, 2002b). As a result it has significant respect amongst young consumers, although this has waned in recent years. Tomorrowland has already moved towards a SPA-like business model and has never had the same following as United Arrows or Beams with consumers. Its main targets are male and female office workers, who prefer safer fashions with just a hint of edgier designs. Baycrews, however, is a world unto itself: the private kingdom of its owner Hiroshi Kubota. Kubota maintains a rigid control over the business and each division is entirely independent of others, each reporting directly to Kubota and his budget team. Divisional performance varies widely but there are some fast growing store concepts in the group such as the Iena format.

While a typical Beams or United Arrows store stocks around 50–60 per cent own brands, Baycrews' ratio of own brand product is usually higher at around 70 per cent with much of the product being made in Asia. This is the current trend throughout the sector as own brands are easier to manage, being mostly basic apparel, and also provide significantly higher margins. While overseas designer labels lure the press, generating lots of editorial, and store window displays by these designers pull in curious consumers, own brands generate the bulk of sales and profits.

However when mass market chains like Uniqlo, Avail and Point improved their merchandise and branding at the low end in the early 2000s, select shop chains struggled to convince consumers that they should pay three to five times the price for a basic own branded garment that looked essentially the same. Given the importance of basic apparel as a component of select shop own brands, this became a serious threat. In response, the select shop chains responded to this by creating more distinctive merchandise. In particular, they created a wider range of store formats to suit more carefully selected consumer targets. Beams, for example, has 14 different formats, each with a slightly different target but still within the core teens to 20s consumer market to which it wants to remain tied. Beams also developed an information service called Beams News as well as a music store called Beams Record.

United Arrows, on the other hand, focused on becoming market leader and a company of serious size (see Case Study 9.3). Accordingly, it expanded its store chain across different generations and types of consumer. The clearest

Case Study 9.3:   United Arrows leads the way

In terms of sales, Beams was the leading group until 2002 when United Arrows, a company that was founded by former Beams staff, usurped its place. United Arrows growth has been the most impressive of all the select shop chains, not only in terms of sales, but also for new stores and new brands (see Figure 9.3). Its merchandising is impressive and well-organized with weekly divisional meetings by all the merchandising and buying staff to review sales and future purchasing. The company operates several fascias, but within overall sales, there has been a gradual increase in womenswear and a reduction in menswear. In 2000, 55.9 per cent of sales derived from menswear but this was down to 50 per cent by 2003. For womenswear, 2000 saw 35.6 per cent of sales from this category, but this had risen to above 37.8 per cent by 2003.

United Arrows operated 63 stores as at March 2004, rising to 73 by March 2005, and up from 37 in 2002. Its stores are located in most major cities in Japan with about 30 per cent of the stores in the Tokyo region. United Arrows continues to produce impressive financial results. For the month of January 2002 alone, the company saw like-for-like sales up 47.6 per cent on 2001, the second largest increase following its record 57.3 per cent increase in August 1999. Overall sales increased 57.3 per cent that year. Its long-term growth is even more impressive: since 1999, turnover has climbed from ¥17 billion to just under ¥43 billion in 2003.

The company is also targeting all of the main apparel markets through different store fascias and concepts. Overall, United Arrows has always been a slightly more upmarket casual fashion chain compared to Beams or Ships, but it has also begun to develop more distinct merchandising policies between its different fascias, making it more attractive to a wider customer base. In general, this has meant a gradual move towards higher prices on the one hand, and fashion basics on the other. The clearest example of the move upmarket is Changes, a concept launched in 2001 that offers quality casual brands for women. Green Label Relaxing (GLR), a family concept offering fashion basics at a low price, best demonstrates diversification. One element of GLR's success is that it is a family store format, taking the select shop idea one step further into a wider market than just that of young fashion. United Arrows saw that the original generation of United Arrows consumers from 1989 onwards, were now parents with different tastes and requirements. Rather than lose them to department stores and SPAs like Gap, the company set up GLR to offer basic and reasonably priced fashion goods for those who used to buy into United Arrows. GLR also includes store branded maternity and childrenswear and a range of imported toys and accessories. United Arrows says it plans to have more than 50 GLR stores open by 2007. It further emphasized its ambitions to become a retail business across all the major consumer markets with the launch of a new brand in Spring 2005. Called Darjeeling Days, the new format was the first United Arrows' concept aimed at men in between the ages of 50 and 55.

United Arrows also took tentative steps into overseas markets with a corner in the Dover Street Market store in London opened by Comme des Garcon's Rei Kawakubo in October 2004. Called Sebiro by United Arrows, the store is just 20 sqm and on the basement level, but is significant as the first overseas venture by the company. Through growth of existing fascias, diversification into new markets as with Darjeeling Days, and continued focus on improving supply chains, United Arrows has a solid base to become one of the largest apparel groups in Japan. The company itself forecasts sales of more than ¥110 billion by 2011. By then, it will no longer be a select shop operator but a fully diversified fashion retailer.

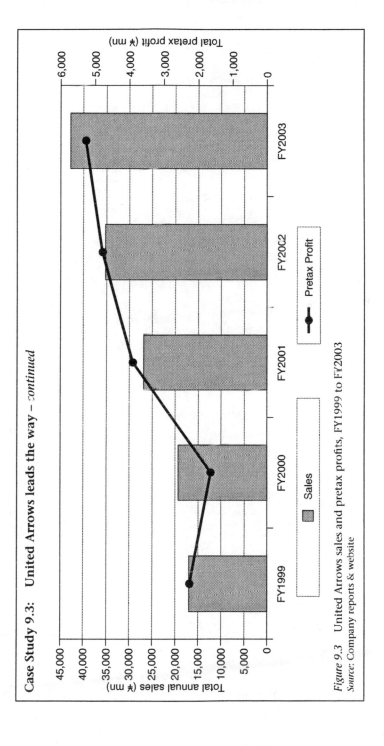

Case Study 9.3:   United Arrows leads the way – *continued*

Figure 9.3   United Arrows sales and pretax profits, FY1999 to FY2003
Source: Company reports & website

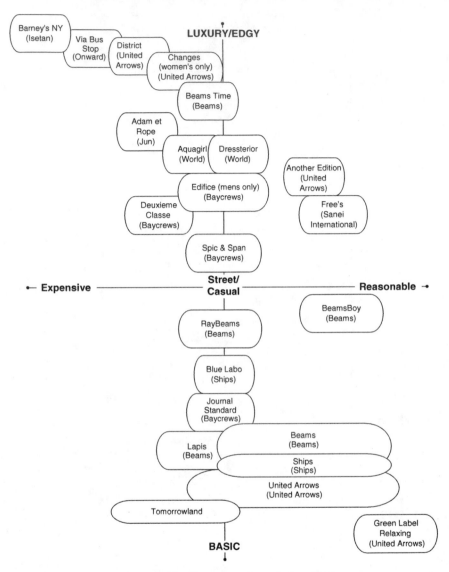

Figure 9.4 Market positions of leading select shop chains, 2004
Source: JapanConsuming (2002a)

example of this was the successful launch of Green Label Relaxing (GLR) in 2002. This fascia saw month-on-month growth of more than 50 per cent for some stores in the first year, and the chain grew to 20 stores as of March 2004. United Arrows also introduced Another Edition in 2001 at higher price points. Featuring up-and-coming casual designer labels from the US and

Europe as well as the store brand, both design and quality are significantly higher than casual apparel from the mass market chains, justifying the much higher prices. The fascia also features a less cluttered merchandise plan to emphasize the higher quality of merchandise on offer. United Arrows also operates a store called Changes which stocks expensive overseas fashion brands and competes with chains like Via Bus Stop.

Although 50–70 per cent of merchandise is own brand for most select shop chains, this ratio is being increased. United Arrows, concerned with building an efficient store operation and raising gross margins, began to expand the percentage of own branded merchandise in most of the main fascias in 2004. The latest fascia, Darjeeling Days that was introduced in 2005, sells some of 80 per cent store brand merchandise. The other main select shop chains are also following this trend.

A bright future for select shop chains

Japan's narrowly focused select shop chains have plenty of life left in them. They have built a tremendous level of trust and respect with consumers. All the main companies are now making efforts to exploit this consumer trust without losing it. One of the key ways is through development of more comprehensive store brands. Another is to follow the brand's consumers as they become older with new concepts that match consumers' changing lifestyles and life stages. At the same time, the select shop chains are adapting existing younger fascias to meet the needs of new generations. These various strategies make a lot of sense in a polarizing market.

3. Traditional specialty retailers

The final main classification of apparel retailers basically includes all those that do not fall under the categories of SPA or select shops. This is the traditional view of apparel retailing, considering each apparel subcategory by target market and merchandise type. There is some overlap with the previously introduced business models in terms of merchandise sold, although those introduced in this final section are generally less innovative and progressive at present. Unlike the SPAs, they all carry a range of brands supplied by wholesalers and manufacturers, but with the benefits of the SPA business model becoming clear, many are attempting to convert to SPA operations.

Menswear

Menswear specialty retailing is dominated by a small number of chains that, together, have divided up the country between them with 52.6 per cent of the market. The main menswear chains are Aoyama Shoji, Aoki International, Haruyama Shoji, Taka Q and Konaka (see Table 9.8). Workman is the fifth largest chain but is focused on work wear such as overalls and uniforms. In the Nagoya region, Torii also has a strong presence but

Table 9.8   Menswear retailers with sales above ¥10 billion (non-consolidated), FY2003

Rank	Company	HQ Prefecture	Sales ¥ mn	YonY %	Pretax Profit ¥ mn	YonY %	Stores
1	Aoyama Shoji	Hiroshima	152,124	3.3	14,391	23.1	744
2	Aoki International	Kanagawa	68,359	0.9	5,122	21.6	281
3	Haruyama Shoji	Okayama	53,425	−6.6	3,810	−27.2	306
4	Konaka	Kanagawa	49,361	5.2	4,424	35.7	290
5	Workman	Gunma	28,640	6.2	3,115	9.6	533
6	Taka-Q	Tokyo	19,090	1.9	255	69.0	154
7	Futata	Fukuoka	11,506	−1.4	151	−	88
8	Lobelto	Tokyo	10,752	−9.2	−	−	103
9	Torii [1]	Aichi	10,665	0.9	−	−	56
10	Mitsumine	Tokyo	10,644	−1.6	−	−	67

Note:
[1] Acquired by Aoki International 200
Source: Company Reports

was acquired by Aoki International in 2003. As with other larger stores and due to the influence of long-term controls on new store development, the differing menswear specialty chains mostly operate in isolation from each other and it is rare to find these stores in competing locations.

While department stores still control the top end of the menswear market, specialty retailers have carved out market share at the bottom end through the introduction of discount suits and higher quality ranges, usually branded as European, targeting the bottom end of the department store suit business. Back in the early 1990s, a "discount" suit at Aoyama sold for ¥39,000. Today, cut-price suits, usually sell at two fixed price points of ¥19,000 and ¥29,000, and are ubiquitous across the menswear specialty sector. These formats are known as "two-price" shops. The boom in low price, low quality office attire has also brought specialty stores and GMS chains into direct competition and since 2000, price points have been falling in many chains. In a bid to win back lost share in apparel retailing, the top GMS chains, Ito-Yokado and Aeon, began offering suits at under ¥10,000 in limited lines and for limited periods, but so far, specialty chains have maintained their lead through better marketing and better ranges of accessories. Some offered a small discount on part-exchange of old suits, while others offered five-point packages including suit, tie, shirt, belt and shoes.

In a sign that the market had reached the natural limit of price discounting, Aoyama Shoji changed strategies in 2003. Instead of attempting to undercut competitors further at the bottom end, it launched new ranges of high price items to compete with the lower price points of department stores. Using European labels like Fariani and Saville Row of London, and often European fabric, the higher priced suits offered better quality and cut but still at competitive prices. As a result, both sales and profits spiraled for Aoyama in FY2003. Consolidated turnover hit ¥186 billion, up from ¥161 billion two years earlier, and pretax profits doubled from ¥8.2 billion to ¥17.3 billion.

In an attempt to catch up, Aoki International acquired Torii in 2003, adding 51 stores to its network and bringing its total chain to 448 stores as at September 2004. As a result, consolidated turnover reached ¥89 billion, but this was still less than half of Aoyama. Aoki also invested heavily in its bridalwear business and even karaoke clubs in an attempt at diversification. Konaka, the third largest chain, made a similar response, becoming sponsor to the ailing Futata menswear chain as a way to boost scale. It also tried to find new ways to generate profits by expanding manufacturing ventures overseas, particularly in India, and also invested in European-style ranges with more fashionable fits and higher prices such as its John Pearse of London and Donato Vinci Moda Milan brands.

In general, prices in mass market menswear retailing stabilized by 2004. High levels of competition from other formats means that margins are no longer as comfortable as they were, but the largest chains now have a firm niche at the bottom and middle of the market. As other, better marketed formats such as SPAs and select shop chains continue to improve, however, mass market apparel retailers of all kinds will look to further increase own-branded product and add greater proportions of directly sourced, low-cost production from China and the rest of Asia, combining this with very fast short-order production in Japan.

With supply chain management streamlined and improved branding and design, the nimbler chains, honed by competition into lean and fit operations, may even be pushed to look at other Asian markets as a way of bypassing intense competition at home. This has already begun with Aoyama, for example, opening four stores in Taiwan and three in Shanghai before 2005 as a precursor to a faster expansion in 2005–6.

Womenswear

In womenswear, the gap between the best performers and the rest is as wide as across the whole apparel retail sector. As Table 9.9 shows, most of the leading mass market chains are contracting, both in terms of store numbers and turnover. Their decline is almost entirely the result of competition from the SPA and select shop operators. In 2003, of 30 womenswear specialty chains with sales of ¥3 billion or more (including SPAs), 15 posted increases in sales of 10 per cent or higher in 2003. Only one of the leading mass market chains, Delica, achieved this and it did so by advancing its shift to SPA operations.

Table 9.9 Womenswear retailers with sales above ¥10 billion (non-consolidated), FY2003

Rank	Company	HQ Prefecture	Sales ¥ mn	YonY %	Pretax Profit ¥ mn	YonY %	Stores 2004
1	Leilian	Tokyo	62,714	–3.2	937	24.3	369
2	Blue Grass	Chiba	40,663	0.1	2,058	39.2	642
3	Sanki	Chiba	31,656	–4.5	1,273	–	82
4	San-ai Group	Tokyo	29,980	–1.3	–	–	174
5	Palemo	Aichi	28,503	7.2	1,506	5.3	409
6	Rio Chain	Aichi	28,248	4.0	2,657	–2.9	256
7	Suzutan	Aichi	25,000	–12.4	176	–56.7	293
8	Cabin	Tokyo	20,197	–6.8	–706	–	181
9	Lobelia	Tokyo	18,820	–1.5	–	–	320
10	Derica	Tokyo	18,719	54.3	3,312	–	79
11	Ginza Maggy	Tokyo	18,500	–	–	–	105

Source: Company Reports

The old, retail only womenswear specialty retail sector now lives in the shadow of SPAs and select shop chains. Chains such as Leilian, Suzutan and Cabin have been in long-term decline since the early 1990s, unwilling to change their business models and unable to come up with new ideas. Instead of adapting, they attempted to continue to sell middle market apparel merchandise at middle market prices in drab and unexciting stores. While these firms sat entrenched hoping for a return to the good old days of high consumer spending, the SPAs ate away at their market.

Since 2000, there have been a few signs of strategies to adapt to new market realities. Among the top eight mass market chains, Cabin and San-ai have shown signs of change, but at a cost. Cabin has cut costs substantially and introduced a series of new fascias, but this has only been made possible by closing stores. By late 2004 Cabin had 181 shops, some 200 fewer than in the mid-1990s. Turnover fell from ¥37.6 billion in 2000 to ¥20.6 billion in 2003 and the company reported losses in FY2002 and FY2003. Similarly, San-ai attempted to climb out of a cycle of poor returns through merger with I-Mario under the supervision of dominant shareholder, Ricoh, the office equipment company. The combined group hoped that a large number of formats and fascias would help provide future growth. However, turnover continued to fall, from ¥35.9 billion in FY2001 to ¥29.9 billion in FY2003. Store numbers were cut from 215 stores in 2001 to 174 as of August 2004, with full-time staff numbers also dropping from 525 to 411.

Japan has many examples of survival despite poor performance, and one of the best is Suzutan. At its peak in the early 1990s, Suzutan boasted 600 stores. By 2004, there were only 293 stores with more than 200 closed in the previous two years. In the 1980s, when consumers would buy almost anything put on the shelves, Suzutan was happy to offer the kind of relatively high priced, medium quality merchandise that dominated Japanese womenswear distribution. When this demand disappeared following the collapse in asset prices, Suzutan still failed to adapt. As a result, turnover fell from ¥70.8 billion in 1998 to ¥25.0 billion in 2003. It is the most visible example and the tip of the iceberg; Japanese retailing has many others.

Leilian remains the largest mass market womenswear retailer, but its history is now similar to that of Suzutan. The chain suffered while main shareholder Renown sorted out its own problems, including 13 consecutive years of losses, and despite other powerful shareholders such as Itochu Shoji and Mitsubishi Rayon, insufficient attention was given to modernize Leilian's supply chain and more importantly, its brand fascias. In 1999, the addition of the select shop format, Anne Recre, did suggest a determination to attract younger women consumers, but in the end even this did not do much to boost sales. Turnover continued to fall, from ¥80.2 billion in 1999 to ¥62.7 billion in 2003.

All of these companies face the same problem: their efforts at reform are coming too late and are insufficient. Unlike the menswear market where the leading chains have managed to find new ways to attract customers and to position themselves away from SPAs and select shop chains, womenswear retailers have shown little such innovation. In most countries, they would have be acquired by more competent management teams, or many of these chains would have simply become bankrupt, whereas in Japan they have been supported by a benevolent banking system. Unfortunately, however, most of the stores they still operate do not make an acquisition attractive even if the owners were willing to sell. These companies are also encumbered with old, poorly located stores, a heavy debt load and piles of inventory. The survival of the likes of Suzutan is a sign that there are still barriers to an entirely market driven apparel retail sector, but with other, new business models succeeding where these firms have failed, it is only a matter of time before they disappear altogether or, at the very least, can be safely ignored.

Casualwear

As with mass market menswear retailers, casualwear specialty retailers have also split between a small number of new, high growth chains and the bulk of older, poorly performing companies. Several of the better companies have already moved to the SPA business model including Fast Retailing, Shimamura, and Point (see Table 9.10).

Fast Retailing, along with its Uniqlo brand, enjoyed such incredible success up to 2001–2 that it has skewed expectations towards this sector as a whole. At one point, press reports were suggesting that three out of four

Table 9.10 Leading casualwear retailers (non-SPA, non-select shop) with sales above ¥10 billion (non-consolidated), FY2003

Rank	Company	HQ Prefecture	Sales ¥ mn	YonY %	Pretax Profit ¥ mn	YonY %	Stores
1	Shimamura	Saitama	276,879	6.7	19,873	9.5	1,060
2	Right-on	Ibaragi	61,381	16.7	5,193	141.0	229
3	Mac House	Tokyo	43,429	3.9	3,529	41.6	393
4	Point	Ibaragi	27,619	33.6	4,235	52.0	206
5	Pal	Osaka	24,114	28.2	1,937	32.9	205
6	Jeansmate	Tokyo	23,887	–3.6	1,949	–1.1	102
7	Cox	Tokyo	20,298	–8.5	526	41.8	175
8	Leo [1]	Tokyo	12,095	–1.6	803	–	73

Note:
[1] Merged into Mac House by parent Chiyoda in 2005
Source: Company Data; JapanConsuming

Japanese were wearing Uniqlo, and that consumers actually became embarrassed to buy the brand. A dip in sales between 2002 and 2004 was, in reality, simply a readjustment down to more realistic levels for the chain, and, to its credit, it has also repositioned itself both in terms of price and a greater emphasis on womenswear compared to its previous unisex casualwear. What sets Fast Retailing apart from other casualwear chains, however, is its use of 100 per cent own brands.

Shimamura is a casualwear chain, sometimes called a discounter, which has a strong emphasis on womenswear. It was the first chain to exceed 1,000 stores in 2003 and had more than 1,110 at the end of December 2004. It has kept up a pace of 100 or more new stores every year from 2000 and plans to continue to do so for the foreseeable future. Although it started out only operating in northern Kanto, it now has stores in every prefecture in Japan. Turnover doubled from ¥155 billion in FY1997 to ¥300 billion in FY2003. The reasons behind its success are common to the other leading casualwear chains and ones we discussed before in talking about SPAs and select shop chains:

- Rationalized supply chains
- Ruthless culling of under performing stores
- A large and increasing ratio of own brands

Shimamura has become a leading exponent of sourcing in China. The primary difference between the casualwear retailers and womenswear chains particularly, has been this willingness and capacity to move production to low cost production centers in the rest of Asia on the one hand, and to develop better merchandise ranges with the brand suppliers on the other. In addition to securing direct manufacturing links with factories near Shanghai and other Asian centers, Shimamura's distribution centers now operate 24 hours a day, seven days a week. As a result, per item shipment costs fell 10 per cent in 2003 and more than 20 per cent in the two previous years.

Most casualwear chains have increased the ratio of own brands in response to the success of Uniqlo. By 2003, Shimamura had 10 own brands contributing just ¥7 billion in revenues but this is expected to increase to double the number of brands and quadruple the turnover by 2006. Another chain, Point, also increased the ratio of sales from own brands by 15 per cent to 90 per cent of sales by 2003, effectively completing its move to become an SPA chain. It grew from a ¥10 billion a year operation in 1999 offering a mix of casual brands from Japan and overseas, to sales of ¥27.8 billion from 206 stores in 2003. Point utilizes multiple fascias including Point, Lowrys Farm, Global Work, Heather, and Eru.

Most casualwear retailers have done similar work on supply chains and, as a result, profitability has improved dramatically since 2000. Point, for example, saw pretax profits increase from ¥2.8 billion in FY2002 to ¥4.2 billion in FY2003. Mac House, a subsidiary of shoe retailer Chiyoda saw pretax profits climb from ¥321 million in FY2001 to ¥3.5 billion in FY2003. Like Right-on (see Case Study 9.4 below), the company focused on culling poor performing stores and new stores are better located in shopping malls rather than in traditional shopping arcades.

Frustrations and bottlenecks remain in the casualwear sector. While Shimamura, Right-on and Point are excellent examples of the new, highly focused and efficient specialty retailers, the rest continue to be a strong a reminder of the old ways. As with womenswear retailers, these chains are ripe for acquisition or will simply fade away over time. Unlike womenswear, however, this is already happening in casualwear. Leo, a

---

Case Study 9.4:   Right-on goes its own way

In 2002, Right-on was beginning to look like one more victim of the onslaught of Uniqlo and Shimamura. It reacted to the threat from these fast growing chains with a plan to fight back on equal terms, developing own brands and cutting prices. That strategy failed but Right-on quickly realized its mistake and, unlike so many of its contemporaries, found a new position where it has performed well.

Right-on started life as a humble casual apparel store in 1980, little different from the plethora of other stores that litter the suburbs and regions of Japan. Today the influence of its early years is still clearly visible but the transformation into a sophisticated, efficient, casualwear retailer has been remarkable. By 2006, Right-on will join the small number of apparel retailers with sales above ¥100 billion, up from ¥28 billion as recently as 1998. For the financial year ending August 2004, Right-on set record sales and profits. Sales reached ¥69.3 billion, up 13.4 per cent, and this produced a pretax profits increase of 43.4 per cent to ¥7.4 billion. During FY2004, Right-on opened 50 stores and closed five, leaving a net 306.

Case Study 9.4:   Right-on goes its own way – *continued*

This is all far removed from the tough start Right-on had on entering the new millennium. At the time, Right-on was facing up to what it thought was its nemesis, Uniqlo. It worked hard to convert itself into an SPA style operation but failed – hardly surprising given Fast Retailing's five-year head start. But Right-on realized its mistake and pulled the plug on that business model, returning Right-on to its original strategy of merchandising famous brands at reasonable prices in suburban locations. In particular, Right-on focused on its family stores, taking a comfortable position between GMS chains and department stores, and working to introduce new efficiencies to a standard formula rather than invent new ones. As a result, the virtuous circle returned: more stores, more sales, more efficiencies, and so more profits to fund more stores. Right-on also worked on improving sales per customer through the introduction of higher priced lines and better store merchandising. Sales rose 2.5 per cent on a like-for-like basis and per basket sales rose 3.6 per cent in FY2003. Overall, gross margins rose to 45.4 per cent and both operating and pretax profit rose above 10 per cent for the first time.

Future growth will also come from store expansion. In 2004, interest from shopping mall developers remained strong, attracted as they were by Right-on's sales numbers and its refreshing store designs. By then 70 per cent of Right-on stores were located in shopping centers with the ratio expected to increase further given plans to open 50 new stores per year in by 2008. The shift from roadside stores to shopping centers, like other specialty apparel chains, was a major factor behind Right-on's more recent growth and will continue to be so.

Further growth can also be expected from the company's second move towards an SPA business model. It may have failed first time round, but in the Fall of 2004, the model was reintroduced to supply two new fascias called Spice Island and Flash Report. Flash Report is positioned to be a tenant in cheaper department stores and lower end shopping malls such as Lalaport, while Spice Island is a casualwear concept for shopping center locations. While Spice Island can leverage the roadside and shopping center knowhow that Right-on has accumulated during its history, Flash Report is a wholly new venture that targets competition directly with the largest apparel conglomerates. The concept offers American style vintage fashions priced around 50 per cent higher than the Right-on average and has a much younger target. Right-on expects to have 30 Flash Report stores open by the end of 2006 along with 50 Spice Island stores. The result: another ¥100 billion specialty chain with a lot of potential.

---

subsidiary of Chiyoda, was merged with another Chiyoda subsidiary, Mac House, in September 2005, creating a ¥50 billion plus retail chain with close to 500 stores. In the case of Cox however, parent Aeon is determined to carve out a share of the casual apparel business and, with profitability improving, looks likely to still be around for some time to come. There is only so much of the market to go around, however, and competition will increase, both within the casualwear sector and across the differing business models.

Other apparel related specialty retail sectors

Finally we take a brief look at the rest of the apparel-related retail sector. In each of the footwear, jewelry and sports categories, Japan has a few relatively large retail firms, but, for the most part, these are sectors that have yet to modernize in the ways seen elsewhere.

Footwear

Specialty footwear retailing is dominated by a single chain: Chiyoda. The sales of the other nine companies in the top 10 only just about add up to its total sales. Until 2000, there was one competing chain called Marutomi, but intense competition forced it into bankruptcy. Since then, Marutomi has undergone rehabilitation, including changing its name to Onezone, and in early 2005, it was acquired by Fast Retailing bringing the possibility for new competition within the sector.

For the time being Chiyoda has an estimated market share of some 18 per cent. It operates some 1,550 stores, the largest retail chain outside the convenience store sector, and backed by this powerful position has also experimented with casual apparel and accessory formats.

Other chains, while much smaller, have sought separate niches in order to compete. The number two firm is ABC Mart, which has been importing and manufacturing shoes since the 1980s. In the early 1990s, ABC Mart changed ownership and the company was repositioned as a specialty sneaker company popular among younger consumers. Having made a success of this market, Chiyoda has since followed suit, using its buying power and store size to tie up exclusive deals such as those with Nike and Dr. Marten's.

The third footwear chain is yet another Aeon subsidiary called NuStep. While currently the third largest footwear retailer, NuStep, is small and its expansion has so far been limited largely to Aeon shopping center developments.

Jewelry

The market for jewelry shrank by a third between 1989 and 2000 from ¥3 trillion to ¥2 trillion (Sensu Report, 2001). The sector has few large retail chains and all of them have been around for a long time. The largest jewelry firm is Mikimoto, which, while having only nine stores, generated sales of ¥31.4 billion in FY2003. This is followed by Tasaki Shinju with ¥27.09 billion from 48 stores. While these two firms lead by sales, both are primarily manufacturers and wholesalers with much larger businesses outside of retailing.

In terms of store numbers, the largest chain is Estelle with 247 stores, most of which are concessions and shopping center tenants. The number three chain, Tsutsumi, along with fifth ranked chain F.D.C. Products are the two most profitable jewelry retailers by far and both grew strongly in FY2003. F.D.C. Products operates a popular fascia called 4°C with 156 stores.

A number of luxury brands from overseas are also active in the market. Tiffany, the US luxury brand, broke away from its exclusive operator, Mitsukoshi, in 2001 but has continued to suffer from deteriorating sales. Japanese consumers now prefer to buy either low price jewels or those at the very top end of the market, and Tiffany, despite its brand name, has found itself uncomfortably between the two. While it has struggled, Cartier, Harry Winston, and Chaumet have all reported growing sales in recent years.

Sporting goods retailing

Sporting goods retailing is a typically traditional sector with, so far, few new initiatives in recent years. The sector has also seen a number of prominent bankruptcies. In February 2002, the fifth largest chain, Minami, went into administration under the Civil Rehabilitation Law, and Victoria, the third largest chain, also fell under the weight of its debt burden and was acquired by Jafco.

The sector is led by Alpen, an Aichi Prefecture based company with sales in FY2003 of ¥154.37 billion from 373 stores. While not unprofitable, Alpen has shown little growth over the past 10 years, and, like Chiyoda in the footwear sector, has enjoyed a strong position largely due to its superior size. Since 1995, Xebio, a Fukushima based apparel retailer by origin, has grown strongly, but with sales of ¥91.7 billion from 140 stores in FY2003, it is still some way behind Alpen. On the other hand, Xebio's pretax profits almost matched Alpen and the company is showing much stronger growth.

The most promising development in the sector, however, is the growth of yet another Aeon subsidiary, Megasports. This chain was developed out of Aeon's joint venture partnership with US chain Sports Authority in Japan. While the joint venture fizzled out, Aeon took advantage of the experience to develop its own remarkably similar format of large, full-line sports stores. In FY2003, Megasports led the sector in terms of growth, recording sales up 22.4 per cent on the year to ¥49.2 billion from just 50 stores.

There are no other sports retailers anywhere near the ¥50 billion sales mark, and most other chains specialize in niche products such as ski or golf equipment. Johshuya, the fourth largest chain, is a specialist fishing goods retailer with a sprawling empire of more than 263 stores catering to Japan's considerable amateur fishing community. The fifth largest chain, Himaraya also used to be a more specialist chain focusing on winter sports but since the collapse in ski sales in the mid-1990s has been converting itself into an all-season sports goods and apparel retailer. Sixth and seventh ranking Niki and Honma Golf are Japan's largest golf goods and apparel retailers.

There are few overseas sporting goods and apparel retailers in the market. REI from the US entered the market in 2000 but pulled out only a year later after opening just one store. The store was sold to Japanese outdoor goods brand, Montbell. Patagonia has its own direct presence in the market with around 12 stores and is a stable and growing operation with a loyal Japanese customer base.

Summary: the SPA model dominates

Specialty apparel retailing and the various related sectors covered in this chapter represent a huge and important part of the overall market, yet it has not before been considered in any depth in Western literature. This is not surprising as small format retailing in Japan was for a long time limited to independent, mom and pop stores. This is no longer the case. In fact, today the reverse is true. In the apparel sector, we are still witnessing the transition from traditional retailing where firms basically source from wholesalers and sell products they find on the market, to one where retailers actually take control of their own merchandise, pricing, and marketing. This came about through the influence of successful examples overseas such as Gap, and led to the popularity of EDASAP, as mentioned at the beginning of this chapter. This process is happening throughout Japanese retailing, but, as evidenced by a few firms in each of the main apparel formats, it is probably most advanced here. Some would even argue that companies like Fast Retailing and Five Foxes were the first to drive towards fully retailer led distribution channels, retail brands, and retail marketing. It is certainly the case that companies such as these have forced others to take a more hands-on and complete view of retailing for the apparel sector as a whole. They have been followed by select shop chains like United Arrows and even by manufacturers like Onward Kashiyama (see Case Study 9.5), all of whom now operate directly in the retail sector and all of whom emphasize unique merchandise and independent marketing.

The apparel sector is worthy of even greater analysis and discussion, but in this quite extensive chapter we have attempted to illustrate not only the worst of traditional retailing, but also the best of the new retail companies. In the following chapters we will again see small groups of retailers that have also taken as much control as they can over their own operations. This all started here in apparel.

Case Study 9.5:   Onward Kashiyama: a fashion conglomerate

When Japan's largest apparel firm launched a luxury brand in 2002, few saw it as the start of a new initiative to become an international leader in apparel distribution. However, Onward Kashiyama's efforts to expand internationally are a long-term strategy and luxury and high end designer brands are very much part of a plan to achieve a strong position in every major apparel market. In the past few years, it has transformed itself into a major distributor of top international brands, an SPA operator, and a supplier to the mass market.

A diversified apparel conglomerate

Onward Kashiyama has moved a long way from its humble beginnings as an apparel manufacturer in 1927 when it was called Kashiyama Shoten. Its original business continues through subsidiaries but the company expanded and diversified rapidly during the 1960s onwards. In 1965, it listed on the Tokyo, Osaka and Nagoya stock markets and established operations in France and Italy two years later. Through organic growth, licensing of key brands such as Polo Ralph Lauren, and acquisitions (it acquired J. Press in 1986 and Chacott in the early 1990s), the company raced past World to become the largest Japanese manufacturing-led apparel company by sales in 2000. Consolidated turnover reached ¥267 billion for the year ending February 2004 (FY2003) up from ¥221 billion in 2000, producing pretax profits of ¥25.2 billion. Retail sales are estimated to account for around ¥190 billion or around 70 per cent of turnover. Although not something widely known even in Japan, Onward operates an estimated 1,200 stores, tenants, and corners and has more than 50 brands under management.

As well as by turnover, Onward Kashiyama is also by far Japan's largest apparel conglomerate in terms of scope. It spans every market from mass market underwear to luxury bags, accessories, and jewelry. In addition to its own successful brands such as 23-ku, it also owns the old Seibu distribution business including Sonia Rykiel and other luxury labels, and the strategically important Gibo manufacturing concern in Italy. It runs 64 Paul Smith Women's stores under license from Itochu and has taken over a large chunk of the Daks operations from owners, Sankyo Seiko. It also has exclusive deals with Calvin Klein and Donna Karan. Onward's main subsidiary, Impact 21, is involved in the licensing and distribution of Polo Ralph Lauren brands in Japan (see Figure 9.5). Onward has five main apparel subsidiaries: Impact 21, Chacott, Donna Karan Japan, Bus Stop, and the Calvin Klein business called On Business Trend.

Success through licensing

Despite its origins as a supplier of more volume brands and generic apparel, Onward's experience as a licensee helped it to see the potential of the upper end of the market. It used this as a tool to gain a foothold in overseas markets earlier than its competitors. In 1995, it launched ICB as its first international brand. At the same time, Onward began a gradual process of acquiring expertise in the marketing and retailing of high end brands. Using its licensing arrangements as a base, Onward set up distribution deals with Paul Smith, Jean-Paul

Case Study 9.5: Onward Kashiyama: a fashion conglomerate – *continued*

Gaultier, Marni and Michael Kors. As a result, the company operates stores in Paris, London, Hong Kong and New York for some of these brands as well as operating its own retail subsidiary, J. Press. This experience was crucial to Onward, both domestically and internationally, helping it to develop from a mainstream Japanese apparel manufacturer into a vertically integrated international fashion conglomerate. At the same time, the company gained experience as a manufacturer of top international brands through its subsidiary, Gibo SpA in Italy. Gibo has been a manufacturer for the likes of Giorgio Armani, Helmut Lang and Paul Smith womenswear since the early 1990s.

International expansion

Yet, until 2002, Onward's international activities remained peripheral. Its core business was still the wholesale and retail businesses in Japan with brands such as 23-ku, Jiyuku, and Kumikyoku along with its substantial licensing operations for Polo, Calvin Klein, Paul Smith Women's, Donna Karan and Jean Colonna. The plan to be a global player only really became official with the launch of a new luxury division within head office in March 2003. Through its luxury division, Onward's international exposure increased dramatically through the acquisition of the import and licensing rights to Sonia Rykiel, Missoni and Gianfranco Ferre following the closure of Seibu's subsidiary Ellebis.

With all this experience of international brands, Onward began to make its move to become a major international fashion company. It launched its own international brand under the Gibo name in 2002. Unusually for a Japanese firm, the new brand was entirely planned and produced by its overseas subsidiary, in this case Gibo SpA. The delegation to Gibo reflected a gradual understanding among Japanese retailers that, to compete on a global basis, they had to incorporate international management teams and not rely on homegrown talent alone. In 2004, Onward launched its own retail stores in Italy under the Via Bus Stop fascia, and existing stores in Paris and New York were converted to the Via Bus Stop name as a precursor to expanding the retail format to other key fashion capitals in Europe, the USA, and Asia.

International retail expansion is not limited to its upscale brands. In addition to the launch of Gibo, Onward Kashiyama is rolling out stores under its main domestic volume brands across Asia and it represents a good example of the serious intent of Japanese retailers to gain a share of the Asian apparel market. Under its medium term plan, by 2006, Onward expects to have a significant presence in all key Asian markets with a focus on mainland China. Already in China, Onward has made headway with its ICB and 23-ku labels with 52 stores operating there by 2004. A brand to target the younger womenswear market was also planned for an Asian-wide launch in 2005.

Onward is a leading exponent of the shift to retailing operations by Japan's most dynamic apparel groups. Since it had strong supply chains in place through its manufacturing and wholesaling operations, Onward was in a good position to undercut competitors with good value merchandise. In the decade to 2005, it acquired retail expertise by converting its wholesale operations to retail chains and through strategic partnerships with international brands. The improvements

Case Study 9.5:   Onward Kashiyama: a fashion conglomerate – *continued*

in profitability provided funding for investment in new brands and expansion of stores to shopping centers and overseas. With a strong portfolio of brands, plentiful funding, global sourcing, and a solid home base, Onward is in an enviable position to develop a global brand business.

Own brands	International brands
23-ku Deux 23-ku 23-ku Sport 23-ku Homme Kumikyoku Kumikyoku sis Kumikyoku FAM. ICB J. Press Jiyuku Suivi. Jane More Prideglide Gotairiku Lakeland Iroiro Sode (kimono) La Beaute Selflex Chacott Noir Robe K-39 Gibo (and others)	Jean Paul Gaultier Gaultier Homme PS Paul Smith Women Cerruti 1881 Joseph Abboud Celine Missoni Gianfranco Ferre Michael Kors & KORS Michael Kors John Varvatos Sonia Rykiel (collections) SONIA Sonia Rykiel Donna Karan New York DKNY Marni Calvin Klein Bernhard Willhelm Jean Colonna Martine Sitbon Viktor & Rolf Tocca Joseph Homme Polo Ralph Lauren (and others)

Figure 9.5   Onward Kashimaya: Main brands, 2005
Source: Company Reports

10
Drivers of Retail Specialization

Japan's move away from general merchandise retailing towards clearly defined retail specialists that are independent of manufacturers and take full responsibility for their own destinies can be seen most clearly in three specialist categories: drugstores, consumer electronics, and home centers. In the early 1990s, all three of these categories already existed as separate retail formats. Home center retailing was still in its infancy, but both drugstores and consumer electronics retailers were the epitome of traditional, manufacturer led distribution channels. Manufacturers created both formats and structured them in the form of chains of *keiretsu* stores.

While their presence has become a point of purely historical and academic interest, the role of retail *keiretsu* is important to note. Retail *keiretsu* consisted of large chains of stores, often numbering 15,000 or so small retail stores per chain, each of which were dedicated to selling the products of a single manufacturer. The manufacturers did not own these stores, nor did they have franchise contracts, but they were provided with store development financing, access to all the latest models, and significant sales support including loaned employees. In the electronics category, young engineers would often be required to work as service and installation personnel at a small retail store as part of their training. In return, the same stores were required to stay loyal to their suppliers, offer local consumers extensive levels of service, and never, ever discount product except with their supplier's permission.

Such chains exist even today, but in terms of store numbers and, much more importantly, in terms of influence as a sales route, they are a shade of what they were as recently as 1990. With large, professional specialty retailers competing in the same categories, along with the improved ability and geographical reach of the general merchandise retailers, even the largest manufacturers could no longer dedicate so many resources to maintaining these exclusive retail channels. You may still see *keiretsu* stores bearing names like Matsushita, Sony, Hitachi, and Sharp in the electronics sector, and Shiseido, Kao, Kose, and Kanebo in the cosmetics sector, as there are still tens of thousands of outlets, but in terms of sales volume, the specialist retailers are now the most important sales route.

In this chapter we take a detailed look at the way these two categories have developed and have become powerful retail sectors. In addition, we also discuss similar developments in the home center format. This is a format that has grown from a handful of tiny, local hardware chains, into yet another large retail sector. Taken together, all three represent a clear trend towards greater specialization and more focused retailing. At the same time, and once again, the presence and influence of Aeon in shaping and developing two of these three categories is also a significant point.

The drugstore sector

Despite the exit from Japan of international retailers like Boots and Sephora after 2000, the drugstore and toiletries sector remains potentially one of the most interesting of all. As with supermarkets and apparel specialists, until recently drugstores were the domain of the small, local independent retailer. As already mentioned, they were also controlled largely by manufacturer *keiretsu* chains. This type of retailing was even the subject of a seminal study by Shimaguchi (1977) that revealed the complex and archaic nature of Japan's distribution system for the first time in English.

Today, however, with the relaxation of laws relating to the sale and display of chemical related products and the growth of a small number of large drugstore chains, the sector has changed at a fundamental level. It is on the verge of becoming a modernized retail category with increasing concentration and a number of outstanding companies taking the lead. Once again, Aeon Group is one of these companies, but it has a strong challenger in the form of Matsumotokiyoshi. Aeon has again taken a cooperative approach to building the first nationwide chain of drugstores, bringing a number of chains into a formal alliance, and Matsumotokiyoshi, itself the largest single drugstore chain, is now following Aeon's lead and building its own alliance. These initiatives alone have pushed the category into a whole new era of competition and have set in motion a process of ever greater consolidation and operational improvements.

Under the watchful eye of toiletry, cosmetics and drug suppliers, until very recently most drugstore chains had little to differentiate themselves other than their name, location, and, possibly store size. New initiatives in retail brands, support from different groups of drug manufacturers, and continued consolidation within the sector as a whole are rapidly changing this situation. Some chains look likely to become more food based (see Figure 10.2), while others will take on the appearance of US style roadside drug emporiums. What is still lacking, however, is the taste of anything truly new or especially Japanese. The chain that comes up with the right marketing initiative could well make a rapid jump to the head of the rankings.

Table 10.1 Drugstore retail sector according to Census of Commerce, 1999 and 2002

	Units	Census Year		Change
		1999	2002	%
Store Numbers	Nos.	10,917	14,673	34.4
Sales	¥ bn	1,495.0	2,495.7	66.9
Employees	People	70,948	116,173	63.7
Sales Space	1000 sqm	1,843	3,227	75.1
Averages				
Sales per store	¥ mn	136.94	170.09	24.2
Employees per store	People	6.50	7.92	21.8
Sales space per store	sqm	168.82	219.93	30.3

Source: METI (2003)

Drugstore retailing becomes concentrated into two main groups

Drugstore retailing, along with home center retailing is now so important as a separate category in Japan that METI included this format for special attention in the most recent Census of Commerce in 2002 (METI, 2003). According to the Census, there were 14,673 drugstores in Japan in 2002, an increase of almost 4,000 on the previous survey in 1999 (see Table 10.1). The only sector to increase store numbers by a higher proportion was home centers. Sales were also up almost 67 per cent, the highest for any retail category, and sales space was up by more than three quarters. As shown in Table 10.1, the average drugstore is getting larger, selling more, and employing more people per store, all indications of a sector in the process of major growth.

The reason behind the phenomenal growth in the drugstore sector in recent years is quite simply one of a new retail professionalism. The changes are being driven by a small number of highly ambitious and skilled drugstore chains, and the amalgamation of chains into a number of key buying group affiliations. This is also leading to significant growth in concentration within the sector.

Table 10.2 provides a full list of Japan's leading 20 drugstore retailers for FY2003 along with 17 smaller chains that are also affiliated with the leading buying groups. Among the top 20 chains, three companies are affiliated to Matsumotokiyoshi including Japan's single largest drugstore chain itself, and six are affiliated to Aeon Welcia Stores, the buying group alliance built by the Aeon Group. There are also two more companies related to both the Cawachi, Sun Drug group, and also to the Seijo, Kokumin group, but the two main groups dwarf both of these smaller

Table 10.2 Leading drugstore chains for FY2003 and smaller chains affiliated to leading drugstore buying groups

Company	Affiliation	HQ Prefecture	Sales ¥ mn	YonY %	Pretax Profit ¥ mn	YonY %	Stores Nos.	Sales per Store ¥ mn
1 Matsumotokiyoshi	Matsumotokiyoshi	Chiba	275,596	3.2	15,490	4.3	632	436.1
2 Cawachi Yakuhin	Cawachi & Sun Drug	Tochigi	180,519	10.0	11,377	6.7	122	1,479.7
3 CFS Corporation	Aeon Welcia Stores	Kanagawa	149,336	-0.5	2,481	-27.2	240	622.2
4 Sun Drug	Cawachi & Sun Drug	Tokyo	122,403	19.2	8,497	15.0	216	566.7
5 Tsuruha	Aeon Welcia Stores	Hokkaido	116,053	14.8	5,141	3.7	408	284.4
6 Fuji Yakuhin		Saitama	104,076	10.8	–	–	–	–
7 Sugi Yakkyoku	Aeon Welcia Stores	Aichi	87,681	10.6	2,323	-9.1	227	386.3
8 Create SD		Kanagawa	71,347	6.2	3,003	-5.5	–	–
9 Segami Medics		Osaka	70,299	10.4	3,008	24.7	290	242.4
10 Kokumin	Seijo, Kokumin	Osaka	66,800	1.5	–	–	–	–
11 ZiP Holdings		Osaka	56,784	19.0	1,806	24.1	184	308.6
12 Sugiyama Yakuhin		Aichi	50,986	5.5	2,503	-1.5	–	–
13 Drug 11	Matsumotokiyoshi	Kagoshima	50,000	–	208	17.5	198	252.5
14 Kirindo		Osaka	48,281	23.3	1283	–	150	321.9
15 Kraft	Aeon Welcia Stores	Tokyo	44,353	16.8	2,327	–	178	249.2
16 Terashima Yakkyoku	Aeon Welcia Stores	Ibaragi	43,986	11.0	1527	–	97	453.5
17 Cosmos Yakuhin		Miyazaki	42,413	89.0	1,107	–	–	–
18 Seijo	Seijo, Kokumin	Tokyo	38,939	9.6	2,142	–	183	212.8
19 Yokohama Pharmacy	Matsumotokiyoshi	Aomori	36,400	–	–	–	37	983.8
20 Green Cross Coa	Aeon Welcia Stores	Saitama	36,087	22.7	1059	–	360	100.2
Smaller Drugstores in the Main Buying Affiliations								
Takada Yakkyoku	Matsumotokiyoshi	Shizuoka	22,400	10.6	–	–	91	246.2
Kusuri no Aoki	Aeon Welcia Stores	Ishikawa	21,600	–	–	–	74	291.9
Sapporo Drugstore	Matsumotokiyoshi	Hokkaido	21,600	–	–	–	86	251.2
Takiya	Aeon Welcia Stores	Hyogo	19,500	–	–	–	72	270.8
Welpark	Aeon Welcia Stores	Tokyo	16,500	–	–	–	57	289.5

Table 10.2 Leading drugstore chains for FY2003 and smaller chains affiliated to leading drugstore buying groups – *continued*

Company	Affiliation	HQ Prefecture	Sales ¥ mn	YonY %	Pretax Profit ¥ mn	YonY %	Stores Nos.	Sales per Store ¥ mn
Drug Fujii	Matsumotokiyoshi	Toyama	16,300	–	–	–	66	247.0
Natural (Drugstore Aomori)	Matsumotokiyoshi	Aomori	16,000	–	–	–	63	254.0
iino	Aeon Welcia Stores	Saitama	12,500	–	–	–	84	148.8
Shimizu Yakuhin	Matsumotokiyoshi	Kyoto	11,000	–	–	–	48	229.2
Kenko Kazoku	Matsumotokiyoshi	Nagano	8,800	–	–	–	27	325.9
Tobu Drug	Matsumotokiyoshi	Saitama	7,900	–	–	–	23	343.5
Medical Ikari	Aeon Welcia Stores	Mie	7,800	–	–	–	52	150.0
Izumi	Matsumotokiyoshi	Hiroshima	7,000	–	–	–	52	134.6
Hiroyo Yakuhin	Matsumotokiyoshi	Osaka	3,800	–	–	–	29	131.0
Itayama Mediko	Matsumotokiyoshi	Yamanashi	3,600	–	–	–	14	257.1
Komeya Yakuhin	Matsumotokiyoshi	Ishikawa	2,900	–	–	–	16	181.3
Powers Drug	Matsumotokiyoshi	Hokkaido	2,000	–	–	–	11	181.8

Notes: Store numbers include franchises

Omitted figures are unavailable where companies are privately owned

Sources: Compiled from Company Reports; NMJ (2004); Asano et al (2004); Ando and Tanaka (2004)

buying alliances. Finally, seven of the leading 20 chains by sales remain independent, although ZiP Holdings in Osaka is itself now attempting to develop its own, local alliances.

Taking the Census figure of ¥2.495 trillion as a rough guide to the total drugstore market in 2002 and allowing for relatively modest growth of 30 per cent since then, the leading 20 chains account for an estimated 52 per cent of total sales for the sector. Add in the remainder of the Matsumotokiyoshi and Welcia alliances, and the figure jumps to nearer 60 per cent of the total.

This new structure to drugstore retailing has appeared since only 2001 when Aeon first formed the Welcia alliance. In essence, the alliance has similarities both to franchise systems and even to the old *keiretsu* system with groups of independent retailers being guided and controlled by a larger concern. Today, such anti-competitive cartels are no longer accepted as openly as they once were, and in Welcia's case, group membership was granted with Aeon taking a share of the member chain, binding group members together in a much more coherent and long term alliance (see Figure 10.1). Welcia was formed with the simple aim to eventually emulate US retailer Walgreen in operation, but take over from the American as the world's largest drugstore operation (see Suzuki, 2002: p. 92). By 2010, Aeon aims to have drugstore sales of more than ¥1 trillion and a market share in Japan of at least 30 per cent. It is well on its way to its goal, with total Welcia Alliance sales reaching ¥748.2 billion in FY2003 from a total of 1,892 stores across all 12 group members.

In reaction to Aeon's Welcia initiative, drugstore chains have had to make clear decisions as to how they intend to compete. Matsumotokiyoshi has long been Japan's single largest drugstore chain and remains so today with sales of close to ¥300 billion from 632 stores, predominantly in Tokyo. Up until 2003, Matsukiyo, as it is universally known, looked to be struggling. While it was the largest single chain, dominant in Tokyo, and the leader of the NID voluntary buying group, it did not have the overall power that Welcia had acquired in a very short time. Matsukiyo quickly realized that Welcia was the single largest threat to its business and has since been working to emulate the Aeon strategy.

By the end of 2004, Matsukiyo had grown its own buying alliance, bringing many NID and Japan Drug Store Chain Association members into a more formal relationship. Unlike Welcia, the alliance is less structured with share ownership not being a feature, although Matsumotokiyoshi as a company has made several acquisitions since 2003. In total Matsukiyo Alliance now numbers some 15 chains, three more than Welcia, and controls 1,393 stores as of FY2003, but total sales still stand at only ¥485.2 billion, a third lower than for Welcia. In addition, more than 50 per cent of this total is made up from Matsumotokiyoshi's sales alone. Aeon Group itself makes up a comparatively small 24 per cent of Welcia Alliance sales.

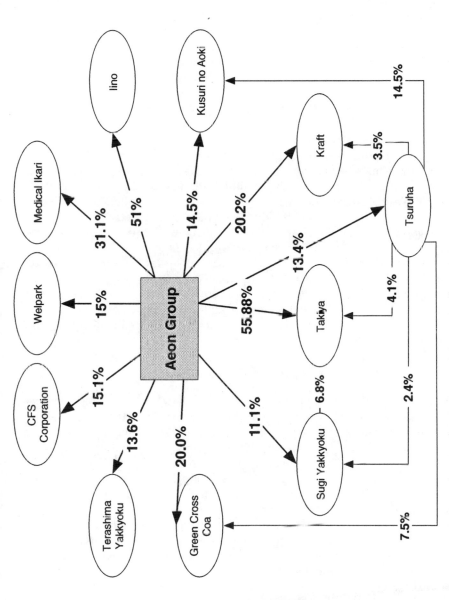

Figure 10.1 Aeon Welcia Stores: Alliance members and shareholdings, FY2003
Source: Adapted from Chain Store Age (August 2004)

On the sidelines, there are also a number of smaller alliances. Second tier drugstore chains Cawachi and Sun Drug, along with Seijo and Kokumin, have each established their own buying alliances, but these are a small fraction of the market held by the two larger groups.

Drugstore retailing is unique in Japan both for the speed of its development and the potential for immediate growth. The race is already down to just two main groups of firms, and the future will depend on which of these two groups manages to entice the remaining independent members to join them. While Aeon Welcia is currently well ahead, Aeon's policy of drawing together drugstore chains through shareholding is a precursor to acquisition and absorption into the Aeon Group as a whole. As Figure 10.1 shows, Aeon already has controlling stakes of more than 25 per cent in Takiya, Iino, and Medical Ikari. While some less successful regional drugstore chains may be glad for Aeon to take over their operations, many will not and this is where Matsukiyo will be looking to make their advantage. By allowing group members to maintain their independence, Matsukiyo can more quickly and easily build its own buying alliance.

In addition, the binding nature of Welcia membership is already causing problems. In 2004, leading Welcia Alliance member CFS Corporation announced publicly that it wanted to withdraw from the group despite the 15.1 per cent of shares owned by Aeon. CFS said it was struggling to cooperate when other alliance members, notably Tsuruha, were operating in similar territories and actually competing for new locations. Aeon, unsurprisingly, rejected CFS's request to leave. This type of issue may well arise again.

Retail brands and prescription drugs

In addition to the question of how quickly the two buying groups can grow and grab overall market share across the whole of Japan, drugstore retailing will be influenced by the growth of two aspects of merchandising: the development of retail brands and the ability to sell prescription drugs.

Both buying alliances are currently developing large ranges of retail brands. In Aeon Welcia's case, for FY2003, the group claimed to have 161 own branded drug and health products, along with 233 food and other products. Most of these carry the Welcia brand, but member chains developed some independently. For the Matsumotokiyoshi alliance, retail brand development is centered on NID, the national independent drugstore association led by Matsumotokiyoshi. Although not all are part of Matsumotokiyoshi's alliance, NID numbers 150 companies in total. In 2004, under its beautifully Japanese English slogan, "A hopeful innovation, that's why it's interesting" (see http://www.nidrug.co.jp), the association began a massive expansion in own brand items including non-drug merchandise such as food and even alcoholic beverages. These included two types of rice wine (*sake*) produced from

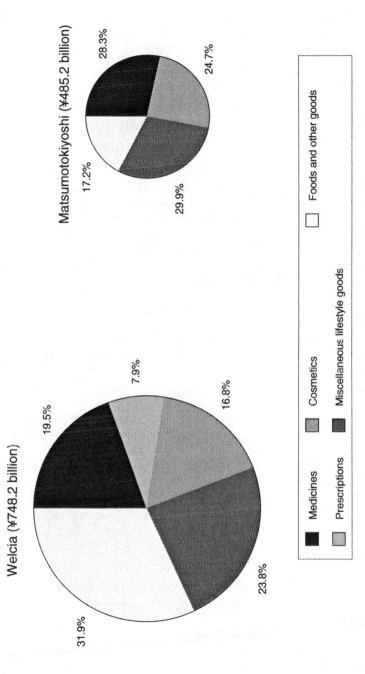

Welcia (¥748.2 billion)

19.5%

7.9%

16.8%

23.8%

31.9%

Matsumotokiyoshi (¥485.2 billion)

28.3%

24.7%

29.9%

17.2%

■ Medicines ▨ Cosmetics ☐ Foods and other goods

▨ Prescriptions ▨ Miscellaneous lifestyle goods

Figure 10.2 Merchandise assortments by proportion of sales for Japan's two leading drugstore alliances, FY2003

Note: Medicine sales for Matsumotokiyoshi include prescription sales

Source: Adapted from Ando and Tanaka (2004)

contracted distillers as well as other Japanese alcohol products such as *shochu* and *mirin*. Total NID procurement for 2004 was around ¥70 billion including both private brands and manufacturer brands. Until now most of this was drugstore merchandise with food accounting for only about 8 per cent, but NID plans to expand food procurement to 15 per cent by 2008, with a future target of 20 per cent. This move towards greater integration of non-drugstore merchandise is a natural progression for the two largest groups and will move drugstore chains into direct competition with convenience stores and supermarkets. Figure 10.2 illustrates the merchandise mix for the two main drugstore alliances as of FY2003.

Second only to their ability to attract new alliance members, however, is the largest drugstore chains ability to attract qualified pharmacists to work in their stores. Until recently, prescription drugs could only be supplied by special pharmacies, usually linked directly with hospitals and medical clinics. Drugstores were required to have a pharmacist on hand if they wanted to sell over-the-counter drugs, but many chains chose to only sell toiletries, cosmetics, and basic medical supplies. As a result, the need for pharmacists remained quite low. Now, drugstores are also allowed to fulfill prescriptions and the largest companies are racing to sign up as many pharmacists as possible.

Once again, Welcia is well in the lead. In FY2003, 42 per cent of Welcia's member stores were equipped to sell prescription drugs, and two chains, Sugi Yakkyoku and Medical Ikari, claimed they could supply prescriptions from each and every one of their stores. Another Welcia member, Kraft, also offered prescription services from 93 per cent of its chain. Even within Aeon's own GMS outlets, prescription drugs could be dispensed from 30 per cent of its stores.

By contrast, Matsumotokiyoshi had only 120 stores out of a total of 632 (19 per cent) that could dispense prescription drugs. For the alliance as a whole, the proportion was only 15 per cent or 208 stores. Of the 15 chains, four had no facilities to sell prescription drugs, and seven chains had fewer than 10 stores with the capability.

Once again, all of Japan's drugstores will be competing to employ both newly qualified and more experienced pharmacists in order to take advantage of the lucrative prescription drugs market.

The immediate future of drugstore retailing

While Aeon's other major goal to build the first nationwide chain of supermarkets continues to gather pace slowly, the battle for the first nationwide drug chain is already moving towards a solid victory. It is likely that more regional chains will join the Welcia alliance in future months and years. Matsumotokiyoshi will do its best to compete, but other groups have little extra to offer smaller chains except the alternative of not tying with Aeon.

There will be a steady and increasingly rapid concentration in the drug-store sector as fewer small, regional chains are able to compete as independents. From the consumers' point of view, this can only be a good thing as the larger chains drag a once traditional and uncompetitive merchandise category firmly into the era of modern, chain store retailing. It is also a good thing for overseas suppliers too, in theory. Large modern retail chains are inherently easier to supply from an overseas base than a fragmented group of regional stores. They are also less dependent on particular manufacturers and so less loyal to domestic firms.

Consumer electronics retailing

While drugstore and consumer electronics retailing are very different in most ways, the current level of change in the former closely mirrors what has already happened in the latter. Whereas change is now being driven directly by a small number of firms in the drugstore sector, similar changes away from manufacturer dominated channels and towards independent, powerful retail chains occurred more naturally and over a slightly longer period of time in consumer electronics. As with drugstores, until the late 1980s, consumer electronics retailing was also largely controlled by power-ful manufacturing interests and their chains of *keiretsu* stores. Since 1990, electrical retailing has been transformed from one of the most traditional and restrictive channels into a modern retail infrastructure.

As already discussed, manufacturers went out of their way to restrict supply of their products, control prices, and dictate customer service options, so keeping retailers firmly in line. In consumer electronics, where arguably manufacturers were most powerful of all, the traditional system was undone by the growth of large retail chains that could reach customers

Table 10.3 Japan's consumer electrical products retail sector, Census of Commerce 1991–2002

Year	Stores	Employees	Sales Area	Sales	Sales per Store	Sales per sqm	Sqm per Store
			sqm	¥ mn	¥ mn	¥ mn	sqm
1991	63,271	237,562	4,730,519	5,796,312	91.61	1.23	74.77
1994	60,592	240,479	5,017,791	5,852,446	96.59	1.17	82.81
1997	58,748	248,102	5,659,397	7,272,476	123.79	1.29	96.33
1999	57,606	270,772	6,617,880	7,699,653	133.66	1.16	114.88
2002	45,414	195,609	5,268,807	5,252,654	115.66	1.00	116.02
Percentage change, 1991 to 2002							
	−28.2	−17.7	11.4	−9.4	26.3	−18.9	55.2

Source: METI (2003)

more cheaply and efficiently than the manufacturers could themselves. By 1990, Daiei was by far the largest seller of so-called white goods (household electronics such as refrigerators, microwaves, and other kitchen appliances) even though it was never listed as a consumer electronics retailer in its own right (see Larke, 1993). At the time, there were only a handful of large consumer electronics specialists and none of them had large sales territories. The largest, Best Denki, was so restricted in the Japanese market that it looked to markets elsewhere in Asia such as Singapore and Hong Kong for means of expansion and remains an important player in several overseas markets even today. Although their resistance was considerable, large manufacturers gradually came to admit that maintaining expensive *keiretsu* chains of shops had little benefit when they could sell greater volume through the largest retail chains. The final straw came in the early 1990s when the newly expanding electronics specialty retailers could actually make more money wholesaling product that they had bought in bulk in order to get sales rebates than they could by selling product through their own retail outlets. It was at this point, that manufacturers realized they had lost control and gave in to the new channel structure. The *keiretsu* chains still exist in a much smaller form, but they are no longer the most important sales route for this category.

Consumer electronics retailing in the twenty-first century

In 2002, the Census of Commerce put total sales in the electronics sector at ¥5.252 trillion (see Table 10.3). This was more than 9 per cent lower than in 1991, but the loss is largely due to the 28.2 per cent fall in store numbers for the sector. A net 18,000 consumer electronics outlets closed in that 11-year period, while at the same time total sales space grew by 11.4 per cent to more than 5.2 million square meters. Most of the decline was in small stores, many of which were *keiretsu* related, and growth has been in larger stores.

Census data omits general merchandise stores and so is understated in this case. NEBA, the National Electrical Buyers Association, estimates the market as closer to ¥7.5 trillion and this is supported by METI's annual retail survey which put machinery and electrical equipment retail sales at just over ¥7 trillion for FY2003. Whereas in the past, the sector was characterized as one of large manufacturers supplying small retail stores, today this huge market is one of large manufacturers and increasingly large retail chains.

Table 10.4 lists the leading electronics retailers for FY2003. The leading 14 chains accounted for ¥4.4 trillion in total sales giving them roughly 60 per cent of the total market. Yamada Denki, the leading chain with sales almost double its nearest rival, alone accounted for around 13 per cent of the total market. The sector has split between older retailers that achieved

Table 10.4 Japan's largest electrical retailers based on sales volume, FY2003

	Company	Note	Operational HQ	Sales ¥ mn	YonY %	Pretax Profit ¥ mn	YonY %	Stores	Sales per store ¥ mn
1	Yamada Denki		Gunma	939,137	18.3	30,652	67.6	193	4,866.0
2	Yodobashi Camera		Tokyo	545,042	5.6	35,810	18.8	18	30,280.1
3	Kojima		Tochigi	476,156	-5.4	3,141	45.1	247	1,927.8
4	Bic Camera		Tokyo	441,555	14.2	-	-	22	20,070.7
5	Edion	1	Aichi	434,166	-	10,207	-	714	608.1
6	Best Denki		Fukuoka	355,204	0.2	3,824	-12.6	613	579.5
7	Joshin Denki	1	Osaka	245,310	9.6	2,013	250.7	164	1,495.8
8	Midori Denka	1	Hyogo	222,210	7.0	7,206	8.9	-	-
9	Gigas K's Denki		Ibaragi	220,000	12.9	6,109	15.6	168	1,309.5
10	Laox		Tokyo	155,147	-7.6	273	-	130	1,193.4
11	Denkodo	1	Miyagi	117,037	-4.2	3,202	-12.2	110	1,064.0
12	SofMap		Tokyo	113,613	-5.9	908	-	43	2,642.2
13	Kitamura		Kanagawa	108,720	-0.4	2,305	-31.9	-	-
14	3Q Group	1	Fukui	92,221	0.2	5,050	14.2	124	743.7

Notes:
[1], Members of Edion led Voice Network buying alliance
'–' indicates unavailable or inapplicable data

Source: Company Reports; NMJ (2004); Asano et al (2004); IT & Kaden Business (2004); Otsuka and Kaneko (2004)

their size at the end of the 1980s under the traditional system, and new retailers that have grown from relatively small, regional chains that as of 1990 were almost unheard of outside their local areas. Among the leading 14 companies, all of the chains except Best Denki and Joshin Denki fall into the category of new retailers. A similar sales ranking for 1990 would not even include Yamada Denki, which was the 264th ranked retailer in the country at that time. In addition, the largest chain from that era, Best Denki, had total sales of only ¥205 billion, lower than the ninth largest chain today.

The growth of firms like Yamada Denki and Edion, and the expansion of Yodobashi Camera and Bic Camera out of their Tokyo markets, is a story of professional retailing taking on the established system. Kojima, which was the fifth largest consumer electronics retailer back in 1990, also expanded through the establishment of a chain of suburban stores around Kansai, abandoning its traditional system of small, city center stores.

Undoubtedly, however, the sector has been led from the front by Yamada Denki. It was the first multiple chain of consumer electronics stores to become truly nationwide in scope. It is also one of the few retailers, along with Ito-Yokado and Fast Retailing, which has emphasized profitability and sales efficiency in addition to expanding volumes. It has achieved its position through a record of excellent retail selling, customer service, store location, store design, and aggressive marketing. It also boosted its capability by acquiring the Daikuma chain of discount stores from Ito-Yokado in 2001, and was the first electronics retailer to insist on large format stores for all its locations.

Yamada Denki, while almost unknown outside Japan, was the most successful Japanese retailer of the 1990s. Even in FY2003, sales increased by 18.3 per cent with pretax profits up 67.6 per cent (see Figure 10.3). The chain is confidently predicting it will be the first specialty retailer in Japanese history to break annual sales of ¥1 trillion in 2005. As with most good retailers, it is a company that has been micro-managed and one that has based its policy on customer service. It has also not been wary about taking on the establishment. In 1996, it offered a limited number of personal computers at just ¥1 a piece as one of Japan's most famous marketing gimmicks. Kojima, Yamada's main rival, responded but by comparison, Kojima's ¥80 PCs were many times more expensive. The profitability of the chain illustrates that it has not simply expanded its chain to gain market share, a limitation that many Japanese retailers have fallen foul to. Despite annual additions to store numbers, Yamada Denki is one of the few chains to have not only increased same store sales, but actually to have improved sales per store annually since 1995. Kojima and Best Denki have seen sales per store dip in recent years (see Figure 10.4).

The other chains to watch, however, are the so called camera retailers. Originating back in the days when Japan's large camera manufacturing

215

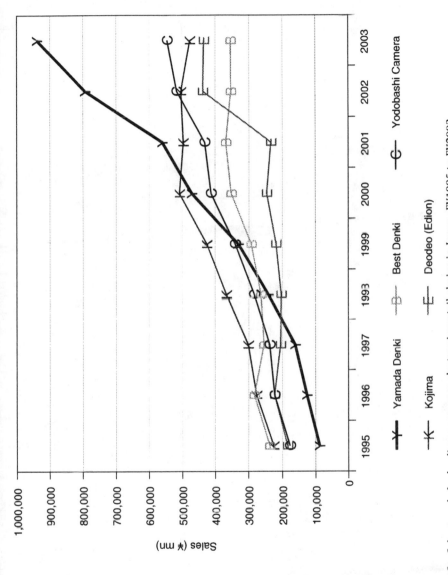

Figure 10.3 Sales trends for leading consumer electronics retail chains in Japan, FY1995 to FY2003

Note: Deodeo merged with Eiden to create Edion in 2002

Source: Company Reports

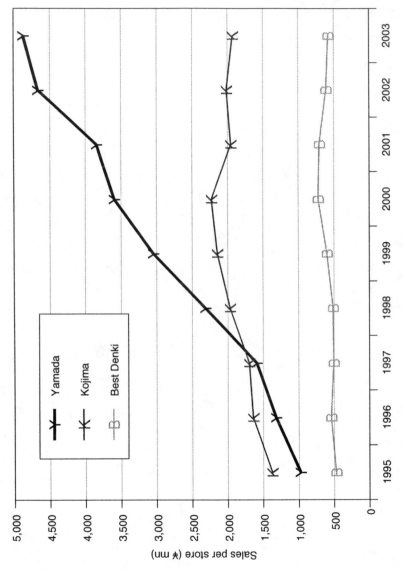

Figure 10.4 Sales per store for leading suburban consumer electronics retailers, FY19995 to FY2003
Source: Company Reports

companies also sold to their own flavor of specialty store format, again employing the standard *keiretsu* systems for much of their sales channel, these retailers are now fully fledged electrical chains selling, in most outlets, a full range of items from cameras to computers and household appliances. Compared to Yamada and other suburban electronics retailers, the big camera stores prefer city center locations. Their stores have always been relatively large, but it is only in the past few years that they have operated outside of Tokyo. Not carrying the overhead of geographically widespread chains, these companies, of which only Yodobashi Camera and Bic Camera are of any significant size, are aiming squarely at inner city locations and opening large stores. Yodobashi and Bic achieve far greater sales densities than any of the other electrical chains.

Both Yodobashi Camera and Bic Camera are still small chain operations with 18 and 22 stores respectively, most of which are located in and around Tokyo. In recent years, they have moved into the largest regional cities with stores from Sapporo to Fukuoka. In Bic Camera's case, it took over two defunct Sogo department store outlets to enter new markets including one in the center of Ginza and another in Sapporo. It also tied up with Odakyu to take over a large section of Odakyu Department Store in the key location of Shinjuku in April 2002.

In the medium term, the fastest growing electronics retailers such as Yamada Denki, along with the so-called camera chains, will continue to grow rapidly. Finding locations is not as difficult as it might seem for large format stores. With landowners, struggling department stores, and shopping centers all assiduously courting these chains, there are a surprisingly large number of options. Electronics retailing will also begin to consolidate. In the face of Yamada's expansion, two regional chains, Deodeo in Hiroshima Prefecture and Eiden in Aichi Prefecture, merged to form the Edion chain in 2002. Edion has since established what it calls its Voice Network, a buying alliance that greatly resembles those developed by the major drugstore chains (see above).

Already, in terms of overall sales, the Voice Network is larger than Yamada Denki. It includes Midori Denka, Joshin Denki, Denkodo, and 3Q among its members. Best Denki was also an original member, but, as with the situation with CFS Corporation and Aeon Welcia in the drugstore sector, Best Denki chose to leave the alliance because of competition between members of the same group. In 2005, Midori Denka, the eighth largest chain, will merge with Edion to create the second largest electronics retailer overall, overtaking both Kojima and Best Denki. This will add to the pressure on non-aligned electronics retailers and create a market very similar to that in the drugstore sector: just two companies competing for the lion's share of the market.

Home center and furniture retailing

The third and final category of new, specialist retailing is home centers. Home center retailing does not bear many of the characteristics of either the drugstore or the consumer electronics sectors whether in terms of market structure or history, but it does represent a type of retailing that is now growing very strongly indeed and one that is being led by retailers rather than manufacturing interests.

The term "home center" is perhaps Japanese in origin. Its nearest equivalent in the West would be a do-it-yourself (DIY) or home improvement store, but this does not accurately describe the origins of the format. Japan has no tradition of DIY, with average consumers preferring to employ professional tradesmen to alter or improve their homes. Home centers originated in two distinct formats:

* As stores catering to the professional trades as a form of wholesaler, usually specializing in particular types of material such as lumber, masonary, plumbing materials, or decorating materials
* As hardware stores, offering deep assortments of household and gardening items to general consumers, and resembling GMS chains in many ways except that they did not sell food

In the early 1990s, home centers consisted of small, regional chains operating one of these two types of formats. In addition, Japan also had a small number of medium sized retailers selling furniture. Furniture was expensive in Japan for a long period due to the high costs of materials and labor as well as high import tariffs. Most furniture retailers operated only a handful of large stores, often resembling warehouses packed to bursting with merchandise.

Today, home centers and furniture retailers have amalgamated into a single format. In addition, the leading retailers in this sector are now large and geographically widespread. Moreover, as with both drugstores and electronics retailers, it is a sector that is showing rapid growth, increasing levels of concentration, and, once again, significant interest from Aeon Group.

As with drugstore retailing, METI considered the home center format (excluding furniture retailers in this case) important enough to receive special attention in the 2002 Census of Commerce. Table 10.5 summarizes the results. The number of home centers grew from 2,911 stores to 4,356 stores between 1999 and 2002. Sales, employee numbers, and sales space were also up accordingly, but sales per store actually declined by 14.5 per cent. The average home center has more than 1,900 square meters in sales space, making it the largest of all the specialty formats.

Table 10.6 lists the leading 20 home center retailers in Japan for FY2003. Several of these companies, notably Nafco, Shimachu, and Otsuka Kagu, are primarily furniture retailers although Nafco and Shimachu are in the process of opening combined furniture and home center outlets. Arguably,

Table 10.5 Home center retail sector according to Census of Commerce, 1999 and 2002

	Units	Census Year		Change
		1999	2002	%
Store numbers	Nos.	2,911	4,356	49.6
Sales	¥ bn	2,402.4	3,073.2	27.9
Employees	People	84,681	128,358	51.6
Sales space	1000 sqm	5,250	8,386	59.7
Averages				
Sales per store	¥ mn	825.28	705.51	−14.5
Employees per store	People	29.09	29.47	1.3
Sales space per store	sqm	1,803.50	1,925.16	6.7

Source: METI (2003)

Table 10.6 Japan's leading 20 home center retailers by sales volume, FY2003

	Company	Notes	Prefecture	Sales ¥ mn	YonY %	Pretax Profit ¥ mn	YonY %	Stores No.	Sales per store ¥ mn
1	Cainz	1	Gunma	245,846	10.2	13,469	23.2	127	1,935.8
2	Kohnan Shoji		Osaka	229,664	17.0	7,539	12.4	171	1,343.1
3	Komeri	2	Niigata	217,922	8.7	13,081	14.6	608	358.4
4	Keyo	3	Chiba	188,842	6.2	1,387	−73.7	154	1,226.2
5	Homac	4*	Hokkaido	187,774	1.3	4,070	−24.6	149	1,260.2
6	Nafco		Fukuoka	181,786	3.9	10,724	15.4	184	988.0
7	Kahma	4	Aichi	125,796	−3.4	4,436	14.4	100	1,258.0
8	Shimachu		Saitama	120,363	1.4	13,945	−3.8	50	2,407.3
9	Daiki	4	Shizuoka	119,943	2.0	2,620	−8.2	82	1,462.7
10	Joyful Honda	5	Ibaragi	110,000	3.4	–	–	13	8,461.5
11	Tokyu Hands		Tokyo	93,439	1.1	1,434	−11.3	16	5,839.9
12	Arcland Salamoto	5	Niigata	80,160	1.8	3,995	12.0	27	2,968.9
13	Tostem Viva		Saitama	79,292	4.4	2,560	10.7	87	911.4
14	Otsuka Kagu		Tokyo	73,102	6.2	6,494	9.5	16	4,568.9
15	Royal Home Center		Osaka	57,226	9.7	–	–	38	1,505.9
16	Sekichu		Gunma	56,329	15.6	465	−40.2	51	1,104.5
17	Loft		Tokyo	50,991	2.5	2,066	52.0	27	1,888.6
18	Juntendo		Shimane	49,575	−3.1	656	−41.8	162	306.0
19	Encho		Shizuoka	48,304	−6.4	838	–	30	1,610.1
20	Yamashin		Ibaragi	43,611	1.1	–	–	34	1,282.7

Notes:
1, Beisia Group subsidiary; 2, Komeri Group parent company; 3, Aeon affiliate; 4, KDH Affiliation and Aeon affiliates (4* Aeon subsidiary); 5, Joyful Honda group and franchise affiliation
Source: NMJ (2004a); Otsuka and Kaneko (2004); Company reports & websites

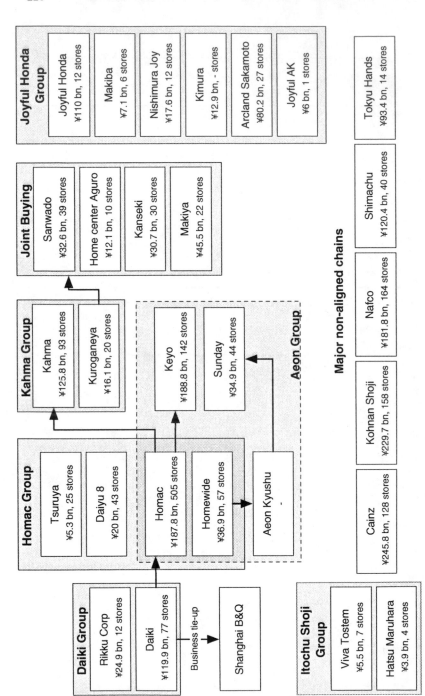

Figure 10.5 Guide to major home center chain groups and relationships, FY2003
Note: Arrows indicate shareholding relationship unless otherwise labelled
Source: Adapted from Chida (2004), sales figures updated where possible

Tokyu Hands and Loft are also somewhat different as they sell a wide variety of merchandise, especially arts, craft, and hobby goods, and are usually located in city centers (see Chapter 11). The remainder of the companies in the table, including the leading five chains, are all home center retailers, however.

Growth rates for both sales and pretax profits in FY2003 confirm the results of the Census that this is indeed a rapidly growing sector. Cainz, the leading chain, saw sales up 10.2 per cent in FY2003, with pretax profits also growing 23.2 per cent. All of the top three companies sold more than ¥200 billion for the year, placing them among the top 50 retail companies overall.

As with both electronics and drugstore retailing, the other major trend in the sector is consolidation. Four of the leading 20 chains are subsidiaries of, or are aligned to, Aeon Group. Homac is a subsidiary of Aeon, operating as the largest home center chain in Hokkaido. In 2003, Aeon agreed shareholding alignments with both Kahma in central Japan and Daiki in southern Japan to form an alliance that covers the whole country. Keyo also became an affiliate in the same year giving the group additional coverage in and around Tokyo. Figure 10.5 provides a simplified illustration of just how the leading chains are related.

Diamond Home Center News (Chida, 2004) estimated the total market for home centers, including furniture stores, in 2003 was ¥3.676 trillion. Based on this figure, the leading 20 chains account for around 64 per cent of the total market. Equally, the four chains connected to Aeon make up the largest alliance in the sector with sales exceeding Cainz, the single largest chain, by about a third. This gives the alliance a current market share of around 17 per cent, with Cainz second at 6.6 per cent. As a result, merger and alliance activity is rampant as companies attempt to keep up with the leaders.

The future of home center retailing

Home Centers are a growing and adapting sector, and there is a lot of room for growth. Ikea, the world's largest furniture retailer, is currently planning to open in two locations in Japan despite numerous setbacks to its plans. A previous attempt ended in failure in the 1980s with the company's unwillingness to adapt to the Japanese market often quoted as the main reason. None of Japan's home center or furniture retailers currently resemble the Ikea model, particularly in terms of pricing and design, so if Ikea's new plan comes to fruition, it could add yet another dimension to the sector.

Equally, Japanese home centers, particularly in the regions, are increasingly adding DIY and professional tradesman services to their assortments. Some stores open as early as 6am to sell to carpenters, plumbers and other building and gardening professionals. There is also a gradual but growing interest in DIY from the general public now that house prices have fallen to more reasonable levels. Given this background, it would not be surprising for major international firms such as Home Depot, Leroy Merlin or B&Q to consider entering the Japanese market.

Meanwhile, in Japan itself, home center retailing will continue along the same path of consolidation and concentration, mirroring the trends already described for the drugstore and electronics sectors. The sector is unusual in having so many large firms enjoying sales growth and that is an indication of how immature the format still is. As elsewhere, however, the influence of Aeon in consolidating through company groupings and buying alliances will further drive the sector towards ever greater concentration.

11
Other Specialty Retailers

Introduction

As noted in the introduction to Part III, specialty retailing is made up of a diverse group of product categories. The previous two chapters covered the most important ones. This chapter looks at those specialty stores that tend to sell a range of merchandise across different product categories but of a similar type. These are variety stores, discount stores, media (books, DVDs and music), and children-related retailing (toys, maternity and childrenswear). Finally, there is a brief section on shopping centers and specialty buildings, the latter being a format that is particular to the Japanese market.

Variety merchandise retailers

In Chapter 10, Tokyu Hands and Loft were mentioned in the home center sector. While a lot of the merchandise sold in these chains overlaps with home centers, along with Ryohin Keikaku and Sony Plaza, they are in reality a separate format, located in city centers and selling a mind-boggling variety of arts and crafts, hobby, interior, gifts, stationery, and gimmicky items (see Table 11.1). The literal variety of merchandise avail-

Table 11.1 Leading variety store chains, FY2003

| Company | HQ | Sales | YonY | Pretax Profit | YonY | Stores |
	Prefecture	¥ mn	%	¥ mn	%	
Ryohin Keikaku	Tokyo	110,702	3.6	8,667	22.2	266
Tokyu Hands	Tokyo	93,807	−4.9	–	–	22
Loft	Tokyo	50,991	2.5	2,066	2.1	25
Sony Plaza	Tokyo	35,244	9.7	1,602	–	60

Source: Company reports; Nihon Keizai Shinbun (2004, p. 162)

able in Tokyu Hands and Loft in particular is so large that it makes classification difficult. Equally, Sony Plaza sells a large volume of both toys and cosmetics, while more than one third of sales at Ryohin Keikaku's Mujirushi Ryohin chain come from apparel alone. Having said this, all four chains are comparable at least in terms of their merchandising.

Tokyu Hands is the most famous of the four, although for anyone not familiar with this small chain of just 22 stores, it is difficult to believe the range of product available in a typical store. Part of the Tokyu Group, Tokyu Hands sells everything from watches and accessories to planks of wood cut to any size on site. It employs DIY (do-it-yourself) and craft experts as sales assistants, and offers numerous services from name card printing to furniture upholstery and picture framing. Formally, the chain has five main merchandise categories: DIY, interiors, hobbies and crafts, variety goods, and stationery. It sells these in large format stores, several of which employ store plans where each floor is split into three separate levels, doing away with the need for an escalator and making browsing around its large merchandise collection that much easier and fun. All Tokyu Hands stores are big shopper destinations at weekends and holidays and, while overall prices are not cheap, the range of low price items is especially popular with younger consumers looking for something different. Tokyu Hands developed in the 1970s and although successful has never grown particularly large. In recent years, sales have floundered somewhat as consumers now have more options, mostly at lower prices. This has led the chain to look at new formats, developing small footprint specialist stores aimed at shopping center tenancies.

Loft is a store concept that was designed to compete directly with Tokyu Hands and shares many of its merchandising characteristics, but with a slightly higher emphasis on arts and crafts products. Originally developed as part of the Saison Group in the early 1980s, again Loft has neither been wildly successful nor a total failure. Due to problems at its various parents over the years, the chain has struggled, however, and in 2002 was taken over by a group of shareholders including Aeon, Sogo and Mori Trust, with Credit Saison, a sister company of Seibu, also still involved. All of these companies have plans to include Loft in their existing and new retail developments. For example, Sogo opened a Loft as an annex to its refurbished Kobe store in 2003. Mori Trust, one of the largest real estate developers in Japan, has several shopping mall interests into which Loft could fit well. The new owners say they will build the Loft chain to the point where it can be taken public.

The remaining companies in Table 11.1 all operate much smaller formats. As already mentioned, Mujirushi Ryohin sells apparel, but also own branded stationery and variety goods. In its larger stores it also offers furniture, some processed foods, bicycles and even some household appliances. Under the name Muji, the chain is also active overseas. Its main selling point is 100 per cent own branded product, all with a very basic design. The store name even means "good merchandise without a brand", and ironically has become one of Japan's more easily recognized brands in itself. Ryohin Keikaku, the brand's owners, has seen profits and sales grow almost constantly since the company's founding by Seiyu back in 1980. After a couple of changes in senior management over the past few years, it has just announced record profits for FY2004, building on the impressive 22.2 per cent increase in pretax profits for FY2003. The chain is currently looking to expand further overseas and is likely to be one of Japan's most international of retailers over the next few years.

In terms of store size and location, Sony Plaza is another variety store that resembles Muji, but it is very different in terms of merchandise. While Muji items are all own branded, almost everything in Sony Plaza is imported from outside Japan. The company looks particularly for items it can license, such as the Sesame Street characters or Harry Potter merchandise. A large proportion of sales space is given over to cosmetics and also to confectionary, but the chain prides itself in selling unusual, gimmicky items, many of which are found by its staff when holidaying abroad as well as its army of traveling buyers. Recently, it has added both a larger and a smaller shop format to its portfolio. Mini Pla, as it is called, aims to open inside high traffic train stations, targeting commuters, while Serendipity is Sony Plaza's new, select shop style format that includes apparel and fashion accessories and targets people in their thirties. The first Serendipity store opened in the Nihonbashi Coredo shopping building in 2004.

The variety store sector is popular and continues to grow because it offers something consumers in Japan get too little of from retailers: entertainment and excitement. Increasingly, however, it overlaps with our next specialty sector, discount stores.

Discount stores

Discount stores are another format that is difficult to classify accurately. As with variety stores, their specialization is not in terms of merchandise, indeed most chains are full-line, but rather, as the name suggests, in terms of price. In the West, what Japan calls general merchandise stores are often called discount stores. In Japan, the lack of price competition distinguishes even these from a handful of other chains that are genuinely cheap. Another feature of Japan's discount store sector is that it is very new indeed.

Japanese discount chains split into two distinct formats: variety discount and ¥100 shops (see Table 11.2). Variety discount stores such as Don Quijote and Daikuma are large format stores selling large ranges of product. ¥100 shops are small formats, and sell large ranges of product but usually at an even lower quality. Both types have been some of the fastest growing of all retailers since the late 1990s.

Table 11.2   Major discount store chains by sales, FY2003

Company	HQ Prefecture	Sales ¥ mn	YonY %	Pretax Profit ¥ mn	YonY %	Stores
Daiso Sangyo	Hiroshima	300,000	6.7	–	–	2,400
Don Quijote	Tokyo	158,043	37.6	10,096	31.9	70
Daikuma	Gunma	116,149	–	103	–	26
Mr. Max	Fukuoka	91,301	1.1	1,444	–11.0	42
JAPAN	Osaka	77,983	0.8	2,325	56.4	136
Direx[1]	Saga	68,643	6.7	1,689	2.9	89
Topos, D-Mart [2]	Hyogo	67,215	–19.6	–	–	18
Rogers [3]	Tokyo	61,332	–0.5	4,060	1.0	10
Can-Do	Tokyo	52,040	26.0	2,076	52.0	618
Trial Company	Tokyo	46,269	–	–	–	26
Seria	Gifu	42,692	13.5	1,213	1.0	690
99 Plus	Tokyo	32,285	39.7	536	–	234

Notes:
[1] Owned by Thanks Japan
[2] Owned by Daiei
[3] Owned by Hokushin Shoji
Source: Company reports; NMJ (2004, p. 162)

Although privately owned and rather secretive, the largest chain is Daiso Sangyo which operates what is generally called by the Japanese the "¥100 Shop". Daiso is still expanding rapidly and the popularity of its low price stores makes finding new tenancies and franchisees very easy indeed. At present it is growing at around 300 stores a year net. Beginning as a deep discount importer of the very lowest cost product from China, Daiso has shifted to become more of a variety retailer and today resembles Sony Plaza in every way except price. Almost all products sold in Daiso stores are now own brand and while most are still ¥105 (including 5 per cent consumption tax), the company also offers a limited range of ¥200 and ¥400 products too. Merchandise ranges from cheap plastic trays, but then goes on to audio CDs featuring out of copyright music, novels, small furniture items, cosmetics, some basic food and drink items, stationery, and even some clothing items and electronics – all with the Daiso brand, and almost all for ¥100. The chain is phenomenally popular with school students and even adults are happy to buy there as, even if the item breaks immediately, the loss is so small that nobody cares.

Daiso and its much smaller rivals Can-do and Seria, are now improving store design and merchandising and look set to be a part of the retail landscape for sometime to come. Daiso has even expanded internationally with franchises in Hong Kong, South Korea, Taiwan, Singapore and even Kuwait.

Don Quijote, Daikuma, JAPAN, and Mr. Max are yet another breed of discounter much more in the mould known in the West. Mr. Max and Trial are actually quite squarely modeled on Wal-Mart style discount stores in the US and, as a result, operate largely in the regions where land is relatively cheap and plentiful. Daikuma, as noted in Chapter 10, is now part of Yamada Denki and is being integrated into Yamada's larger electrical outlets in order to diversify merchandise ranges.

Don Quijote, however, is another major Japanese success story. Beginning as a low cost buying operation selling basically anything the owners could procure cheap enough, it has grown into an almost nationwide chain of 70 outlets and has a very unique format somewhat like the one used by Tokyu Hands. Don Quijote believes in high density merchandising, very high density merchandising. It operates two formats: one a shopping center concept called PAO which includes a number of service tenants and usually a small supermarket, but its main format is usually a multistory building, into which it packs as many products as possible. There is some organization of product category between floors, but this is far less important than volume. And it aims to sell everything, from apparel to electronics to drugs and cosmetics, confectionary, sex aids, toys, gadgets, and, usually on the top floor, parallel imports of top luxury brands such as Louis Vuitton and Gucci. Don Quijote's other claim to fame is its long opening hours. Stores usually open at 11am and stay open until 6am next morning, making them very popular with young consumers out late at night.

While not a major part of its business, the recent opening of a Don Quijote store just south of the exclusive Ginza area in Tokyo has added a new dimension to the chain. Selling top designer labels on its top floor, the store is popular among local bar hostesses who think nothing of taking their slightly tipsy and bonus rich male guests shopping to get them to buy gifts of Chanel, Prada, and Louis Vuitton. It is equally easy, however, to take the same gifts the next day to Don Quijote and exchange them for money, so allowing Don Quijote to get them back on display ready for the evening's rush. Thus, Don Quijote has come up with a whole new way of recycling.

Amusing anecdotes aside, Don Quijote, Mr. Max, JAPAN, and the ¥100 shops are all very successful and continue to grow rapidly. They are some of the few chains in the country that offer genuinely low price merchandise at the cost of lower quality, and although some foreign retailers have been accused of being "too cheap for Japan", such criticism has never been leveled at these domestic chains.

Toys, childrenswear and maternity retailers

Until 1990, Japanese toy and children's apparel retailing was a close-knit and cozy sector dominated by the large local toy and apparel manufacturers, and lacking even one large retail chain. Today, the childrenswear market is still the same although two companies, Nishimatsuya Chain and Akachan Honpo are now growing. The toy market, however, has been revolutionized by the arrival of Toys 'R' Us. When the company announced its intention to open in Japan in 1989 it caused a huge negative outcry. Opposition came not only from politicians, retailers, and housewives, but most of all from local manufacturers.

More than 15 years later, Toys 'R' Us is a fully integrated chain in the Japanese retail landscape with over 140 stores nationwide and is totally accepted. For a number of years, Toys 'R' Us worked within the Japanese system, allowing domestic manufacturers to impose pricing and supply channels, but within five years of opening, it had expanded to such a size that the tables were turned. Manufacturers must now cooperate with the retailer if they want to put their products on its shelves. With sales for FY2003 of ¥189.09 billion it is more than times 14 times larger than its nearest domestic rival. Some Japanese academics still label Toys 'R' Us as an industry wrecker and revel in the term "category killer", but its story proves just how backward Japanese retailing used to be. Today consumers are able to buy reasonable priced products, with an excellent range of merchandise, and can enjoy doing it. It is only surprising that there are so few examples of similar upheavals in other sectors.

There are only two large childrenswear retailers, Akachan Honpo, a manufacturer and wholesaler, and Nishimatsuya Chain, a company established in the 1950s but which has begun to grow strongly. In 2003, Nishimatsuya had 364 stores and was opening around 50 stores a year. Sales grew 22.1 per cent to ¥77.8 billion in FY2003. One of its strengths is the development of own brands sourced from Asian factories and a focus on lower cost suburban centers. This kind of cost-cutting helped raise pretax profits to ¥7.04 billion. In the same year, Akachan Honpo struggled, seeing sales fall 4.3 per cent to ¥103.15 billion, and it barely broke even with pretax profits down to just ¥553 million.

Non childrenswear specialists are now taking a larger share of the market. In particular, Fast Retailing, Shimamura and the Aeon are expanding their apparel offer for kids and becoming much more sophisticated at developing areas for families to shop. Shimamura for example has expanded play areas for children and introduced slightly more fashionable lines. Select shop chains are also active with United Arrows' fascia Green Label Relaxing selling both childrenswear and imported toys as well as basic fashion for parents.

At the higher end of the market, Miki House and the department stores have dominated Japanese childrenswear retailing. Recently however, overseas competition has come in the form of CWF, a French company that is the largest childrenswear licensee in the world with brands such as Kenzo and Timberland. In 2002, CWF set up a joint venture with Ma Mere, an Osaka-based childrenswear retailer. The first store was opened in Hiroo in 2002.

While relatively small, Narumiya International is a Tokyo based childrenswear retailer that is now using its focus and brand marketing capabilities to drive growth. It has developed a stable of brands such as Mezzo Piano, Angel Blue and Pom Ponette that cater to the early teenage market for fashionable apparel and accessories. For the year ending January 2004, Narumiya International's sales grew 19 per cent to ¥35 billion from 900 shops, up from 586 shops in 2002 and including stores in Korea. As a result of its success, it listed on the Jasdaq Securities Exchange in March 2005.

Specialty books, music and video

Until the 1990s, Japan's music retailing sector was dominated by a group of powerful music distributors, while the retail sector had no powerful players. The sector was then shaken up by the entry of overseas retailers in the form of Tower, HMV and Virgin Megastores. Tower and HMV began to import CDs and other media directly into the market, undercutting local competition by as much as 25 per cent and expanding rapidly. By 2003, Tower had more than 50 stores, HMV 36 and Virgin 30. These chains seem insignificant compared to number one ranking domestic firm Shinseido with 300 stores, but many of these are small format and in outlying suburban locations with much lower sales densities. Tower Japan is now independent from its US parent, MTS; in early 2002, Tower Japan was sold to management in a deal financed by Nikko Cordial.

The music industry has tried to protect itself from low-priced imported CDs by lobbying the government to introduce a monopoly on imports for copyright holders. Of particular concern was the re-import of CDs of popular Japanese music from other Asian markets. Asia has increasingly taken to Japanese popular music and production has been localized. Unfortunately for Japanese music distributors and retailers who maintain recommended prices, this has meant an influx of CDs at low prices.

In the print sector, while overall sales of published material managed to grow 1.2 per cent due to strong sales of magazines and comics (manga), book sales fell for seven consecutive years between 1997 and 2003 (NMJ Trend Joho 2005). There are few large book chains, and marketing of books remains at a very basic level in Japan. The leading chain, Kinokuniya, has 59 stores across the country. A notable new entry into the top 10 is Book Off Corporation which has built a chain of more than 750 stores selling second-hand books, CDs, games and other merchandise. Kinokuniya has a few stores overseas, mainly catering to Japanese expatriates, but Book Off has even trumped this with its first store in Paris in 2005.

A major event in the otherwise highly regulated book market was the entry of Amazon in 2000. Beginning with books alone, but quickly expanding into audio CDs, games, and software, Amazon has been a success in Japan despite the market restrictions and despite numerous local online book sellers. It now offers electronic books, along with a number of specialty categories such as adult books and videos. The Japanese arm is reported to have achieved profitability in 2003. Although book prices are protected in Japan, Amazon competes by offering free delivery on orders over ¥1,500, whereas most of its competitors charge a fee unless orders are ¥10,000 or more.

Shopping buildings

Calling the majority of shopping centers in Japan "buildings" rather than "malls" reflects the fact that most of them are multistory and located in city centers. Recently, companies like Aeon and Mitsui Real Estate have opened large, Western style malls in the suburbs, but these are still in the minority. It is worth considering each type in turn.

1. Specialty Buildings
2. Shopping Malls: Japan also has Western style malls like those found in the US and Europe and include both covered malls centered round an anchor such as a supermarket, department store or GMS, and outdoor malls such as those specializing in factory outlet stores.

Specialty buildings

There are actually two main types: station buildings and fashion buildings. Both are vertical shopping malls, usually covering five to eight floors with multiple tenants on each floor. Station buildings are located near or at railway stations and have a mix of tenants ranging from fashion through food to services like travel agents. Fashion buildings, or *Fashion Biru* in Japanese, are usually comprised of a minimum of 70 per cent fashion tenancies and are not restricted to station buildings.

Fashion buildings are popular shopping destinations and have become one of the most characteristic aspects of Japanese retailing, but today, with the growth in out-of-town centers, only the best locations continue to prosper. In the 1970s and 1980s, a number of fashion building chains emerged including Parco (then Saison Group), Vivre (then Mycal Group), 109 (Tokyu Group), Lumine (JR East Group), and Forus (Aeon Group). All continue to operate but both Parco and Vivre are now under new management. Each had a different profile and positioning. Parco buildings for example are generally regarded as upscale while the 109 buildings cater for a very specific type of young female fashion consumer. Within the 109 portfolio, however, locations are segmented, to create buildings with very defined consumer targets. In Shibuya the main 109 building caters for late-teen girls and young women whilst 109-2 focuses on younger teenage children.

The other type of specialty building, the station building, takes full advantage of its proximity to key transport nodes in the main city centers. This has a lot to do with their ownership. Around Shinjuku Station for example there are four main specialty shopping buildings as well as annexes and department stores. Most are linked to railway groups that operate from the station.

The specialty buildings are dominated by just six groups, themselves linked to larger retail, railway and property conglomerates (see Table 11.3). The largest chain is Parco, which today is controlled by Mori Trust with a 25 per cent shareholding. Parco was the first specialty shopping building and remains the standard model with key developments in Shibuya, Ikebukuro, Osaka, Sapporo and Nagoya. Second is Lumine, owned by

Table 11.3 Japan's largest specialty buildings by sales, FY2002

	Company	Building	Prefecture	Sales ¥ mn	YonY %	Sales space sqm	Sales density ¥ mn/sqm
1	Parco	Nagoya Parco	Aichi	40,891	−0.7	33,236	1.230
2	Kintetsu	† Prats Kintetsu	Kyoto	35,951	–	38,700	0.929
3	Lumine	† Tachikawa	Tokyo	35,440	−2.6	20,597	1.721
4	Lumine	† Omiya	Saitama	34,504	−2.1	34,504	1.000
5	Shinjuku Station Bldg	† MyCity	Tokyo	30,105	−1.6	18,322	1.643
6	Parco	Ikebukuro Parco	Tokyo	30,105	9.6	19,059	1.580
7	Okadaya	Okadaya Moas	Kanagawa	29,508	0.2	25,867	1.141
8	Kawasaki Station Bldg	† Kawasakai BE	Kanagawa	29,091	1.4	21,865	1.330
9	Kichijoji RonRon	† Kichijoji RonRon	Tokyo	28,242	3.9	13,189	2.141
10	TMD	† Tokyu Dps S.C.	Kanagawa	27,500	14.6	48,576	0.566
11	Lumine	† Yokohama	Kanagawa	26,675	−0.8	15,425	1.729
12	Lumine	† Shinjuku	Tokyo	26,382	1.8	17,718	1.489
13	Lumine	† Kita-senju	Tokyo	24,020	0.8	13,801	1.740
14	TMD	Shibuya 109	Tokyo	22,900	1.8	10,220	2.241
15	Parco	Shibuya Parco	Tokyo	22,127	−6.8	20,696	1.069
16	Parco	Sapporo Parco	Hokkaido	21,449	0.9	13,993	1.533
17	Parco	Chofu Parco	Tokyo	20,747	0.6	15,378	1.349
18	Vivre	† Yokohama Vivre	Kanagawa	19,648	−6.0	14,300	1.374
19	Flags	Flags Shinjuku	Tokyo	17,228	5.7	9,799	1.758
20	Jujiya	Canal City	Fukuoka	16,726	4.8	19,157	0.873

Note:
† = 2000–01 sales
Source: NMJ (2003, pp. 241–9)

JR East, the largest railway company in Japan. TMD, which operates the famous 109 buildings, is a subsidiary of Tokyu Department Stores, itself a subsidiary of railway to property group, Tokyu Corporation. Vivre is now part of Aeon following the collapse of Mycal.

In general, specialty building operators offer a standard tenancy contract based on a percentage of sales with a minimum monthly payment. Percentages vary widely depending on the type of tenant. The costs of shop fit used to be paid outright by the tenant but in recent years, this condition has become more flexible.

Comparatively high land costs mean that specialty buildings are not as popular for new developments as larger, out-of-town centers. Many existing buildings are also in need of improvement in both management and tenant mix. Parco has benefited from a sudden boost in investment in the early 2000s after changing ownership. In 2001 for example, the company posted pretax profits up 14 per cent to ¥7.1 billion and pretax profits have continued to improve reaching ¥7.79 billion in 2003. Improvements in profits came at the expense of turnover as Parco cut underperforming peripheral businesses. It leased some of its less attractive buildings, divested Wave, a CD store, and Libro, a book store, as well as restaurant businesses. As a result, sales fell from ¥312 billion in 2001 to ¥283 billion in 2003.

Outside of Tokyo, most station buildings were developed locally and had something of a dreary reputation in many places. Today, however, compared to department stores and less well located buildings, station buildings have two major advantages: great locations and a flexible tenancy structure for popular specialty chains. In some cases, such as Shinjuku in Tokyo, Umeda in Osaka, and Nagoya station, footfall is quite astounding, numbering more than a million people a day, 3 million in Shinjuku's case. Both railway operators and retail developers are keen to make better use of this asset. The largest example is JR East, a company which claims it is one of the top 10 retailers in the country (see JR East's website: http://www.jreast.co.jp).

JR East's retail building operations used to be a labyrinth. Until 2003, its station building division consisted of 56 companies managing 101 buildings with sales of ¥960 billion. It began overhauling its station buildings in 2001 under its three subsidiaries, Lumine, Atre and S-Pal. Other station buildings were slowly folded into these three companies in order to streamline the retail developer business and give it focus. It is a slow process, however, with consolidation expected to continue until 2007. Most buildings continue to operate as separate businesses, but under the centralized management system, store chiefs at the best buildings are being given responsibility over more than one location. Building management and information systems are being amalgamated under JR East subsidiary companies. Perhaps most important of all, the railway is hoping to build a pool of experienced building managers who can work in various locations, and who know the industry rather than just a single shopping center.

Parts of this portfolio have seen strong growth. Until 2003, Lumine Shinjuku posted 24 months of continuous sales growth while the Yokohama building had positive growth for 28 months. The Shinjuku buildings Lumine 1 and 2 benefited from refurbishment and from longer operating hours, extending to 10 pm, as well as the introduction of new brands. JR East also leveraged the 600,000 holders of the Lumine store card with special offers and discount periods of four days, four times a year. It is now capable of attracting popular specialists such as United Arrows.

Not every station building is enjoying similar success, however, and many of the private railway companies are as burdened by debt as any of the worst cases in retailing, making rebuilding almost impossible. But with Japan's need for major commuter hubs unlikely to change in the near future, there are still significant opportunities at many urban stations around the country.

Case Study 11.1:   The outlet boom

Japanese business has never been keen on discounting of any kind, leading to amazement about prices when Japanese travelers visit factory outlet malls in the US and Europe. As a result, there is now a growing demand for factory outlets in Japan too.

This has affected to a significant degree the way consumer goods in Japan are distributed, particularly for apparel. Many retailers are now ready to take on the risk of inventory now that they have a legitimate route to offload the stock in a way that does not damage their brand image. More importantly, the growth in retailers using the SPA model and others using own brands (see Chapter 9) has meant that unsold stock can no longer be passed back down the distribution channel. In the past, sale or return contracts were common because it was the only way department stores would do business. Manufacturers were happy that prices were not being discounted and retailers felt they could avoid the risk of unsold product. SPA chains have no recourse to wholesale suppliers in order to reduce inventory risk, and even other retailers now realize that a little risk can actually provide a lot more freedom to operate more efficiently and effectively.

Another important factor behind the growth of outlet malls in Japan has been the success of luxury brand retailing. International firms like Louis Vuitton Moet Hennessy (LVMH) and Prada have invested heavily in opening their own stores in Japan, and in taking control of department store concessions. Rather than sending unsold inventory home, the Japanese subsidiaries of these companies have found that it is much better business to sell the stock in Japan through outlet stores. In many cases this causes little harm as it provides an attractive and promotional venue to offload relatively less popular items.

The leading outlet mall developers include Mitsui Real Estate, the real estate arm of Mitsui Bussan, and Chelsea Japan, a joint venture between the US firm of the same name, Mitsubishi Estate and Sojitz, a trading company. Chelsea Japan operates successful outlet malls in Gotenba (Shizuoka), Rinku Town (Osaka), Sano (Tochigi) and Torisu (Saga). The company has expanded its highly successful Rinku Town outlet mall near Kansai International Airport to 28,000 sqm from 23,400 sqm, making it the largest outlet mall in the country.

Shopping malls

Western style shopping malls located in the suburbs and designed to attract shoppers mostly by car are only now beginning to grow in number. Regulatory restrictions on suburban developments, along with the relative ease of developing malls at railway stations caused demand to be limited in the past. But as large retailers like Aeon now find their independence, shopping malls have become a retailing model with potential. Perhaps one of the most striking features of Japanese shopping mall development is the dominance of just a few players. Trading houses are prominent, cleaving out yet another level of influence in the distribution system, with Mitsubishi Shoji and Mitsui Bussan the most active. In addition to the activities of its real estate arm, Mitsubishi is the joint owner of Diamond City with Aeon, as well as owning a third of the business of Chelsea Japan, the leading developer of outlet malls in Japan.

Aeon operates two separate development businesses, Aeon Mall and Jusco, and is itself one of the largest operators of shopping malls. In 2004, it opened 17 shopping centers through one of its three development businesses. These included the Aeon Sennan center in Osaka with 75,000 sqm of gross space, as well as 11 other centers over the 30,000-sqm mark. As noted in Chapter 6, a large proportion of Aeon's sales and profits come from leasing space in these centers rather than through its own retailing operations. For example, in November 2004, Aeon re-opened a shopping center in Kita-Toda in Saitama, north of Tokyo. At the time, Aeon said it expected total sales of ¥28 billion in the first year but its direct retail operations would only contribute ¥12 billion, less than 50 per cent of the total.

Shopping centers have been the focus of developer investment and are a further indication of buoyancy in the retail market since the early 2000s. According to the Japan Shopping Center Association (see JCSA website: http://www.jcsc.or.jp), 62 new shopping centers opened in 2004, 15 more than in 2003 (see Table 11.4 for notable developments). This was still fewer than before the Large Store Location Law was implemented in 2000, but the first time since then that the number had exceeded 50 in one year.

The expansion reflects the incursion of specialty retailing on the traditional territories of regional department stores. Since specialty retailers are continuing to expand, demand for new shopping center development has risen. According to the JSCA, of 47 new shopping mall developments in 2003, 70 per cent were designed solely for specialty store tenancy and the ratio for 2004 was similar.

Although large scale malls are increasing in number, the biggest increase has been in medium sized malls away from train stations. The average size of shopping malls opened in 2004 was 28,071 sqm, slightly smaller than in 2003. This was because many of these were more cen-

Table 11.4 Leading shopping mall developments, 2004

Opening	Name of shopping center	Area	Prefecture	Developer	Store Area sqm
19 Feb	Lumine Kawagoe	Kawagoe	Saitama	Lumine	2,900
3 Mar	Atre Shinagawa	Shinagawa	Tokyo	Ekibiru Development Co.Tokyo	5,200
3 Mar	Diamond City Hana	Kyoto	Kyoto	Diamond City	22,000
3 Mar	Kawasaki LeFront	Kawasaki	Kanagawa	Mitsubishi Jisho Group	10,600
12 Mar	Tosu Premium Outlets	Tosu	Saga	Chelsea Japan	8,400
19 Mar	Lala Garden Tsukuba	Tsukuba	Ibaraki	Mitsui Fudosan	18,000
March	Diamond City Soleil	Fuchu	Hiroshima	Diamond City	64,500
March	Diamond City Nara Kashihara SC	Kashihara	Nara	Diamond City	39,000
30 Mar	Coredo Nihonbashi	Nihonbashi	Tokyo	Mitsui Fudosan etc.	10,000
7 Apr	Yu-Sui-Chi-Mikitei	Yokohama	Kanagawa	Tokyu Dentetsu	3,120
Spring	Omiya Miyahara SC	Saitama	Saitama	Mitsui Fudosan	142,000
April	Minamisenjyu SC	Arakawa	Tokyo	Mitsui Fudosan	9,171
April	Aqua Kisarazu	Kisarazu	Chiba	Nihon Sogokikaku	43,000
28 Apr	Karuizawa Prince Shopping Plaza New East	Karuizawa	Nagano	Kokudo	7,383
Spring	Outlet Concert Nagara	Nagara	Chiba	Nagara Shopping Resort	16,500
June	Diamond City Kisogawa SC	Kisogawa	Aichi	Diamond City	48,000
June	Diamond City Fukuoka Kasuya SC	Kasuya	Fukuoka	Diamond City	69,000
July	Marinoacity 2nd term	Fukuoka	Fukuoka	Marinoacity Fukuoka	6,760
August	Utsunomiya Bell Mall	Utsunomiya	Tochigi	Miya Group	42,000
August	Marunouchi 1 Cho-me Area Development Project	Marunouchi	Tokyo	Mitsubishi Jusho	–
September	Katakura Shintoshin Mall	Saitama	Saitama	Katakura Kogyo	33,300
October	Kojunsha Building	Ginza	Tokyo	Mitsui Fudosan	22,000
Fall	Aeon Sennan SC	Sennan	Osaka	Aeon Mall	75,000
Fall	Nishi Kagoshima Eki Building	Kagoshima	Kagashima	JR Kyushu	30,000
Fall	Toki Premium Outlets	Toki	Gifu	Chelsea Japan	19,000

Table 11.4 Leading shopping mall developments, 2004 – *continued*

Opening	Name of shopping center	Area	Prefecture	Developer	Store Area sqm
Fall	Diamond City Sakai Kitahanada	Sakai	Osaka	Diamond City	55,000
Fall	Hanshin Park Atochi SC	Nishinomiya	Hyogo	Mitsui Fudosan	49,000
Fall	Mori Town New Mall	Akishima	Tokyo	Showa Hikoki Kogyo	21,000
Fall	Minatomirai 21 Central 53 Area	Yokohama	Kanagawa	Yokohama Road King Group	17,000
December	Keio Takahata Building	Hino	Tokyo	Keio Dentetsu	16,000
December	Vivit Square	Funabashi	Chiba	Pacifica Malls	37,000

Source: JapanConsuming (2004)

trally located within cities, or designed around key transport points. Mitsui Real Estate, in competition with what is happening at Aeon, is a key developer in this area, opening the Lala Garden in Tsukuba and the LaLa Terrace in Minami Senju, with gross space of 18,000 sqm and 9,200 sqm respectively in 2004.

The JSCA is predicting a continuing general trend of mid-sized, more convenient shopping centers in the medium term. It notes the aging of society, a falling off in shopping by car, and demand for more specialist retailing as being key drivers behind this trend. Consumers are less inclined to choose a huge, one-stop-shop center unless the transport links are just right.

There are also plenty of large sites available. This is partly the result of manufacturing moving to other parts of Asia, leaving many factory sites in city suburbs, or even in the centers, standing empty. Many of the developments coming to completion since 2000 were formerly occupied by factories or dowdy office buildings. The land is often cheap and sometimes comes with development grants from local governments keen to revitalize run-down parts of their jurisdictions.

Summary

Japan has the usual full range of specialty retailing, some of it traditional and not far removed from mom and pop stores, other parts highly professional and growing strongly. There are also still areas where further modernization and development is sorely needed. Books and footwear retailing both spring to mind.

Many visitors to Japan have the sense that Japan is already over shopped. Japan does after all have more shops than the US with less than half the population. But this would be to miss the point. Much of the current retail development is actually replacing redundant retail operations, in particular the large swathe of mom and pop operations that continue to make up around 70 per cent of stores by number. Specialty store centers are also replacing struggling department store operations particularly those of regional department store companies. As long as demand for well-produced and entertaining national chains in local areas continues, shopping mall development is likely to continue at the same relentless pace.

Part IV

Future Developments

12

Internationalization of Japanese Retailers

"Overseas retailers cannot succeed in Japan" (sic)

East Asia is experiencing an influx of retail companies from the West. Locally, politicians, academics and journalists are not too happy about this, although the majority of consumers do not seem to mind. Japan too has seen its fair share of overseas retailers entering the market, and it is one of the places where opposition to Western firms is strongest. But the question is, as they too expand into East Asia, how do Japanese retailers fit into this situation? Yes, they represent East Asia and are subject to the same competition with so-called global retailers like Wal-Mart, Tesco, and Toys 'R' Us in their own market, but they also originate from the second richest market in the world. Japan would be the first to insist it is very much a first world country, and, at least privately, most Japanese would admit they enjoy an economy far more advanced than that of the rest of Asia. When it comes to international expansion around the Asian region, should Japanese retailers be seen as Asian, or just another example of large, ambitious retailers powering their way into underdeveloped markets? The truth is, there is very little difference between companies from Europe, North America and Japan when it comes to taking over markets in the rest of the East Asian region.

As is well known, the Japanese postwar economic miracle was built almost entirely on exports, particularly of technology. Large parts of the economy are geared solely towards this aim, and everything from education to politics have evolved to support the system. Equally, Japan built a reputation as a difficult, inscrutable, and very expensive market to enter. Some of this reputation was well deserved, at least for a time, but much of it was myth and little more than reiteration of Japanese fundamental belief that its culture is uniquely different and therefore impossible to understand except by the Japanese themselves. Occasionally, politicians and academics restate this thesis, but whether accurate or not, the size and attractiveness of the Japanese market and, much to its supporters' dismay, a significant drop in the country's business influence, has made more than a few

Western firms take a closer look. Too many Westerners still fail, but an increasing number find success and stay long term.

Although there are a lot of mature domestic retail companies in Japan, levels of competition remain extremely low in many sectors. In many places, large retailers were protected by store development regulations that allowed them to openly veto the building of competitors' stores in their catchment areas, and manufacturers and politicians protected small retailers at the expense of a free market and at the expense of consumer interests. True, this also resulted in a complex, inefficient, and anticompetitive distribution system, much of which still exists and with which new entrants to the market, be they domestic or foreign, must still contend, but to suggest non-Japanese retailers failed in the market due to its advanced nature or high levels of competition is simply giving in to the traditional myths.

This mindset is the biggest barrier to entry faced by any non-Japanese firm. Even without ever seeing Carrefour's stores, many consumers were adamant that the French retailer was unsuited to the Japanese market and would fail. In the end, they were right, and Nihon Keizai Shinbun was vehement in its attack on all overseas retailers, going so far as to suggest that they simply were not good enough to "crack" the Japanese market (see Nikkei Weekly, 2005). How ironic then that Aeon has openly stated that it aims to develop store formats and, at the most fundamental level, an operating system that is virtually identical to that used by Carrefour, and, lo and behold, that Aeon should be the company to acquire Carrefour's stores in Japan.

Today, when Japanese academics discuss retail internationalization elsewhere in Asia, the common view is that overseas retailers help to "create" distribution systems. When the same academics talk about Japan, however, overseas retailers are seen as damaging the distribution system and being directly responsible for the breakdown, and therefore decline, of traditional distribution systems in Japan (see, for example, Takayama, 2001). Of course, local academics in the rest of Asia probably talk in the same way. The difference is, of course, increasingly it is not only Western firms entering and creating local distribution systems in the rest of Asia; Japanese are being equally creative.

Japanese retailers taking over Asia

No matter how unfairly Western retailers are treated by Japanese press, it is equally true that Japanese firms making their way overseas are treated as heroes. There are actually a lot more of them than even Japanese consumers realize. In 1996 one report (Mukoyama, 1996) found almost 300 retail stores operated by Japanese firms outside Japan but even this did not include investment companies and other non-retail companies operating

Table 12.1 International spread of Japanese retailers, circa 1996

	Stores	% of Total	Year of Entry (where known)			
			1960s	1970s	1980s	1990s
Specialty Stores	135	46.2	0	3	25	107
Department Stores	81	27.7	1	14	30	36
Supermarkets	76	26.0	0	3	24	49
Total	292	100.0	1	20	79	192
Asia	243	83.2				
Hong Kong	82	28.1	1	3	25	53
Taiwan	51	17.5	0	0	6	45
China	35	12.0	0	0	2	33
Singapore	30	10.3	0	2	11	17
Thailand	18	6.2	0	0	7	11
Malaysia	17	5.8	0	0	8	9
Macao	4	1.4				
Indonesia	3	1.0				
Brunei	1	0.3				
Australia	2	0.7				
Europe	25	8.6				
UK	10	3.4				
France	8	2.7				
Spain	2	0.7				
Germany	2	0.7				
Netherlands	1	0.3				
Austria	1	0.3				
Italy	1	0.3				
North America	24	8.2				
USA	22	7.5				
Canada	1	0.3				
Costa Rica	1	0.3				
Total	292	100.0				

Source: Compiled from Mukoyama (1996, pp. 75–81)

retailing overseas. Significantly, however, more than 83 per cent of the stores found in the study were based in Asia, and two thirds had opened after 1990 (Table 12.1).

In reality, Japanese retailers have the same competitive characteristics, with the same potential as both distribution creators or breakers, as retailers from Europe and North America. This is borne out by a second study (Kawabata, 2000), which showed a continued expansion of

Table 12.2   Stores opened and closed by Japanese retailers by region, 1995–1999

Supermarkets	Department Stores					
	Total 1955 to 1999	Stores Opened	Stores Closed	Total 1955 to 1999	Stores Opened	Stores Closed
Asia	87	21	15	252	129	103
China	7	2	2	66	59	43
Hong Kong	12	1	7	20	6	9
Taiwan	23	10		99	40	24
Singapore	19	2	2	14	4	6
Thailand	9		2	23	12	8
Malaysia	14	4	2	24	6	8
Indonesia	3	2		2	1	2
Others	0			4	1	3
Europe	23	0	7	1	0	1
UK	4		2	1		1
France	8		3			
Italy	2		1			
Germany	4					
Spain	4		1			
Austria	1					
Americas	12		2	19	1	14
Australia	3	1		0	0	
Other	0			8		2
Total	125	22	24	280	130	120

Source: Compiled from Kawabata (2000, pp. 70–75)

Japanese retailers in the late 1990s, and, again, a concentration on Asia (Table 12.2). In the period between 1995 and 1999, Japanese retailers opened 22 department stores and 130 supermarkets overseas, but of these, only one department store and one supermarket opened outside Asia. Clearly, it was not just Westerners invading Asian markets from overseas.

In the same period, Japanese firms closed 31 department stores, half of these in Asia, along with 121 supermarkets, again 103 of which were in Asia. By contrast to the 1996 study, which found only 35 stores in China, the later work discovered 73 new stores in China, including 61 after 1995, and these results only considered department stores and supermarkets. The same figures suggest a complete drop off in new stores being opened in Europe and America as would be consistent with declining business confidence in Japan itself, but interest in Asia remained high.

At the same time, the 2000 study pointed out that most Japanese firms made little attempt to develop their businesses once a store opened overseas. According to the study, many saw their overseas stores, particularly in Asia, as easy, cash-generating machines, with profits being quickly repatriated back to Japan. As a result, there are relatively few cases of Japanese retailers becoming part of the local market, preferring instead to target tourists, and often they were quickly closed when results turned bad. There are some very important exceptions to this conclusion, notably Aeon, Takashimaya, and Muji, but it is a claim that is in stark contrast to the operations of most Western firms in Asia – except, Japanese journalists would argue, in the cases of those that failed in Japan.

Trading firms spearhead expansion

Since the turn of the century, however, Japanese retailers have been expanding in Asia with the same vigor and the same long term goals as those shown by any retailer originating from an advanced economy. Retailing has become an important new part of Japan's export business, so it comes as no surprise that the *Sogo Shosha*, Japan's trading companies, are heavily involved. As Table 12.3 illustrates, the largest trading houses, along with a small number of other consumer goods wholesalers, have huge interests throughout Asia. Their overseas subsidiaries include a majority of manufacturing companies, but the total ranges across a multitude of trading, procurement, logistics, and consulting businesses. Overall, the types of businesses operated by the trading houses cover every industrial sector, and, in recent years, increasingly include retailing.

As described in Chapter 4, the same trading houses control the majority of brand licenses currently being imported into Japan, although in this case, as master licensee the trading house facilitates production and distribution through subsidiaries and intermediaries. Similarly, the same trading houses are acting as facilitators for Japanese companies, from all industrial sectors, seeking to enter markets elsewhere in Asia. They provide financial, logistics, and local knowledge support, and in some cases also organize license businesses. In the case of Itochu Shoji in South Korea, for example, the trading house holds a 49 per cent stake (44.1 per cent Itochu Shoji, 4.9 per cent Itochu Korea) in Italian fashion brand Bvlgari's retail operations (see Shukan Toyo Keizai, 2004b). In China, Itochu's subsidiary, Itochu Seni Boeki, supplies womenswear and sportswear to Japanese apparel firms, home furnishings to the US, and suits to Europe. Sales are now estimated at US$700 million. Itochu is also expanding the Familymart chain of convenience stores in Taiwan, South Korea, and in Shanghai. Including its interests in Renoma and Descente's Le Coq Sportif business, it has nine companies currently in China and is expecting sales of US$1 billion by 2006.

Table 12.3 Japanese trading companies in Asia, 2003

Trading Company	Taiwan	China	South Korea	Thailand	Malaysia	Indonesia	Singapore	Hong Kong	Vietnam	Philippines	Others	Total No Companies
Itochu Shoji	7	62	2	16	2	16	9	18	2	3	6	143
Sumikin Bussan		19	1	4		1	1	3	1			30
Sumitomo Shoji	8	37	1	25	12	26	15	8	7	7	3	153
Marubeni	4	42	1	11	4	11	7	9	1	8	5	101
Mitsui Bussan	4	27	2	25	8	13	14	20	2	1	5	121
Mitsubishi Shoji	6	30	2	34	6	11	5	14	5	9	5	127
Yagi Tsusho		3						1				4
	29	220	9	115	32	78	51	73	18	28	26	679

Source: Shukan Toyo Keizai (2003, pp. 1190–1334)

Mitsubishi has expanded its Chinese business following the creation of a Hong Kong subsidiary called Tredia Fashion in 2004. The Shanghai business, called Tredia Fashion Shanghai, saw sales reaching US$390 million in 2004. Similarly, Mitsui's Alta Moda International Shanghai office had turnover of US$150 million, and Sumitomo's Sumitex also increased sales. All three of these businesses are still very new and can be expected to grow rapidly in the coming years.

There are also numerous cases of trading houses becoming involved more directly in retailing. Itochu owns and operates 70 per cent of the Paul Smith operation in Hong Kong, is a major supplier to department stores, supermarkets, and convenience stores in Taiwan and Singapore, and is a major textile and apparel manufacturer throughout the region for both local sale and for import into Japan. Sumikin Bussan provides procurement and logistics services to retailers in Hong Kong, Thailand, and Singapore, as does Sumitomo Shoji throughout the region, as well as being the main sales agent for Honda and Ford automobiles in Thailand. Mitsui Bussan and Marubeni also operate a full range of companies that aim to provide upstream services for Japanese and other retailers, but Mitsubishi Shoji goes one step further, operating food supermarkets itself in China (in joint venture with Daiei) and in Vietnam (joint venture with Seiyu), and at least one chain of restaurants in Shanghai (joint venture with House Foods).

Japanese retailers in Asia

The extent of Japanese retail penetration in the region is also much greater than it appears from considering just the largest firms. Toyo Keizai's directory (Shukan Toyo Keizai, 2004b) lists 97 separate, retailer-operated companies in Asia, of which 72 are confirmed store or mail order operations (see Table 12.4). These are concentrated in China and Hong Kong, with 12 in Singapore – a country where the Japanese retail presence is immediately and clearly visible through two major department stores and numerous specialty store chains. The numbers in the Toyo Keizai directory were collected in 2002–3 and newspaper reports suggest that there has been considerable growth since then, particularly in China. Ito-Yokado, Aeon and Lawson have all been active in store expansion, and a number of specialty chains, such as Comme Ca, Narumiya, Daiso Sangyo, World, Sanei International and others have begun to open stores across the region. With growing competition at home, fashion chains have been expanding into new markets overseas.

The competitive advantage for Japanese fashion SPAs is of course their supply chain system (see Chapter 9) along with the growing devotion to Japanese fashion among young Asian consumers. These strengths are helping them to expand into markets they know well, notably China, Taiwan, Hong Kong and Korea and making substantial investment in locations and supply.

Table 12.4 Japanese retailers in Asia, 2003

Retailers	Taiwan	China	South Korea	Thailand	Malaysia	Indonesia	Singapore	Hong Kong	Vietnam	Philippines	Others	Total No Companies
Aoyama Shoji	1	1										2
Akachan Honpo		2						2				4
Aeon	1	2		2	2							7
Ito-Yokado		2										2
Isetan	1	3		1	1		1	1				8
Cabin	1	2					1					4
Seiyu		1					2	2				5
Senshukai		1		1				1				3
Takasho		2										2
Daiei		4								1		5
Daiki		2										2
Takashimaya	2			1				1				4
Tokyu Department Store				1								1
Tokyo Megane	1			1	1			1				4
Nissen		1						2				3
Nisshin Shoji				1	1							2
Parco							3					3
Hasegawa		1					2		3		1	7
Fast Retailing		2										2
Family Mart	1		1	1								3
Lawson		1										1
Best Denki					1		1	1				3
Belluna								2				2
Mycal	1							1				2
Mikimoto	1		1									2
Ministop		1								1		2
Paris Miki	1	1			1		1	2				6
Mitsukoshi		1						2				3
Meitetsu Pare											2	2
Ryohin Keikaku								1				1
Total companies	10	30	2	9	7	0	12	19	3	2	3	97

Source: Shukan Toyo Keizai (2003, pp. 1334–1348)

A good example of this is Itokin. Following the successful opening of an Itokin branded fashion building in Shanghai in 1999, it continued to expand widely in China. Three fashion buildings were opened in Qingdao, Dalian and Tianjin by 2002. The Qingdao store comprises more than 20,000 sqm and the second store in Dalian has over 30,000 sqm. These fashion buildings house a range of Itokin apparel and store brands and include tenants that complement the Itokin brands with accessories and related fashion merchandise.

At least in the apparel sector, one of the primary motivations for expansion in Asia is growing competition in the home market. Mokumoku launched the successful Olive des Olive brand in Asia in 1999, primarily through Japanese department stores in Taiwan, Hong Kong and South Korea. It was one of the first SPA operators to venture into other Asian markets, strongly supported by main trading company Itochu Shoji. As of 2003, Mokumoku had around 140 stores in Japan and overseas, including 45 stores in Korea under joint venture and 20 stores in Taiwan. In 2004 alone, it opened 25 more Olive des Olive stores in Taiwan and 15 in Korea as well as new stores in Shanghai and Beijing. By the end of 2005, Mokumoku will have more than 200 stores outside Japan, more than in the home market.

Japanese companies are no stronger than other international competitors – yet. Penetration of Japanese firms is, however, much larger than previously recorded. They are easily keeping pace with the internationalization of retail markets across Asia as instigated by Western entrants. The firms with the ambition and ability to operate overseas are the largest and most sophisticated firms in the Japanese market. They are eminently capable of success in the rest of Asia and may even possess certain competitive advantages based on better cultural understanding as they originate from Asia themselves. Aeon and Ito-Yokado certainly believe so and target European and North American competitors specifically in their PR.

Looking at each market separately makes this clear. Naturally, the best example today is China.

Japanese activity in China

Table 12.5 lists 21 retail companies set up by Japanese firms in China by 2003. Things are moving so quickly in the Chinese market, however, that these numbers are undoubtedly now out of date. By the Beijing Olympics of 2008, the picture will be totally transformed, but these statistics do show the beginning of the trend. Until 2004 when ownership and operating restrictions were lifted in China, most overseas firms had set up multiple companies in different locations. A glance at the table suggests that this build up has been going on for some time, with Isetan establishing businesses in Shanghai and Tianjin as long ago as 1993, but there has been a recent upsurge. Ito-Yokado, while establishing its Chengdu operation in 1998, opened its first store in 2000 and still only had three GMS outlets in 2004, with plans for at least five more by 2008 (Fok, 2004). At the same time, Ito-Yokado as a group is developing both its Seven-Eleven convenience store chain, the first of which opened in Beijing in 2004, and York Benimaru supermarkets. It aims to blanket cover areas of Beijing with these three complementary formats by 2008. In addition, it signed a joint venture with Beijing Shoulian Group and the China National Sugar & Alcohol Group Corporation in order to expand Seven-Eleven in and around Beijing with 500 stores forecast by 2008.

Lawson, now owned by Mitsubishi, while opening its first store in 1996, had fewer than 50 stores up to 2002. This jumped to almost 200 in 2004 and Mitsubishi is planning to expand at a rate of some 100 stores a year from now on. Lawson operates entirely in the Shanghai market, keeping it well away from competition with Ito-Yokado's Seven-Eleven chain.

Similarly, a number of prominent companies are absent from the table due to lack of data. Familymart operated a single store in Shanghai, but owner, Itochu, was planning a rapid expansion in 2005, and auto-parts retailer Yellow Hat announced in April 2004 that it would be expanding its own franchise chain of stores in the next few years, also with the help of Itochu. In 2004 it had three stores in China.

In China, Japanese retailers may be behind in terms of store development as compared to Carrefour, Auchan, and Wal-Mart for example, but they are expanding fast. A number of companies, Aeon in Shanghai, Daiei in Tianjin, and Ito-Yokado in both Chengdu and Beijing even claimed that they entered China after invitations from government officials. Similarly, while Chinese consumers are not at all similar in terms of tastes and behavior as compared to Japanese, these firms are happy to suggest they can understand the practices and demands of the Chinese market due to the relatively close cultural proximity of the two countries. Another key advantage is the strong link between Japanese manufacturers and retailers both operating marketing in China, and the use of Japanese consultants and logistics and transport firms when setting up in the country. Sales volumes remain small, with the largest, Ito-Yokado, generating only about ¥25 billion in sales, or about the same as one large store in Japan. Carrefour is eight times larger, with Wal-Mart and Metro already three times larger.

Pitfalls abound, however. Many retailers complain bitterly about the "old fashioned" and "opaque" nature of Chinese business practices, notably the use of long payment periods and large, volume buying rebates, and the close involvement of national and local government within the distribution system. These are genuine concerns to be sure, but it is ironic that these are the very same practices so bemoaned by overseas retailers and distributors entering Japan even as recently as the 1990s (see Miwa, 1992; Larke, 1994).

Table 12.5 Japanese retailers in China, 2003

Japanese Retailer	Shareholding %	Location	Retail sector	Entry date Yr.Mth	Sales ¥ bn	End sales period Yr.Mth	Net Profit ¥ mn	Stores	Employees
Isetan	63.0	Shanghai	Department store	1993.01	2.76	2002.12	−45.0	1	172.00
Isetan	75.0	Tientsin	Department store	1993.01	4.12	2002.12	34.0	1	447.00
Isetan	80.0	Shanghai	Department store	1997.03	5.48	2002.12	197.0	1	311.00
Ito-Yokado	51.0	Changdu	GMS	1997.11	9.00	2003.12	20.0	2	1,028.00
Ito-Yokado	36.8	Beijing	GMS	1998.04	16.00	2003.12	32.0	3	1,399.00
Aeon	65.0	Beijing	SC	1995.10	75.00	–	P	5	2,144.00
Aeon	60.0	Tsingtao	SC	1996.03				2	896.00
Seiyu	42.0	Beijing	SC	1996.06	1.60	2003.12	OK	1	546.00
Daiei	95.0	Tientsin	Supermarket	1995.05	3.60	2002.12	–	12	1,000.00
Heiwado	75.0	Tientsin	SC	1998.11	7.50	2003.12	55.0	1	1,134.00
Lawson	49.0	Shanghai	CVS	1996.02	3.39	2003.12	L	153	149.00
Komeri	70.0	Luta	Home center	1996.03	2.23	2002.12	L	2	29.00
Itokin	100.0	Shanghai	Women's apparel	1997.07	–	–	–	1 flagship per company, 67 concessions, 66 franchise stores	216.00
Itokin	97.0	Tsingtao	Women's apparel	1995.12					
Itokin	100.0	Luta	Women's apparel	1993.10					
Itokin	95.0	Tientsin	Women's apparel	1997.00					
Aigan	45.0	Beijing	Eye wear	1954.10	0.26	–	–	8	90.00
Paris Miki	100.0	Shanghai	Eye wear	1993.08	1.41	–	P	89	133.00
Paris Miki	48.0	Shanghai	Eye wear	2000.10					
Aoyama Shoji	54.0	Shanghai	Menswear	1994.09	0.18	2002.12	L	3	369.00
Fast Retailing	71.4	Shanghai	Apparel retail	2002.09	0.56	2003.06	−680.0	6	–

Key: '–' not available; P: Profitable; L: Loss making; OK: undisclosed but acceptable
Source: Compiled from various press reports

Japanese retailers in the rest of the world

In Europe, the record of Japanese retailers is patchier. Department stores were again present in the first stage of Japanese retail expansion overseas. Many set up branches of their stores in London for example including Mitsukoshi, Yaohan, and Sogo. As in Asia, the primary purpose of these stores was to cater to Japanese tourists, and most had closed by 2003.

The only recent Japanese presence in these two markets has come from the apparel retailers. Japanese fashion is popular in Asia, but the same fashion trends and brands are now also common in London, Los Angeles and New York. The first specialty retailer to take advantage of the enthusiasm for Japanese design was Ryohin Keikaku. The company began its Muji operation as a joint venture with Liberty in 1998, but then established its own subsidiary later. It expanded and contracted haphazardly, ending with a total of 13 UK stores and three Paris stores by the beginning of 2002, down from 23 in total the year before. In 2001, sales reached ¥2.6 billion in the UK and ¥600 million in France, but the European operation was still making a loss of close to ¥60 million. By the end of 2003, the company had added three more stores overseas but had also been forced to close some of its European outlets. It did sign a franchise deal for the Irish and Swedish markets and added one UK store, but for the most part it shifted its focus to Asia. Total overseas stores stood at 27 in 2004 (see Figure 12.1) but after 13 years, the European business finally posted a small but promising ¥150 million profit in 2003. As a result, Ryohin Keikaku said in 2004 it would look to have stores open in all the key European markets within three years (Nikkei Weekly, 2004).

Another specialty retailer, Fast Retailing, established a UK operation in September 2001 and quickly opened 21 stores, only to then close all except five in 2003. Fast Retailing blamed UK management culture on the initial collapse rather than its own failure to understand the market. In early 2002, Tadashi Yanai, the president of Fast Retailing, said he had been surprised by how difficult it was to transfer Uniqlo's business model, particularly Japanese personnel standards, to the UK. His main contention was the UK's management culture, particularly the strict demarcation between managers and other staff. In reality, the Uniqlo brand was positioned to compete below the prices offered by Gap, with Japanese management overlooking the strong trend towards much cheaper apparel prices at other retailers. The company's insistence on keeping product pristinely folded and displayed in stores also put off many consumers.

Fast Retailing's strategy of such a rapid rollout of stores was based purely on the success of the same tactics in Japan, and, in hindsight, showed a distinct lack of understanding of retailing in the UK. To its credit, the company has not pulled out completely, and after some study and reconsideration is planning to open more stores in 2006. By August 2004, Fast

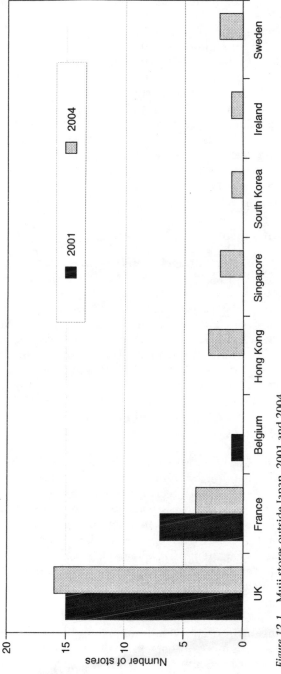

Figure 12.1 Muji stores outside Japan, 2001 and 2004
Source: Company Reports

Retailing's UK operation turned a small pretax profit of ¥20 million on sales of ¥1.8 billion.

In addition to the UK, Fast Retailing also opened in Shanghai in 2003. By contrast to the UK, the Chinese operation has had immediate success with sales of ¥1 billion in the first full year. Fast Retailing is using a store unit profit system, and has already closed one of the original eight opened in Shanghai. In late 2004, it also established a subsidiary in the US and said it expected to launch Uniqlo stores there in the near future.

Examples of Japanese retail expansion into Europe and the US remain few in number, and as yet there are no examples of long-term success. However, as retailers establish profitable systems, for example as is happening in apparel retailing with SPAs, there is every likelihood that there will be more attempts to tackle these lucrative markets, particularly following consolidation in Asia.

Three stages of expansion

The extent of Japanese retail operations overseas has a long history and has passed through three distinct phases. The first was one of mostly department store expansion, and was motivated by increased numbers of Japanese tourists going overseas. Even when overseas, the preference of Japanese consumers to shop at Japanese retailers was once an important trait but is now waning overseas as consumers become more international in thinking. Naturally, stores with no other target soon closed. The second phase was a brief hiatus when Japanese retailers were struggling to come to terms with domestic problems caused by the worst of the Japanese economic slowdown in the second half of the 1990s. The third and current phase is a new and rapid re-expansion, again in line with improved business confidence in Japan itself. This phase is just beginning.

Although there have been one or two incursions into Europe and the US, Asia has been the main region of interest for the majority of retailers. This has now become even more concentrated on China alone. The key to the current phase is the establishment and strength of supply and support firms in the same East Asian region. In addition to manufacturers that have developed a solid history within the region, largely as a base to produce consumer products for the Japanese market, Japanese firms are also supported by logistics and transport companies and, most importantly, by the powerful and knowledgeable trading houses.

Except in Malaysia, where Aeon is the number two retailer, no single Japanese firm is prominent in the main markets of East Asia but Japanese firms are significant in their overall number and presence. With various sources placing the number of separate retail companies already operating in China alone between 20 and 40, and with at least 97 overseas retail operations established by some 30 firms across the East Asian region, Japanese firms are highly prominent and, overall, are ahead of any one Western country.

Quite correctly, managers in Japan are keen to emphasize the cultural proximity of their business systems and expectations as compared to the rest of Asia. The current numbers are clearly just the beginning. Japanese retailers are set to further expand in China and the rest of Asia.

Conclusion

13

Japan: A Modern Retail Superpower

The study and analysis of Japanese distribution has passed through several distinct stages, and mostly without tangible result. It was not the aim of this book to consider older, academic work, but rather to show that retailing and distribution in Japan is now quite similar to that in other industrialized nations. Many, and in particular Japanese academics, would argue that Japanese distribution is culturally based and therefore unique by definition. This is of course partially true, but the importance and extent of this uniqueness extends only as far as micro level store operations, some business customs and, in a few cases, consumer tastes. Whereas up to the early 1990s distribution in Japan was largely a manufacturer-controlled system entirely dependent on structures and procedures that over time had become almost tradition, the same is certainly not true today. Scholars may continue to claim that Japan is unique, but companies such as Aeon, Fast Retailing, Yaoko, and Onward Kashiyama all share the same objective: profit through successful supply of consumer needs. No matter how much this is disturbing to the more traditional observers and commentators on Japanese distribution, it is equally undeniable that in this sense the modern system is no different from that in any other.

In this book we have presented the current situation in all of the major distribution sectors. In each and every one of these there are some clear and overwhelming developments, all of which have occurred since 1990 and most of which have only really become apparent since 2000.

First, manufacturers have been supplanted by retailers as the leaders of distribution channels in almost every single major merchandise category. The details are slightly more complicated in some cases as, particularly in apparel and increasingly in food distribution, the leaders of the category originated their business either in manufacturing, or wholesaling, or both. Even in these cases, however, the lead in the channel is now coming from the retail end of the chain. In other words, power is now in the hands of companies actually operating the retail stores themselves. These are not manufacturers operating stores by proxy, as was the case with the often-quoted *keiretsu* chains of stores, or wholesalers that organize branding and production but outsource store operation to others; they are genuine retailers. These are the same companies that are growing and leading the industry for the simple reason that they have direct contact with, and understanding of, consumer demand.

Traditional manufacturers would argue that they too operate based on consumer demand, but as has been shown in every advanced retail industry in the world, retailers that control consumer information and proactively seek to understand and meet consumer needs are often better positioned to comply to those needs than manufacturers. Even in Japan, where an estimated 10,000 new food products are offered to convenience store chains every year by the various manufacturers, most are based not on consumer trends or tastes, but rather on the improved engineering and product development capabilities of the manufacturers themselves. At the same time, convenience store chains are themselves offering more retail brand products that are developed specifically based on observed consumer demand.

Secondly, in every major sector there is a growing trend towards consolidation and concentration. With the exception of the convenience store, consumer electronics, and drugstore formats, overall levels of concentration in Japan remain low by international standards. This picture is distorted because many of the larger retail groups operate a large number of different formats, most of which exist as separate and sometimes non-consolidated subsidiaries or affiliated companies. This effectively hides the true level of concentration, but the picture is becoming clearer as retail firms begin to concentrate on specific, profitable formats and actively avoid the older trend towards multiple format businesses. Adoption of international accounting standards has also helped analysts unravel more of the true extent of the influence held by some firms.

The picture is also clouded by the continued existence of very large numbers of small, independent retail stores. These were the main subject of much of the early research and commentary on Japanese distribution and have been used by some academic writers as an effective smokescreen to cover up opportunities in the market, but today are, in reality, largely irrelevant. Even in Japan, the survival and support of small enterprise retailing and wholesaling is no longer a major issue because the industry has shifted towards genuine, corporate systems.

Despite these problems of analysis, however, by observing the top companies in all of the main merchandise categories it is clear that concentration levels are increasing and at a growing pace. With retailers controlling the channel, this is a completely natural development as professionally managed companies seek to grow market share and take a larger stake from their competitors. Merger and acquisition activity is growing in every sector; as is the plight of less successful companies that have become available for takeover as a result of being unable compete alone. Again, there is not a single sector that has not seen this trend occur.

Concentration levels will continue to increase. Already, Aeon Group in particular is the leading company in at least four of the formats that it operates and is growing in market share in every one of them. In consumer electronics, the rise of Yamada Denki has been a phenomenon in itself. Finally in food retailing, while Aeon again stands out as the first company in Japanese history to be developing a nationwide chain of food super-markets with significant buying power and market share, behind the scenes, the general trading companies or *Sogo Shosha* are amassing a huge wholesaling capacity. Even here, whereas in the past the wholesaler-retailer demarcation was largely maintained, the same *Sogo Shosha* have also direct control of major retail firms through acquisition and so are also being led by their interest at the retail end. No one company has a significant share of food distribution at present, but the trends towards greater concentra-tion, and the aims of the companies driving these trends, are the same as in all other sectors.

Thirdly, there is a move away from general merchandise retail formats such as department stores and GMS chains, and a move towards specialty retail formats. Despite continued insistence on the traditional Japanese-ness of the system as a whole, much of the old retail system is now being dismantled. Department stores continue to survive, but the only firms displaying any degree of success are increasingly moving towards central-ized management systems and towards brand development, becoming by turn both chain store style operations and more clearly specialist in certain merchandise categories, notably apparel. GMS chains are also part of the traditional system. Hailed as "revolutionary" when they first appeared in the 1960s, these firms were, in reality, merely a more mass market version of their department store predecessors and, although marginally cheaper, still suffered from the same inefficiencies. The con-tinued intervention and channel leadership asserted by manufacturers even in their dealings with GMS chains led to the same levels of woefully poor customer focus. Today, again, the surviving GMS chains have devel-oped more Westernized styles of centralized management, logistics, and information systems in order to control costs. As part of this they are now just beginning to also control their own supply chains and move away from the influence of manufacturing concerns.

GMS chains have to make this change because they too are being sup-planted by specialty retail companies that focus on much narrower mer-chandise categories. Today, only four GMS chains still exist, with a fifth, Daiei, currently considering whether or not to move to a food-only specialist operation. The remainder have each survived through different means: Ito-Yokado by maintaining an upscale, mass merchandise offer with high levels of cost control; Seiyu through takeover by Wal-Mart; Uny through regional isolation; and Aeon by emulation of cost effective, direct channel control strategies used by the leading companies in North America and Western Europe. In this sense, Aeon is the only remaining

GMS chain that continues to grow and develop a general merchandise format as a major part of its business.

On the other hand, in every single merchandise sector, there are three or more companies that have risen from the ranks of regional players to become major national retailers in their own right. In almost every case, direct control of channels, retail branding including branding of their actual stores, significant consumer focus, and the goal of profitability set these companies apart from more traditional, supplier reliant firms of the past. The biggest change in Japanese retailing since 2000 is that in each sector, the traditional firms have at last made way for these new firms and they all lead their own particular categories.

Finally, in response to each of the above three trends, there is a positive change in consumer thinking and reaction. Consumer demands and tastes are indeed a cultural phenomenon. Although it might seem absurd to argue that Japanese people prefer smaller houses, more expensive food and clothing, less leisure time, and random levels of after service compared to consumers in other advanced economies, this is in fact what many Japanese politicians, academics, and, especially, manufacturers have argued in the past. Manufacturers additionally insisted that as the people they employed also represented the consumers that bought their products, they were as close as necessary to the market that they served. Loyalty to the company remains as strong as ever for many Japanese, but today, because of retailers that have given consumers that much more in terms of quality and value for money, even the most ardent salaryman now looks forward to more brands and lower prices.

The result is a completely new distribution system in Japan. The process of change is far from complete in the mid 2000s. Wholesaling and physical distribution in particular are still changing and will take some time to catch up with developments at the retail stage. Similarly, larger manufacturers continue to cling to their traditional leadership roles, and while concentration remains as low as it is, still dominate the many small and medium retailers that continue to survive. At the same time, there are some signs that manufacturers increasingly view the larger retailers more as competitors than as clients creating new levels of friction. Unfortunately for them, however, retailers are now able to simply bypass such problems altogether, either by taking up the excess production capacity at smaller manufacturers in order to make their own retail brands, or more usually, moving production and procurement entirely outside Japan to low cost centers such as China. Too many manufacturers remain unwilling to admit that survival is more likely through cooperation and better products than through dictating prices and sales terms to retailers.

A further result is that the best retailers are now as good as any. Consumer focused companies are no longer second tier, they lead their merchandise sectors and are primary companies in their own right. Most have retail brands of their own, and, to the delight of traditional observers, have even developed management systems for merchandising, branding, and even product supply, that are particular to Japan. Even more exciting, these same companies are now secure enough in their domestic market to take their skills overseas. Companies like Fast Retailing, Ryohin Keikaku, Aeon and Ito-Yokado are all very active on the international stage. In the cases of the first three of these companies, they even have existing interests in Europe and North America. Their strength and ability in Japan, along with a traditionally lenient and export supporting banking system, means that the potential for taking their new concepts and systems overseas has only just begun. The growth of these and other leading Japanese retailers overseas is no longer probable, it is inevitable.

International retailers in Japan

This book has focused on the development of domestic retailers in the Japanese market with only passing reference to the entry and results of overseas retailers operating in Japan. In truth, the increase in number of overseas firms operating retail stores in Japan since 1990 has been so rapid and so far reaching that it is only the most stringent conservatives that would deny that it has not been a factor in changing the system overall. Of course, Japan has plenty of stringent conservatives, but even taking their views into account, once again Japanese consumer reaction to overseas retail stores speaks for itself. The popularity of overseas retailers, most notably upscale apparel and accessory brands, is accepted by all. The argument that these represent only a small niche market overlooks the fact that Japan alone accounts for a significant share of the global market for these brands. In addition, the similar degree of popularity displayed towards other companies disproves the idea that this is a random phenomenon. A short list of examples include Gap, Toys 'R' Us, Starbucks, HMV, Virgin, Tower, Apple, Barneys New York, J. Crew, Chelsea Outlet Malls, Vivit Square, and even McDonalds.

Yet the standard press and academic line is that Japanese consumers are different and, by definition, overseas retailers cannot understand them and are actually bad as they confuse consumers. Unfortunately, companies such as Boots, Dairy Farm, REI, Sephora, and Carrefour have provided fuel to this argument by conspicuously pulling out of the market. Wal-Mart and Tesco, two more of the world's largest retail companies with significant international interest remain in the market and struggle on a daily basis with such journalistic reaction. Operating in the FMCG (fast moving consumer goods) and food sectors, these companies are at the very grass roots level, a long way away from the luxury end of the market that everyone agrees is suited to Japan and Japanese consumers. In addition, with Carrefour announcing its exit in 2005, they face tremendous pressure to follow the French firm into retreat.

But this view is also distorted by the traditionalist perspective and overlooks just how much impact a company like Carrefour or Wal-Mart can have on a retail industry that clings to outdated forms of distribution. Carrefour may have pulled out but it can equally be argued that its very presence in Japan further advanced the trends that were discussed above.

It is easy to misunderstand why Carrefour did not succeed in Japan. It is still the second largest retailer in the world, growing in China, already the fifth largest retailer there overall, and is a leader in Taiwan, Brazil, and a number of other less developed countries. It is also the market leader in France. The Japanese press was unanimously delighted with the announcement of Carrefour's withdrawal from Japan in March 2005 as it confirmed journalist rhetoric that had appeared since the company first began operating in the country. Numerous reasons were put forward for its exit including a failure to understand the market; a failure to meet consumer needs; having stores too big; making stores too French; not making stores French enough; being too aggressive with suppliers; and so on. Among the reports, the more ridiculous even made claims that Carrefour was too expensive, too low quality, or, our favorite, didn't carry enough merchandise. In the end, however, it can be concluded that as the first overseas FMCG retailer to attempt Japan, Carrefour was just too foreign.

All such views were, however, far more designed to bolster previous arguments against overseas retailers and to polish public opinion than to present any true research or actual facts. As analysts outside Japan were well aware, Carrefour's exit was due largely to pressure on its main board to focus on improving performance in its home market in the face of aggressive discounters, and cut any overseas ventures that were not already fully developed. Carrefour's Japan operation faced precisely the problem that dogs so many overseas firms coming to Japan: time. Eager shareholders often simply cannot wait for expected performance to materialize. As a result, Carrefour left not only Japan, but Mexico as well and, in mid 2005, was facing rumors of further retreats from countries such as South Korea. In addition, and as with many other firms, Carrefour saw China as big enough in itself and could not justify spending extra investment money in Japan when the same money could be spent on the opposite side of the East China Sea.

Despite what Japanese journalists may have believed, Carrefour actually achieved good results in Japan, at least in terms of how it changed the market around itself. Before the Fall of 1999, Japanese retailing had not changed to any significant degree since Daiei opened the first full-line GMS outlet back in the 1960s. On 12 December 1999 when Carrefour opened the first foreign operated hypermarket on Japanese soil, it marked the first time in recent history that academics could accurately use the term "revolution". It represented a company that was prepared to make demands of wholesale suppliers and, in contravention of traditional distribution practices, insisted on its right to decide final retail prices, ignoring wholesalers' recommendations. As we saw in Chapter 6, Japanese firms like Aeon and, in its heyday, Daiei, had made tiny stabs at manufacturer power in the channel, and Ito-Yokado had caused a few waves by forcing Seven-Eleven suppliers to jointly pay for logistics costs (see Chapter 8), but basically suppliers still ruled the channel up until this point. Kokubu and Cupie, both major food companies, are just two suppliers that were reported as refusing to deal with Carrefour outright. The CEO of Nihon Shurui Hanbai, Japan's largest liquor wholesaler, was quoted publicly as saying he was happy to deal with Carrefour as long as Aeon and Ito-Yokado didn't object and the French chain didn't undercut his wholesale prices (Nikkei Ryutsu Shinbun, 2001). Open market? Not a chance. It was even common for students, who had never even seen a Carrefour store, to tell us that the French firm would clearly fail because it did not understand Japanese consumers and, anyway, it was bad for Japan to have the company in the market. With opposition like this, even good retailing is not enough.

It is equally wrong to say Carrefour failed at store level. Early stores floundered after an initially positive consumer response. It had attempted to source product mostly from local suppliers, because, in addition to the cost benefits, it logically believed that Japanese opinion would be more amenable to a company that did not sell a large proportion of imports. Unfortunately, with local suppliers unsympathetic, it could only offer second tier brands, which consumers saw as low quality, meaning they were far less impressed with Carrefour's lower prices. In addition, consumers naturally expected a French retailer to stock French product and were disappointed that there was so little. To its credit, however, Carrefour addressed both of these problems and many more in its second round of store openings. Whereas early stores were relatively poorly received, the later stores that opened in Kansai were reengineered for Japan. The company as a whole still faced the same obstacles in the supply chain, but its stores were packed with product, bustling with customers, and everything a retailer should be. They were also the first of their kind in Japan, combining a very large GMS with a well targeted shopping center that could produce a high level of footfall throughout the week.

Carrefour's story should be essential reading for any overseas firm, both those looking to enter the market or even those already working there. Regardless of how well it actually performed as a retailer, the public vitriol poured on the chain by the Japanese press, encouraged by the distribution establishment, showed very clearly that, at least in terms of PR, Carrefour did not do a good job at all. This in itself is a significant lesson for any firm looking to succeed in the consumer market. What Carrefour failed to realize is that retailing, perhaps in Japan more than most places, is as much about hearts and minds as it is about products and profits. It is equally certain that by not bending to the myth that overseas companies must follow traditional Japanese distribution rules and customs, Carrefour proved that retailers can take control of markets. Aeon, the company which bought Carrefour's eight stores, announced its own strategy of global scale in 2001, two years after Carrefour's initial entry. As described in Chapter 6 and in subsequent chapters on drugstore and home center retailing, Aeon's strategy and its way of achieving it is focused on economies of scale and control of its own supply chains. This is precisely what Carrefour introduced to Japan and remains its legacy.

The future

Japanese retailing is not about to change or undergo a so-called revolution. It has changed already. The traditional customs and mechanisms that once made distribution in Japan a subject of academic study around the world, as well as a point of contention in international trade talks, are now rapidly being dismantled. Manufacturers are no longer the leaders of distribution channels, having been supplanted by retailers with better marketing, branding, and consumer knowledge. While some continue to cling to the traditions of the past, in reality the market has moved on and these same retailers are now firmly in control. It is only the lower ranked, smaller retail companies that still suffer the domination of manufacturers and suppliers and this is purely because they are in no condition not to. As they too decline, the transition to a modern, retailer and, consequently, consumer led distribution system will be complete.

References

Abegglen, James C. and George Stalk (1987) *Kaisha: The Japanese Company*, Tokyo, Tuttle Books.

Ando, Takashi and Hiroyuki Tanaka (2004) Analysis of publicly listed drugstore company accounts 2004 [Jojo doraggusutoa kessan bunseki 2004] *Chain Store Age*, 15 August, pp. 66–71.

Asahi Shinbunsha (2004a) *Population Power 2004 [Minryoku 2004: Chiiki Deta Besu]*, Tokyo, Asahi Shinbunsha.

Asahi Shinbunsha (2004b) *Japan Almanac 2005 [Asahi Shinbun Japan Arumanakku]*, Tokyo, Asahi Shinbunsha.

Asano, Kyohei, Ichiro Yamada, Kazushige Tsuji, Satoshi Ota (2004) Intermediate Distribution Company Ranking for Japan: top 1000 firms [Nihon no chukan ryutsu 1000 sha rankingu], *Chain Store Age*, 15 September: pp. 20–42.

Chida, Naoya (2004) Specializing Home centers [Bunka suru home center] *Ryutsu to System*, No. 118, January, pp. 10–15.

Czinkota, Michael R. and Masaaki Kotabe (eds) (1993) *The Japanese Distribution System*, Chicago and Cambridge, Probus Publishing Company: pp. 123–36.

Doi Takeo (1973) *The Anatomy of Dependence*, Tokyo, Kodansha International.

Fields, George (1983) *From Bonsais to Levi's*, London, Futura.

Fields, George (1986) *The Japanese Consumer Market*, Tokyo, Japan Times.

Fok, Simon (2005) *Assessment of China's retail logistics market*, Unpublished presentation, Said Business School, Oxford University.

Hoshino, Shigeru (1990) For Quality-Conscious Japanese Consumers Low-Prices also Matter, *Tokyo Business Today*, September, pp. 50–2.

IT & Kaden Business (2004) Top 6 firms total market exceeds ¥3 trillion for super oligopoly [Joi 6 sha gokei de 3 cho en oba no cho-kasenka], *IT & Kaden Business*, August, pp. 70–79.

JCCI (Japan Chamber of Commerce and Industry) (1989) *Distribution System and Market Access in Japan*, Special Report, Tokyo.

JETRO (Japan External Trade Organisation) (1987) *The Japanese Market: A Compendium of Information of the Prospective Exporter*, Tokyo.

JapanConsuming (2002a) *Retail Japan 2003*, Tokyo, Sensu.

JapanConsuming (2002b) Cashmere: the new luxury market, *JapanConsuming*, 3 (11) November, pp. 13–14.

JapanConsuming (2004) Special Focus: 2003–4 Retailing in Japan: Japan's new stable retail industry, *JapanConsuming*, 5(8) August/September, pp. 13–17.

JapanConsuming (2005) The fate of Japanese wholesaling, *JapanConsuming*, 6(1) January, pp. 13–16.

Kawabata, Moto (2000) *The Overseas Expansion and Strategy of Retailers*, Tokyo, Shinhyoron.

Kenrick, Douglas Moore (1990) *Where Communism Works: The success of competitive-communism in Japan*, Tokyo, Tuttle.

Kerr, Alex (2002) *Dogs and Demons: tales from the dark side of modern Japan*, Tokyo, Hill and Wang.

Kingston, Jeff (2004) *Japan's quiet transformation*, London, RoutledgeCurzon.

Kokuritsu Shakai Hoken Jinko Mondai Kenkyusho (2001) *Japan's Population: Future Projections*, Tokyo.

Larke, Roy (1991) *Consumer Perceptions of Large Retail Stores in Japan*, unpublished PhD. thesis, University of Stirling.

Larke, Roy (1994) *Japanese Retailing*, London, Routledge.

Larke, Roy (2005) Retailer-supplier relationships in Japan: restructuring the wholesale industry. Paper presented at the *3rd Asia-Pacific Retail Conference*, Sookmyung Women's University, Seoul, 15 March.

METI (2003) *Census of Commerce Advanced Report 2002 [Heisei 14 nen Shogyo Tokei Sokuho]*, Tokyo, METI.

METI (2005) Website: http://www.meti.go.jp/, 1 April 2005.

Maruyama, Masayoshi, Yoko Togawa, Kyohei Sakai, and Nobuo Sakamoto and Masaharu Arakawa (1989) Distribution System and Business Practices in Japan, in *EPA International Symposium Structural Problems in the Japanese and World Economy*, Economic Planning Agency, 12–13 October, Tokyo.

Meyer-Ohle, Hendrik (2003) *Innovation and Dynamics in Japanese Retailing*, London, Palgrave.

Meyer-Ohle, Hendrik (2004) Walking with Dinosaurs: general trading companies in the reorganization of Japanese consumer goods distribution, *International Journal of Retail & Distribution Management*, 32 (1), pp. 45–55.

Miwa, Yoshiro (1992) Japanese Business Trading Customs [Nihon no Torihiki Shukan], Tokyo, Yukaikaku.

Mukoyama, Masao (1996) *Towards the establishment of pure global*, Tokyo, Chikura Shobo.

NMJ (2003) *Distribution Economics Notebook 2004 [Ryutsu Keizai no Tebiki 2004]*, Tokyo, Nihon Keizai Shinbun.

NMJ (2004a) 37th Nikkei Ryutsu Shinbun Survey of Retailing, *NMJ*, 24 June, pp. 1–10.

NMJ (2004b) *Distribution Economics Notebook 2005 [Ryutsu Keizai no Tebiki 2005 nen]*, Tokyo, Nihon Keizai Shinbun.

Nakajima, Kiyoshi (2004) Japan Chain Stores 1000 firm ranking [Nihon chen sutoa 100 sha rankingu], *Chain Store Age*, 1 September, pp. 38–83.

Nakamae, Tadashi (1998) Views from 2010, *Economist*, 19 March.

New Frontier (2004) *The New Image of Trading Houses [Shosha no Shin-Jitsuzo]* Tokyo, Nikkan Kogyo.

Nihon Keizai Shinbun (2004) *Distribution Company Yearbook 2005 CD-ROM [Ryutsu Kaisha Nenkan 2005 nen CD-ROM]*, Tokyo, Nihon Keizai Shinbun.

Nikkei Ryutsu Shinbun (1991) *Distribution Economics Notebook 1992 [Ryutsu Keizai no Tebiki 1992 nen]*, Tokyo, Nihon Keizai Shinbun.

Nikkei Ryutsu Shinbun (2001) Asking top wholesaler executives about the true trading conditions with French Carrefour, 23 January, p. 11.

Nikkei Weekly (2004) Muji comes back to life overseas, *Nikkei Weekly*, 31 May.

Nikkei Weekly (2005) Carrefour exit marks tough road for foreign retailers, *Nikkei Weekly*, 14 March.

Ohmae, Kenichi (1991) The mind of a strategist: the art of Japanese business, McGraw-Hill.

Otsuka, Takashi, Noboru Kaneko (2004) Accounts for 181 Chain Stores [Chen sutoa 181 sha dai kessan] *Hanbai Kakushin*, July, pp. 94–131.

Shibata, Mutsumi and Tomoko Tsumoto (2004b) Aeon's Blindspot [Ion no shikaku], Shukan Diamondo, 27 November: pp. 30–41.

Shimaguchi, Mitsuaki (1977) *Marketing Channels in Japan*, Michigan Mass., UMI.

Shukan Toyo Keizai (1999) *Overseas company data CD-ROM 2000 [Gaishikei kigyo deta cd-rom 2000 nenban]*, Tokyo, Toyo Keizai Shuppan.

Shukan Toyo Keizai (2003) *Companies operating overseas 2004 [Kaigai Shusshin kigyo deta 2004 nen]*, Tokyo, Toyo Keizai Shuppan.

Shukan Toyo Keizai (2004a) *Economic Statistics Yearbook CD-ROM 2004 [Keizai tokei nenkan cd-rom 2004 nenban]*, Tokyo, Toyo Keizai Shuppan.

Shukan Toyo Keizai (2004b) *Japanese Company Groups 2004 [Nihon no kigyo group 2004 nen]*, Tokyo, Toyo Keizai Shuppan.

Somucho (2001) *Population Census 2000 [Kokusei Chosa Heisei 12 nen]*, Tokyo.

Somucho (2004a) *Record of Population Movement 2004 [Jumin Kihon Daicho 2004]*, Tokyo, Nihon Tokei Kyokai.

Somucho (2004b) *Survey of Household accounts [Kakei chosa 2003 nen]*, Tokyo.

Store Japan Online (2005) Website: http://www.sji.gr.jp/, 1 April 2005.

Suzuki, Takayuki (2002) *The Reformation of Aeon Group [Ion Gurupu no Dai-Henkaku]*, Tokyo, Nihon Jitsugyo Shuppan.

Takayama, Kunisuke (2001) The Impact and Reaction within the Japanese distribution industry of the overseas expansion of Western retailers [Obei kourigyo no kaigai shinshutsu ga, waga kuni ryutsu-gyo ni ataeru inpakuto to taio] *Ryutsu to System*, 108, June: pp. 3–11.

Yahoo! Japan (2005) Website: http://www.yahoo.co.jp/

Company Index

NOTE: Page numbers in italics refer to tables and figures

Subject Index

NOTE: Page numbers in italics refer to tables and figures

Printed in the United States
56108LVS00003B/3